BUILDING A PARTNERSHIP

THE CANADA-UNITED STATES FREE TRADE AGREEMENT

Mordechai E. Kreinin, editor

Michigan State University Press/East Lansing

University of Calgary Press/Calgary

Copyright 2000 by Michigan State University

Paper used in this publication meets the minimum requirements of ANSI/NISO Z39.48–1992 (R 1997) (Permanence of Paper).

Published simultaneously in the United States of America by Michigan State University Press and in Canada by the University of Calgary Press

05 04 03 02 01 00   1 2 3 4 5 6 7 8 9

The contents of this volume were selected from the transcripts of presentations delivered originally at the "Tenth Anniversary Conference of the Canada–U.S. Free Trade Agreement," 11–12 September 1998 at Michigan State University's Kellogg Center. The conference was co-sponsored by the James A. Baker, III Institute for Public Policy of Rice University and Michigan State University.

Library of Congress Cataloging-in-Publication Data

  Building a partnership : the Canada-United States Free Trade
Agreement / Mordechai E. Kreinin, editor.
    p. cm.
  Selected papers presented at the 10th Anniversary Conference of the Canada-
U.S. Free Trade Agreement, held Sept. 11-12, 1998, at Michigan State University.
  Includes bibliographical references.
  ISBN: 0870135376 (alk. paper)
  1. Free trade--North America— Congresses. 2. Free trade— United States—
Congresses. 3. Free trade— Canada— Congresses. I. Kreinin, Mordechai
Elihau, 1930- II. Anniversary Conference of the Canada-U.S. Free Trade
Agreement (10th : 1998 : Michigan State University)
HF1746 .B85 2000
382'.973071— 21

                                                                99-086819

Cover design: Jesse Howard
Cover photograph of the Internationaltional Bridge between Sault Ste. Marie, Ontario,
and Sault Ste. Marie, Michigan, by Chris Smith (Courtesy of the Michigan
Department of Transportation)

Visit Michigan State University Press on the World Wide Web at:
http://www.msu.edu/unit/msupress
Visit the University of Calgary on the World Wide Web at:
http://www.ucalgary.ca/UofC/departments/UP/

Contents

A Reunion of Trade Warriors from the Canada–U.S. Trade Negotiations: Remembering How it Happened

Peter McPherson[*]

Ten years ago, Canada and the United States, the world's two biggest trading partners, put together an agreement of historic importance. For the U.S. the pact was precedent–setting. Except for an agreement with Israel, its successful negotiation marked the first time the nation had entered into a *regional* free trade treaty. Recently, a conference held at Michigan State University celebrated the tenth anniversary of the negotiations that led to this historic understanding. The gathering in East Lansing, a decade after the actual events, presented negotiators, scholars, and observers with a unique opportunity to re–visit a landmark in U.S.–Canadian trade relations.

In the late 1980s, I was fortunate to be Deputy Secretary of the U.S. Treasury and involved in discussions that led up to the Canada–U.S. Free Trade Agreement. Those of us who participated in those negotiations, as well as in the conference, remembered the good times and the struggles, but mostly we are pleased with what was achieved.

This volume contains a number of presentations from the 10th Anniversary Conference, held on the Michigan State University campus in the fall of 1998. It addresses fundamental questions faced by negotiators. Why, for instance, did the agreement come about? The U.S., for its part, was already quite open to imports from its northern neighbor; Canada simply wanted an agreement to prevent a retreat from that position. Urgency was heightened in Canada by protectionist talk in the American Congress. Canada, on the other hand, was not nearly as open to U.S. imports, and American officials wanted to roll back trade barriers.

Both parties really desired an agreement. And the Canadian government had taken a large political risk by entering into the negotiations. No doubt,

*Peter McPherson has served as President of Michigan State University since 1993. From 1987 to 1989 he was Deputy Secretary of the United States Treasury focusing on trade, tax, and international issues. He was a senior negotiator during the Canada–U.S. Free Trade Agreement negotiations.

the U. S., too, would have paid a price if the negotiations had failed. But beyond these broad objectives, parties to the negotiations faced hard choices, choices central to political and policy issues that stood between them and a successful agreement.

Canadians believed that, in order to assure the openness of the U.S. market, the United States should agree to modify its anti-dumping and countervailing duty laws regarding Canada. But U.S. negotiators feared that Congress was in no mood to approve such sweeping changes— and Congress is a real partner with the U. S. executive branch on all trade agreements.

On the other hand, the U.S. felt that Canada should reduce or eliminate its tariffs, as well as constrain various subsidies that were given to its citizens and businesses. Without such discipline the U.S. argued, there would not really be an open market. The Canadians had major problems in this regard, particularly with regional subsidies. Canada argued that it should not have to control subsidies, especially since the U.S. did not want to modify subsidies that it, too, provided to certain sectors of its own economy. The U.S. negotiators countered that American subsidies did not affect Canada–U.S. trade in a significant way.

Although much was accomplished during the long months of discussion in 1988, these two issues continued to pose problems as a negotiation deadline imposed by technical rules within the U.S. Congress began to loom. The U.S. executive branch had to submit a statement to the legislative branch on or before midnight 2 October 1988 declaring that a basis existed for an agreement.

It is worth noting here that the U.S. negotiator, Peter Murphy, felt captive to events. He could not give in to Canadian wishes without alienating the U.S. Congress, and he could not say "no" absolutely to his Canadian counterparts without breaking off the negotiations. In any event, Murphy felt that major concessions had to be made at a higher level within the U. S. government, probably as part of the endgame.

Then, on 22 September 1989, the Canadian delegation walked out of the negotiations. In retrospect, this breaking off of talks can be seen as key to the final success of the Canada–U.S. Free Trade Agreement negotiations. Breaking off negotiations is usually dangerous and often unproductive, but in this case the Canadian walk–out focused energies at the highest levels in the United States. It galvanized both parties.

In the end, there was an agreement around a proposal suggested by Sam Gibbons, Chair of the Trade Subcommittee of the Ways and Means Committee of the U. S. House of Representatives. His idea was somehow to sidestep the issues of countervailing duties, anti–dumping provisions, and subsidies. Each country would keep its trade laws, but there would be a bi-national panel to review decisions made by whichever was the "importing country." The panel would apply the laws of the importing country to decisions made by that country, that is, the panel would review and apply American law for U.S. decisions regarding Canadian imports to the U.S.

As the deadline approached, tensions increased, once again, when a last minute issue arose. It was settled only a few minutes before the Congressionally imposed deadline of midnight, 2 October. The problem was whether the United States could continue to change its laws. The U.S. felt that Congress would insist upon that prerogative. And although the U.S. delegation argued that the bi-national panel would, of course, have the authority to continue to interpret and apply laws as they were changed, the Canadians said this solution would not work for them. In the end, negotiators decided that *both* Canada and the United States could change their laws, but that any changes had to be compatible with the "objects and purposes" of the General Agreement on Tarrifs and Trade (GATT) and the Canada–U.S. Free Trade Agreement (CUSTA). If the change of a law was not compatible, as determined by the panel, then the legislation had to be changed, once again, or the affected country could retaliate.

These were not just "technical" issues; they went to the heart of whether or not a trade agreement between Canada and the United States could be crafted. Given both the difficulties encountered, as well as the promises for rewards that the agreement held out for both sides, I think everyone involved can be proud of what was achieved.

As the papers contained in this volume recreate the tense climate in which negotiators, at once fierce nationals and sincere diplomats, did battle, they also demonstrate the insightfulness and dignity with which these "trade warriors" approached the task at hand. We also hope they will convey the excitement inpired at the 10th anniversary conference in East Lansing and that they will engage your interest.

THE SUCCESSFUL QUEST FOR A CANADA–UNITED STATES FREE TRADE AGREEMENT

Roger B. Porter[*]

The negotiation of the Canada–United States Free Trade Agreement was a singular accomplishment at the time it was concluded and remains a remarkable achievement when viewed from the perspective of a decade. The agreement represents a significant development in the relationship of Canada and the United States and strengthened the economic ties of the world's largest bilateral trading partners. Moreover, the pact proved a crucial first stage in the subsequent negotiation of the North America Free Trade Agreement and has served as a model and encouragement for other regional trading arrangements. Not least, this was a creative agreement going beyond merely resolving differences and reaching compromises. The Canada–U.S. Free Trade Agreement embodies a novel approach to the challenging task of resolving disputes, a mechanism that has proven useful in subsequent agreements.

Viewed from the perspective of ten years, the Canada–U.S. Free Trade Agreement enjoys widespread support in both countries and seems natural, even inevitable. Few, if any, seriously question its value. The absence of controversy is striking. Yet, the process of negotiating the agreement was controversial and uncertain, and required considerable political courage and the expenditure of much political capital.

Indeed, given the repeated failures of previous attempts to forge such an agreement, a puzzle remains: What factors explain the success of the

---

*Roger B. Porter is IBM Professor of Business and Government at the Kennedy School of Government, Harvard University. He served as Assistant to the President for Economic and Domestic Policy during the Bush Administration and as Deputy Assistant to the President and Director of the White House Office of Policy Development during the Reagan Administration.

agreement signed by President Ronald Reagan and Prime Minister Brian Mulroney on December 31, 1988?[1]

Fear and Opportunity

Perhaps more than other factors, the combination of fear and opportunity played a powerful role in bringing the agreement to a successful conclusion. Each element was present in different ways on both sides of the border. For decades, a sense of vulnerability and dependence has characterized the outlook of Canadians, particularly with respect to Canada's economic future. The U.S. economy is ten to twelve times the size of Canada's. The U.S. market receives the overwhelming bulk of Canada's exports and by the late 1980s that share was rising from two-thirds to nearly three quarters.

This increased reliance on the U.S. market came at a time when security of access seemed threatened. U.S. trade policy officials faced aggressive pressure from domestic industries exhibited, among other ways, in the form of antidumping, countervailing duty, and escape clause petitions. These officials also felt the heat of unhappy and assertive members of Congress. The softwood lumber countervailing duty case, begun in 1982 during a recession and involving Canada's third largest industry, provided a tangible, highly visible reminder of the potential for legally imposed restraints on trade. Canadian business leaders were particularly active in expressing their fear of what they viewed as the misuse and politicization of U.S. trade laws. From their vantage point, they felt there was no realistic avenue of relief in U.S. courts and no useful international review in the GATT. Some type of discipline was needed to prevent actions which could lead to downwardly spiraling trade with the U.S.

Canadian officials, however, were driven not only by the fear of a deteriorating trade relationship, but also by the element of opportunity—the prospect of unfettered access to the U.S. market beckoned. For Canada, a major challenge was to enjoy greater security of access to the U.S. market and benefit from the spur of healthy competition while preserving Canadian culture and sovereignty.

---

1   A useful brief account of previous efforts is found in Raymond Vernon, Debora L. Spar, and Glenn Tobin, *Iron Triangles and Revolving Doors: Cases in U.S. Foreign Economic Policy Making* (New York: Praeger, 1991), pp. 22–23. Ronald Reagan signed Executive Order 12662 "Implementing the U.S.–Canada Free Trade Implementation *Act*" on December 31, 1988. *Public Papers of the Presidents of the United States, Ronald Reagan 1988–89* Book II (Washington, D.C.: United States Government Printing Office, 1991), pp. 1666–67.

The impetus for developing an initiative took the form of a "Trade Policy Review" led by a Ministry of External Affairs official, Derek Burney, the Assistant Under Secretary for trade and economic policy.[2] The interagency review ultimately led to the adoption by the Cabinet of its recommendation to undertake a series of bilateral sectoral negotiations modeled after the successful auto pact negotiated in the mid-1960s. U.S. Trade Representative William Brock, after securing interagency approval, responded positively and in the spring of 1984 the low-key negotiations began but with limited success. The potential for significant trade-offs was severely constrained by a sectoral approach and within a few months the effort was quietly abandoned.

In September 1984, the political landscape in Canada changed with the stunning victory of the Progressive Conservative Party. The new Prime Minister, Brian Mulroney, publicly supported establishing closer ties with the United States, a relationship made more difficult in recent years by a series of measures advanced by the Trudeau government to reduce Canada's economic vulnerability, not least by limiting U.S. ownership of Canadian industries and natural resources. Trade policy had not played a prominent role in the election campaign, although Mulroney had pledged to oppose any free trade negotiations with the U.S.

Soon after coming into office, the Mulroney government set out on a new course. Encouraged by a business community eager for assured markets and fearful of U.S. industry-inspired trade actions against Canadian enterprises, and with support from permanent government officials, particularly those in the Ministry of External Affairs, the new government moved to commence discussions designed to lead to a free trade agreement with the U.S.

One of the challenges and benefits of summit meetings between heads of government is that they serve as action-forcing events, the life-blood of policy entrepreneurs. Brian Mulroney seized the opportunity occasioned by his first summit meeting with Ronald Reagan to seek agreement to set the two governments on a course that would lead to a free trade pact. The March 1985 "Shamrock Summit" communique included the commitment Mulroney sought: "We have today agreed to give the highest priority to finding mutually-acceptable means to reduce and eliminate existing

---

2   See Brian W. Tomlin, "The Stages of Prenegotiation: The Decision to Negotiate North American Free Trade" in Janice Gross Stein, ed., *Getting to the Table: The Process of International Prenegotiation* (Baltimore: John Hopkins University Press, 1989).

barriers to trade in order to secure and facilitate trade and investment flows."[3]

Fear and opportunity also played a prominent role on the U.S. side of the border. Trade policy making is a genuinely shared enterprise in the United States. Congressional prerogatives are jealously guarded, especially during an era of divided government.[4] The 1980s was a restive time in U.S. trade policy driven largely by continuing sizeable trade deficits. Unilateral action by Congress, while ultimately constrained by the hurdle of having to overcome a presidential veto, was nonetheless a persistent threat and influenced the thinking and behavior of executive branch officials.

The level of congressional involvement in shaping trade policy, the scope of discretion accorded the executive, the willingness to give further grants of authority depend on a variety of factors— current and prospective conditions, personal relationships, and the perceptions of an administration's strategy. Large trade deficits had strained the credibility of U.S. trade policy on Capitol Hill. While congressional policy prescriptions vary enormously, they usually partake of a common element — activism.

The Administration felt the need to conduct an activist trade policy— initiating Section 301 actions; successfully administering trade remedy cases; resolving bilateral disputes with Japan and the European Community; and seeking to advance the multilateral Uruguay Round. No single approach was considered sufficient. A three-pronged strategy with bilateral, plurilateral, and multilateral elements evolved as senior officials sought to maintain control and guide the direction of policy.

But fear of losing control of policy was merely one side of the coin; the opportunity for an agreement with Canada represented the other side. U.S. officials wanted an activist approach that was positive, that held out the promise of opening markets rather than constantly threatening and sometimes taking retaliation.

Overcoming Differences

Successful negotiations face a host of barriers that extend beyond the differences in objectives and priorities of the parties. The Canada–U.S.

---

3   Joint Canada–United States Declarations on Trade and International Security, March 18, 1985, *Public Papers of the Presidents of the United States, Ronald Reagan, 1985*, Book I (Washington, D.C.: United States Government Printing Office, 1988), pp. 307–308.

4   During the two decades preceding the signing of the Canada-U.S. Free Trade Agreement, divided government, with the President facing opposition majorities in one or both houses of the Congress, was the norm during sixteen of the twenty years.

Free Trade Agreement illustrates the point. Its negotiation revealed sharp contrasts in organization, constraints, and strategy—differences that required skill and patience in bridging.

Organization • Despite their geographical proximity, the U.S. and Canada could hardly have organized for the negotiations more differently. The Canadian approach reflected the priority attached to the effort by the Prime Minister and the Cabinet. A special negotiator, not tied to a departmental or ministerial bureaucracy, was appointed and given frequent, direct access to the Prime Minister. Simon Reisman, a former government official, seasoned, tenacious, sometimes volatile, and experienced in negotiating with the United States was appointed as the special negotiator. He operated with a relatively large, high-quality staff seconded for the effort from ministries across the government. Reisman quickly assembled a staff of roughly 110 of whom forty were professionals, demonstrating early the depth of the Canadian commitment to the effort.

The U.S. organization for the negotiations provided a sharp contrast. No seasoned former official was assigned the task. No large staff was assembled. No regular, direct access to the President and his senior officials was considered vital. Peter Murphy, 37 at the time of his appointment as the U.S. negotiator, had served for four years in Geneva representing the United States at the GATT. Well-liked and regarded within the Office of the U.S. Trade Representative (USTR), Peter Murphy's Geneva assignment had not given him a high profile within Washington. Calm, composed, meticulous, and respected, he was not well known at senior levels in the U.S. Government. The staff assigned full-time to the negotiations was Spartan, totalling four including Murphy and his able deputy Bill Merkin. Instead of a large USTR-based staff, Murphy relied on a loose interagency collection of sub-cabinet political appointees and civil servants, which came to be known as the "core group," drawing expertise and analysis from across the executive branch.

The differences in organization contributed to an underlying tension that emerged periodically during the negotiating process. From the Canadian viewpoint, the low-level, skeletal organizational arrangements conveyed the appearance that the U.S. did not take the negotiations seriously. This impression was reinforced by the limited visibility accorded the negotiations in the public press and in statements by senior government officials. Likewise, there was a feeling in Canada that the U.S. was insensitive to Canadian public opinion which followed the negotiations closely.

CONSTRAINTS • The constraints operating on the two governments again illuminated significant differences. For the Canadian government, the first constraint was to reverse past positions and to overcome the legacy of the past. The Progressive Conservative Party had opposed an agreement in public discussion preceding the September 1984 election. The conversion to seek an agreement, what one senior Canadian official referred to as "a road to Damascus reversal," was aided by encouragement from the Canadian business community, and by support within the upper reaches of the Canadian civil service.

The decision by the new Prime Minister and Cabinet to seek an agreement, however, was a modest hurdle compared with the need to convince a skeptical public with understandable concerns over such an arrangement with a larger, more powerful partner. The visibility of the issue in Canada sensitized political antennae across the country.

In the United States, the constraints were less public and more intragovernmental. In accordance with statutory provisions, President Reagan notified Congress in November 1985 of his intention to commence negotiations with Canada on a free trade agreement. While positive congressional action is not required, either house, looking to the Senate Finance Committee and the House Ways and Means Committee, has sixty days in which to vote a resolution blocking the commencement of such negotiations.

USTR officials considered a hearing before the Senate Finance Committee as an appropriate forum in which to outline the administration's objectives. They discovered that protectionist sentiment was stronger than they had anticipated. One recalled that a private canvassing of members found fourteen of the twenty Senate Finance Committee members opposed to the negotiation. Irritation over softwood lumber, textiles, footwear, and subsidies had eroded the administration's credibility with the Congress. Only a concerted bipartisan effort, including presidential importunings and skillful advocacy by David Boren (D-Oklahoma), led four Senators to shift their votes, producing a 10–10 tie that allowed the negotiations to begin with a somewhat less–than–ringing endorsement.

STRATEGY • The U.S. and Canada similarly took very different approaches to the structure and pace of the negotiations. The Canadian negotiators led by Simon Reisman, with access to and encouragement from the highest levels of the government, at the outset sought to resolve large conceptual issues that would form the basis for a comprehensive agreement. The Canadian approach was driven by an overall vision and confidence that, if the agreement as a whole was satisfactory, it would command a majority in Parliament and support by the public.

The U.S. strategy, sensitive to the wake-up call delivered by the Senate Finance Committee, rested on carefully managing relations with Congress and not letting the negotiations get ahead of the political process of patiently building a coalition in support of such an agreement. The approach was to work away at the micro-level, tackling the task piece by piece, consistent with the organization of the "core group." It called for methodically removing sectoral irritants first and keeping open the largest issues for the end game.

Peter Murphy understood the task, his role, and the limits on his mandate as a negotiator. He would leave to his boss, Clayton Yeutter, the U.S. Trade Representative, and to James Baker, the Secretary of the Treasury and head of the Economic Policy Council, resolution of the final issues. Understandably, this approach left Simon Reisman and his highly organized and eager Canadian negotiating team, frustrated with the pace and content of the negotiations.

Individuals and Ideas

Accounting for the success of the Canada-U.S. Free Trade Agreement negotiation given the differences in organization, constraints, and strategies, requires more than a recognition of the combination of fear and opportunity. People, moments, and ideas also played a role and the reflections of the negotiators a decade after its signing helps illuminate many of those contributions.

For Canada, the agreement loomed large on the political horizon, an issue on which the government could rise or fall. Few characteristics are so cultivated by elected officials as a reputation for consistency, particularly with respect to campaign promises. Launching the negotiations required a change of course from its campaign rhetoric by the first Mulroney government, a shift made early in its life when the honeymoon provided by the flush of victory often eases such moves. Greater courage was required as the process labored on and another election was required before the agreement was finally implemented after the second Conservative election victory in the fall of 1988.

Simon Reisman also played a pivotal role, not merely as an indefatigable negotiator but by lending his reputation for integrity and high standards to the outcome. At a crucial moment in the negotiations, on 23 September 1987, with the clock ticking on the congressional grant of authority for the U.S. negotiators, the talks reached an impasse prompting Reisman to seek and gain approval from his Canadian masters to walk out of the negotiations leaving the next steps in doubt. In the end, the event signaled an elevation of the negotiations. When the talks resumed they actively engaged Mulroney's chief of staff, Derek Burney, and U.S. Treasury Secretary James Baker. Reisman's role, now diminished, was not extinguished. His reputation and extended visibility combined with the divisions within the Canadian electorate on the issue left him with a de facto veto. Close observers of the process on both sides of the border have suggested that had Reisman opposed the agreement as finally negotiated, it would have been virtually impossible for the Mulroney government to secure the approval of Parliament and the country. His support for the final agreement proved crucial.

Not least, Derek Burney played a pivotal role early and often. As the Ministry of External Affairs official entrusted with organizing the "Trade Policy Review" that led to the initial Canadian initiative, to his reassurance of a new Prime Minister that launching the effort at the Shamrock Summit was both economically and politically wise, to his concluding the negotiations with senior U.S. Treasury and USTR officials, Burney provided remarkable continuity and commitment to the effort. Elected officials need those around them in whom they can repose confidence and who have the ability to close deals. For Brian Mulroney, Derek Burney was such an aide. Finance Minister Michael Wilson, who accompanied Burney for the final negotiations and provided reassurance throughout the process, was another.

The U.S. government was also filled with individuals who contributed greatly to a successful outcome. Much has been written about the crucial role of Congress and the bipartisan nature of the support the pact received. David Boren (D–Oklahoma) led the way in corralling Democratic support for permitting the negotiations to commence. Bill Bradley (D–New Jersey) and Daniel Patrick Moynihan (D–New York) helped secure agreement to support the new binational dispute resolution panel.

At pivotal points, President Reagan gave direction to his team and used his political capital with reluctant members of Congress. Reagan's support for such an agreement originated well before his assuming the Presidency. Close associates recall his having discussed with them in the mid–1970s the idea of a free trade agreement involving Canada and Mexico. As in many policy arenas, Reagan was blessed with a sense of timing, understanding the gestation period of an idea or initiative. Some of his most cherished accomplishments such as tax reform and the Canada–U.S. Free Trade Agreement came during his second term in office.

The team at the Office of the U.S. Trade Representative— Clayton Yeutter, Peter Murphy, Bill Merkin, Alan Holmer, and Judy Bello—

skillfully orchestrated the drama being played out in multiple arenas. Though small in number, whether dealing with the large, determined Canadian negotiating team led by Simon Reisman, or coordinating the multitude of executive departments represented on the "core group," or cultivating support for the pact with members of Congress, they succeeded in every act of the drama.

In closing the deal, the Department of the Treasury, led by James A. Baker and his deputy Peter McPherson, proved crucial. Baker had a remarkable relationship with Ronald Reagan, gaining his trust and confidence while serving for four years as his first White House Chief of Staff and then as Secretary of the Treasury. His negotiating skill rested in part on his acute sense of the shape of the possible and on his sensitivity to congressional interests and concerns that inspired trust on both ends of Pennsylvania Avenue. Baker's comment to his Canadian counterpart, Michael Wilson, in April 1987, that the real action would commence in the final days leading to the October deadline proved prophetic. It also revealed his exquisite understanding of the ebb and flow of a successful negotiation.

Great undertakings, when tenaciously pursued, acquire a sense of momentum— a strong vested interest in completion, especially at the end of an administration. This momentum generated within the government and business communities in both the United States and Canada sustained the process at crucial moments. Persuaded of the economic benefits and encouraged by businesses eager to maintain competitiveness in a global marketplace, officials in both countries persisted in their quest to produce a mutually beneficial pact, in the process devising a dispute resolution mechanism that has proved durable and a model for subsequent agreements. The negotiation demonstrated that both people and ideas matter.

Many consider the statements of public officials little more than inflated rhetoric. The conclusion of Ronald Reagan's statement on 4 October 1987, however, is one that has stood the test of time:

> "I congratulate Prime Minister Mulroney for his courage and foresight in seeking this free trade area. It will strengthen the bonds between our nations and improve the economic performance and competitiveness of both countries. The agreement will provide an enduring legacy of which both nations can be proud."[5]

---

5   Statement on Canada–United States Free Trade Agreement, 4 October 1987, *Public Papers of the Presidents of the United States, Ronald Reagan 1987*, Book II (Washington, D.C.: United States Government Printing Office, 1989), p. 1132.

Part One

THE NEGOTIATIONS

It is my privilege to introduce a man who had a pivotal role in American politics in the 20th century. James Baker III has served in senior government positions under three United States presidents. He served as the nation's 61st Secretary of State from January 1989 through August 1992 in the Bush administration. During his tenure at the State Department, Secretary Baker traveled to 94 countries, as the United States confronted unprecedented challenges and opportunities in the post-Cold War era. Prior to assuming the role of Secretary of State, he served as Secretary of the Treasury— the 67th Secretary— in the Reagan administration in the years 1985 to 1988. And prior to that, he had served as Chief of Staff to President Reagan from the beginning of his Presidency in 1981. He even has a Michigan connection because his distinguished record of public service began in 1975, when he served as Under Secretary of Commerce in President Ford's Administration.

Much has been written and said about Secretary Baker. In his book Politics of Diplomacy: Revolution, War, and Peace, 1989-1992, *he reveals a secret to the high achievement in life: "Personally and professionally, for as long as I could remember, my inclinations were to go out and get things done, rather than sit around and think about them." That quality was much on display as he led the way in Washington. Secretary Baker practiced law with the firm of Andrews & Kurth from 1957 to 1975. Early on, he was a Princeton graduate. He was an officer in the Marine Corps. He received his J.D. with honors from the University of Texas Law School in 1957. That is something that Michigan's First Lady, Michelle, is proud to share— a degree from the same law school in Texas. In 1991, Secretary Baker was awarded the Presidential Medal of Freedom for "Outstanding contributions to the security or national interests of the United States and to world Peace." He has received many other awards for distinguished public service and numerous honorary academic degrees. Today, he serves as honorary chairman of the James A Baker III Institute for Public Policy at Rice University, a distinguished public policy institution. He is also senior partner in the law firm Baker & Botts, and Senior Counsel to the Carlyle Group, a merchant banking firm in Washington, D.C.*

One of Secretary Baker's finest accomplishments is the Canada–U.S. Free Trade Agreement. When President Reagan signed that historic agreement 10 years ago, he said: "This is a moment future historians will sight as a landmark— a turning point in the forward march of trade, commerce, and even civilization itself." And Secretary Baker played a key role in bringing that about. When Secretary Baker stepped down from the Treasury, Business Week *said this about him: "Baker's skill at the game is what will ensure his place in history. He will be remembered for recognizing that the U.S. had lost the power to dictate economic policy for the industrial world. Through negotiations, the pragmatic and wily Baker not only eased the way into a new era, but usually emerged with the lion's share."*

John Engler
Governor of Michigan

PRESENT AT THE CREATION: THE U.S. SIDE

James A. Baker III*

Thank you, Governor Engler, for an overly generous introduction. I am delighted to be here today, and particularly delighted that Peter McPherson called me some time ago and said "How about jointly sponsoring with us at Michigan State— a conference on the Tenth Anniversary of the Canada–U.S. Free Trade Agreement?" I quickly said that yes, we at the Rice Policy Institute would be delighted to do that. It is apparent to me that Peter, as he usually does, has put together a first–rate conference.

I want to begin by paying my respects to two people that you will hear from during the course of this conference. Ambassador Derek Burney, who was instrumental in the negotiation of this agreement on behalf of Canada. He was Brian Mulroney's chief of staff at that time and, like myself, got involved perhaps a little late in the process. He was able, and had the ear of the Prime Minister, to help push that agreement through. Mike Wilson who was the finance minister of Canada at the time, was equally heavily involved. Mike has just returned from several days of fishing with me at my ranch in Wyoming. While we had a tough time bargaining and negotiating the Trade agreement, some of the friendships that formed during the course of negotiations lasted until this day.

When you have served as long as I have in Washington, D.C., and in the jobs that I held, you become reasonably well known to people in this country. And having served for four years as Secretary of State, you get to be pretty well known across the water too, because our Secretaries of State tend to get a lot of coverage on TV. So it used to be that whenever I walked down an airport concourse some people would recognize me or they'd come up and either cuss me out or say something nice, depending upon what they thought about the job I had done. After having been out of office for five and a half years it doesn't happen quite as often. Yet it still happens on occasion. And not long ago I was walking down some

*James A. Baker III, is Senior Partner in the law firm of Baker & Botts and a Senior Counselor to the Carlyle Group. During the Reagan Administration, he served as Secretary of the Treasury and chair of the President's Economic Council from 1985 to 1988. From 1989 to 1993 he served as President Bush's Secretary of State.

concourse and I could tell that this guy recognized my face, but he had no idea who it was. Still, he did a little double-take as people will do after they pass you and recognize the face. He looked at me and said, "I know you. You're Jim Baker." Well, I swelled up with pride and said, "Indeed, sir, I am Jim Baker." This guy never batted an eyelash and said, "I knew it. And how's Tammy Faye?" So you see, Governor Engler, what awaits you when you've been out for five and a half years.

Looking around this room, I am struck by how distant the Canada–U.S. Trade Agreement seems today. It's not just a matter of how much older we veterans of the negotiation have become. But it's also because so much has happened since the 1985–1988 timeframe, when many of the individuals in this room worked so long and hard to make the dream of that free trade agreement come true. In the economic arena alone, the years since the FTA have been years of extraordinary change and dramatic progress. The agreement itself has been expanded by NAFTA to include Mexico. The Uruguay round of GATT has been completed, and we've seen the establishment of the World Trade Organization. We've even seen an agreement, in principle, by the countries of North and South America to create a hemispheric free trade zone, and last but not least, the pace of globalization has accelerated, ushering in an era of unparalleled economic integration globally.

Far from diminishing the importance of the FTA, these developments point to the real significance of this agreement. This is because the agreement represented an important mark in the then-emerging global trend toward liberalization of trade and investment. So I submit that the FTA was historic in ways that were not fully realized at the time.

But historic or not, I'm here to tell you, and I'm sure my Canadian colleagues will second this, that this agreement very nearly didn't happen. When looking back, there is a natural tendency to imbue decisive events like this agreement with an aura of inevitability. The Agreement was anything but inevitable. Michael Hart, who has written a book about it, echoed the Duke of Wellington's comment on the battle of Waterloo when he described the agreement as a near-run thing. And as those of us who were involved remember very well, the negotiations leading up to this agreement were protracted, they were very painful at times, and more than once, they collapsed. The fact that there was an agreement at all is testimony to the personal commitment and the physical stamina of negotiators on both sides.

Speaking from my personal experience, I had been involved with the general course of the negotiations from the beginning, first, as President Reagan's White House Chief of Staff and later as Treasury Secretary. But my role changed dramatically in the month prior to the deadline for submission to our Congress, when President Reagan asked me to be the point-man on the Agreement. My mandate was clear: If a reasonable agreement were at all possible, get it. I had been engaged in intensive negotiations before that, having been a business lawyer for 20 years, and also having served four years as White House Chief of Staff and a year or two as Secretary of the Treasury. And I was gonna undertake some additional sensitive negotiations as Secretary of State during the Bush administration. From that background of experience I can tell you that very few negotiations compared in complexity of the material, or the contentiousness of the issues with what we confronted in late September and early October 1987. Many of the people present here were participants in that last weekend marathon of negotiations in Washington that led us to a final agreement. It was an experience that I will never forget. I remember all those hectic, hurried, and harried, down-to-the-wire meetings with our American team in my office, following which we would wander across the hall and have the same kinds of discussions with our Canadian colleagues in the conference room. I clearly remember the emotions I felt when the agreement was finally struck. It was a strange mix of elation and exhaustion that I suppose was shared by everybody present. We had persevered and we had succeeded.

I would like to tell you why we were able to succeed against some extraordinary long odds, and then venture a suggestion as to what that success has meant, both for the United States and Canada, and perhaps even for the rest of the world. Let me first turn to the 'why.' First and foremost is the imperative of leadership at the very top. As important as the work of the negotiators was, the FTA was really ultimately the creation of two men: Ronald Reagan, and Brian Mulroney. Only these two individuals could commit their respective bureaucracies to the very difficult process of negotiating this pact. And only they could provide the vision necessary to bring public opinion behind the agreement. Only they could make the hard political decisions required to reach an agreement. Now Brian Mulroney and Ronald Reagan were and are quite different men—by age, by background, and in many other respects. But both of them shared, first of all, a profound belief in the importance of free trade, and secondly, the political courage to pursue that belief in the face of significant domestic opposition. That commitment and courage were perhaps most clearly articulated in March, 1985 at the Quebec city summit when President Reagan and Prime Minister Mulroney pledged themselves to freer trade and investment between Canada and the United States. But they were also to prove critical in the difficult years of negotiation that followed. Both of them placed the Free Trade Agreement at the very top of their administrations' respective agendas. And if they had not done this there would be no FTA. As with all major foreign policy initiatives, active, sustained leadership at the top was truly indispensable.

A second lesson to draw from the negotiations is the importance of political pragmatism. I readily admit to a personal bias. I am an unabashed pragmatist, albeit, a principled one. During my entire public life I have been criticized, sometimes harshly, for my supposed preference for a deal over the ideal. I plead guilty. But I plead guilty only so long as the deal in question gets us closer to the ideal we desire. And that's why I call it principled pragmatism—because it is a pragmatism that doesn't abandon principle. In my experience, pragmatism, which is really a way of recognizing political limits, is a prerequisite to any successful negotiation. From a negotiators point of view, that pragmatism has to be twofold. First, the negotiator has to be aware of the political dynamic within his or her own country. This dynamic is all the more complicated in a democracy, where interest groups are varied and vocal, and power is divided and diffuse. Such complexity is particularly acute in the United States, where in contrast with the parliamentary system such as Canada's, party discipline is weak and authority is shared by the executive and legislative branches of government. It is even more acute when the United States has a divided government (such as we have today, and as we had back then when we were trying to negotiate this agreement), where Congress is controlled by one party, and the White House controlled by another. A pragmatic sense of what will or will not sell politically, is absolutely key. I spent much time and effort during the negotiations gauging Congressional opinion and cultivating bipartisan support from the friends of free trade on Capitol Hill.

But the negotiator must also be aware of the political constraints under which his or her counterparts labor. Here I suspect that our Canadian friends came to these negotiations better prepared than we were. I think there is a tendency, regrettable but real, for Americans to take their northern neighbors for granted. Canadian politics, like our very own, are complex, contentious, and prey to all the contradictory influences of an open society. But if we were a little slow at the beginning to grasp Canadian sensitivities, we had become, by the end of the negotiations, experts by necessity. In such decisive and divisive areas as subsidies or dispute settlement, a sense of just how far our Canadian counterparts could go politically proved critical in hammering out the final compromise.

That brings me to what I consider to be the third lesson from the FTA experience: the importance of proactive policy making. We would be wise to remember just how strong the protectionist sentiment was in both of our countries at the time this treaty was negotiated. Here in the United States, our large trade deficits—larger as a percentage of GNP than they are today—resulted in many Congressional calls for punitive measures against major trading partners. There was political pressure on the Reagan administration to do something and we were constantly responding to various protectionist initiatives coming from the Congress. That put us in the position of occasionally taking action that we might otherwise have avoided, in order to avert even more dangerous measures on the hill, particularly in the area of exchange rates. The FTA, like NAFTA later on, allowed us to move beyond political passivity, by changing the terms of the debate from specific trade figures and individual industries to broader national interests and more open trade and investment. Perhaps the same thing held true for our Canadian counterparts. The importance of a proactive trade and investment policy holds true today, but the current administration failed to address that over the last couple of years. The President's decision not to seek fast-track negotiating authority prior to the 1996 election, because of pressure from the protectionist wing of his party, was counterproductive; it is certain to embolden precisely the protectionist interests that he's seeking to placate. As the FTA reminds us, it is simply not enough for supporters of free trade and investment to put their fingers in the dike when it springs a leak caused by protectionist pressure. Instead, we must build new dikes that open up ever more of the world economy to free trade and investment. The best defense is a good offense. And the FTA is a dramatic and educational case in point.

Let me conclude with a consideration of what the FTA has meant for our two countries and indeed for the world. First is the two-way increase in trade and investment that the agreement has fostered. Like any major effort at economic liberalization, the agreement has no doubt created both winners and losers. But on balance, the winners have clearly outnumbered the losers, and the net effect of the agreement has been to increase trade and investment. The result: higher economic growth, and with it, more jobs and higher wages in both the United States and Canada. Secondly, the FTA set the stage for NAFTA, and thereby the creation of a free trade area of 370 million inhabitants, reaching from the Yukon to the Yucatan. In some ways the issues in negotiating NAFTA were more difficult than those of our bilateral FTA. For all of our differences, and there were plenty, the economies of the United States and Canada are fundamentally similar in terms of per capita output and sectoral composition. By no stretch of the imagination could the same be said of the Mexican economy, on the one hand, and the United States and Canada on the other. That

NAFTA was negotiated, and was negotiated so quickly, was due, in large part, to the lessons learned from the negotiations leading up to the FTA.

Third, the FTA and its direct descendent NAFTA, have laid the groundwork for a hemispheric free trade zone. We should all be deeply disappointed by the lack of progress since the agreement, in principle, to establish a hemispheric FTA at the Miami summit back in the mid-1990s. The Clinton administration mishandled the request for fast-track trade negotiating authority from the Congress. That, coupled with the President's reluctance to take tough positions with Congress, given his current troubles, and coupled with the fact that the Vice President has to keep his eye on an important Democratic constituency as he looks to the nominating process in the year 2000, does not bode well for fast-track trade negotiating authority any time soon. It is very important to the United States that Congress give the President that authority. And it will have to be a bipartisan effort. There were many positive Republican votes on the failed attempt of last year, but not many Democratic votes. We need to bring along the Democrats and also to get even more Republican votes. But the above reasons raise serious doubts about whether we can look for fast-track trade negotiating authority in advance of the 2000 presidential election. I'm still enough of an optimist to believe that a hemispheric free trade zone will ultimately be created, if only because it is so obviously in the interest of all the countries involved. And I know that such a zone is even conceivable today because of the earlier successes of the FTA and NAFTA.

Fourth, the FTA demonstrated that regional arrangements, if they are properly crafted, need not be in conflict with broader efforts to liberalize trade and investment. Far from undermining the GATT-Uruguay round as some had feared at the time, the FTA actually complimented it. This is an important lesson in a world where the possibility of competitive trading blocs remains a constant threat to further progress toward free trade and investment.

Fifth, and perhaps the most important lesson, the FTA recommitted both Canada and the United States to openness and to the optimism that have always been our greatest strengths. After all, we're both relatively new nations, we are both largely populated by immigrants, and we are both dedicated to the democratic ideal. This openness to the new, whether new citizens or new ideas, is a powerful common tradition, and also a compelling call to joint action. By committing our countries to look outward rather than inward, by fostering self confidence instead of fear of competition, the FTA symbolized and strengthened, in a way that transcended economics, the very best of our respective national characters.

Chesapeake Bay in late July is normally a very hot place to be on a boat. But 31 July 1985, proved to be an exception. Ambassador Burney had called me earlier in the month to see if we could meet somewhere to talk about the future of Canadian–U.S. trade relations. And, ever eager to escape Washington, I suggested that we meet on my boat, a 34-foot Sabre Sloop, Wind. To my pleasant surprise, Derek accepted and we agreed on the 31 July date.

But between the earlier discussion, which had taken place in Hull, Quebec, and our scheduled meeting on the Bay, the political leadership in Canada changed. So when Derek called and suggested that we get together again because of some "changed circumstances," I immediately agreed, and hence came the meeting on Chesapeake Bay. We hoisted the sails, cut the motor, and for the next six hours had one of the finest sails on the Bay I have ever experienced. And after a delicious lunch, and while still tearing up and down the bay at a good seven and a half knots, Derek turned to me and said, "Well Mr. Ambassador, it's time we get down to serious business."

With that, Derek broached the notion of a full free trade agreement; none of this sectoral partial stuff. He stated that the new Prime Minister had personally examined Canadian trade flows and had come to the obvious conclusion: Canada's trade was inexorably tied to that of the United States. Hence, it was in the economic interest of Canada that a closer trade relationship be established forthwith, with its biggest market. Derek said that, in suggesting the full-fledged free trade agreement, the Canadians would want just two things: Exception from the application of U.S. Dumping and Anti-Subsidy laws, and a gradual phase-in, indeed a back-end loading, of tariff eliminations. I responded by saying that the U.S. would have two demands: Immediate abolition of the infamous Herb Gray Investment Board, and a faster implementation of Canadian tariff reductions, given the fact that Canadian tariffs were already higher than U.S. tariffs. And that is how it all started; It was born on my boat named Wind, now sold to an owner in Portland Maine.

Sure he's been Ambassador to the United States, Chief of Staff to the Prime Minister, the Canadian Sherpa, etc. But in my view, history books of another generation will cite his most remarkable contribution as the originator of the Canada–U.S. Free Trade Agreement, all of which began on that hot, delightfully windy day in the Chesapeake Bay.

Michael B. Smith
Former Senior Deputy
United States Trade Representative

PRESENT AT THE CREATION: THE CANADIAN SIDE

Derek H. Burney[*]

It's true Mike and I were both involved at the beginning, first with the limited sectoral approach, which didn't get off the ground because it was too limited. And second, on the famous boat trip in which we tested the water on the prospect of a broader negotiation. But I will give a little more diplomatic spin on it. We did make it clear that some relief from unilateral U.S. trade remedy would be the best for Canada, and Mike was equally explicit about seeking relief from Canadian restraints on American investment. As it turned out, these were fundamental keys to success for both sides. And in the end what was negotiated was a compromise on both: A limited but binding dispute settlement mechanism to satisfy our objective, and increased ceilings for review of U.S. investments coming into Canada.

Mike and I went on to other things and left the heavy lifting to the hearty professionals, many of whom are here tonight. I am pleased to be here to join in the tenth anniversary commemoration of this trade agreement and I want to add my congratulations to our host, Peter McPherson, to Charlie, Nancy, and their associates at Michigan State for taking the initiative and for assembling such an illustrious audience of trade warriors from the past and present. I have a minor complaint, and that's about speaking after dinner. That's a deadly chore for anybody. I learned that very quickly in my assignment in Washington because one of my first speaking engagements was a dinner speech to the American Association of Newspaper Editors and Publishers. As I began to speak there was a guy at the table right beside me in the front who started to speak at the same time in a very loud voice. So I tapped the mike to make sure I got his attention. It didn't work. I then turned to the person next to him and said, could you please shut him up? Nothing. Finally I gave up and leaned into the mike and started speaking very loudly in the hope that

---

[*]*Derek H. Burney is President and CEO of CAE, Inc., in Toronto. Burney was Ambassador to the United States from 1989 to 1993; from 1990 to 1992 he was the Prime Minister's personal representative in the preparation for the Houston, London, and Munich G-7 economic summits.*

it would carry. At the end of the speech, I was standing at the exit and I could see this guy stagger towards me and I thought: he is coming up to apologize. And he came up, grabbed my hand, and said, "Mr. Ambassador, I just want to tell you one thing. I love Canada."

Unlike Mike, I came back to the free trade negotiations. Free trade was a very key issue on our Prime Minister's agenda and I was obliged, as his Chief of Staff, to monitor the negotiations very closely. I had been involved in the preparation of the meetings between the President and the Prime Minister, including the one in Quebec in March of '85 which also helped launch the initiative. It was eleven years ago this month that I met Jim Baker and we had our first real discussion about the free trade agreement. At that time, the formal negotiations had been going on for about 18 months and they were making little headway. Frustration was setting in. We met at the annual IMF–World Bank meetings in September 1987, together with our Finance Minister Mike Wilson and our Ambassador Allan Gotlieb. I had been asked by the Prime Minister to convey a message of urgency to the Secretary of Treasury. Actually it was an attempt to get him involved. To give you a sense of the drama, if not the urgency of the moment, I recall asking Jim how it was that the Americans could contemplate concluding a nuclear arms reduction agreement with the Soviet Union, as it was then, but were unwilling to test the Congress with a free trade agreement with Canada. I thought it was a performance worth an Oscar. But it failed to move the distinguished Secretary—for a while anyway. And shortly after, as many of you in this room know, the formal negotiations ran aground, and then the fun began. Calls came from the White House, the other Baker, Howard, to try to restart the process. The major sticking point for us at that time was the issue of dispute settlement or, more generally, relief from unilateral trade remedy actions. Many formulas had been floated. All had sunk. Some with good cause.

For Canada, the prospect of eliminating our tariffs (higher on average than those of the U.S.) without some form of relief from unilateral trade action, was not affecting. The action that had bedeviled our exports of softwood lumber earlier in the 1980s was simply not worth the political price. In any event, when the formal negotiations broke down in September 1987, the Prime Minister instructed me to get directly involved. I had a very concentrated session with Simon's negotiating team and with individual Canadian ministers, including the Minister for Culture. That eventually led to the October weekend, the weekend after which U.S. negotiating authority would expire. In Canada, we knew what we could and could not accept. We knew, for instance, that an agreement which did not temper the unilateral, if not arbitrary, nature of U.S. trade remedy actions would not be saleable in Canada. As it was, there were expectations of total immunity which were impossible to attain, so we sought a respectable compromise. And in the end, thanks in large part to the tenacity of Jim Baker, Clayton Yeutter, and their officials, as well as some Canadian stubbornness, that is what we concluded.

There were, of course, other objectives from the Canadian side. For one thing, there had been calls from many quarters to "get things right" with the United States. That was seen as a litmus test for Canada, even though the definition of what was meant by getting things right was often more elusive than the objective. Many of us in the Canadian government had concluded further that if Canadian industry and our exporters were to be more successful globally, they needed, first of all, to have a stronger base for success here in North America. Adjustments were needed, not least in dismantling artificial barriers to effective competition and productivity within Canada. Above all, we sought a rules-based platform for our most crucial trade relationship, one which would reflect not simply a tariff-free regime, but would provide, as well, a greater degree of certainty for Canadian exporters. Trade and cultural products was a Canadian hot button, as Jim Baker confirmed to you this afternoon. But to say that this was not fully appreciated by our U.S. counterparts would be an understatement. Movies are a part of culture, and President Reagan was quite emphatic about the access he wanted for those. As for Jim Baker, at one point he told me bluntly, "In Texas, Derek, sugar is culture." No wonder we had such difficulty with definitions. So we tried to avoid sensitive terminology. In Canada we talked of freer trade. The Americans talked about free and fair trade. Euphemisms and labels gradually gave way to negotiations.

But the result triggered emotions in Canada on a scale no one had anticipated. As students of Canadian history, we knew the issue would be politically sensitive, after all, free trade had been attempted twice before. It defeated one liberal government in 1911. It intimidated another from going beyond very private, exploratory discussions in 1948. What made it politically more palatable for us in the mid 1980s were, first of all, the increasing importance of trade with the United States, and the particular success of the Auto Pact. Forty years of GATT negotiations provided an umbrella for a steady liberalization of Canada-U.S. trade. This meant that the concept of free trade was, in fact, a logical, and certainly not a radical extension of the prevailing trend. Equally, this trend placed a higher premium on the need for Canada to protect and preserve our existing access to the U.S. market, and to dampen concerns about U.S. trade remedy actions. A strong endorsement of free trade in September of '85 came from MacDonald Royal Commission appointed by the Trudeau government and headed by a former liberal cabinet member. And I might add the compelling rationale offered to the Prime Minister in a private memo by a retired, but certainly not retiring, public servant named Simon Reisman. And finally, but crucially, the firm support for free trade from Quebec and the liberal provincial government of Robert Bourassa. The concept of free trade had always been popular in western Canada; much less so in Ontario and Quebec. So the change of heart in Quebec was pivotal. Mr. Mulroney's government, although it had significant representation from all regions, was based on particularly strong support from the west and from Quebec.

Canadian support was one thing. U.S. interest was quite another. It was anything but a sure thing, especially at the outset. You may recall the first key vote by the Senate Finance Committee in Washington. It was a 10–10 tie, and very few of those votes had much to do with free trade with Canada. That day, I can recall vividly, began predictably in Ottawa, with about 20 people gathered in the Prime Minister's board room in anticipation of a good–news event. As the day progressed and the bulletins from Washington became more bleak, a contingency mentality took over. Messages in response to a defeat were hastily drafted. As the hours ticked by and the result became even more uncertain, the audience dwindled sharply. At one point, only Don Campbell and I were left in the room. Don't you dare leave, I suggested. He stayed, and when the verdict came in, the 10–10 tie, a tie meaning support, he and I celebrated quietly and the room quickly filled, once again, and the noise level increased. Proof positive that failure is often an orphan. Later on, there were times in the Canadian Cabinet, when had there been a vote, it would've probably been 10–1 against, but the one carries. The real point is that an agreement was negotiated, signed, and ratified by both governments.

We had an election in Canada over it because the senate refused at first to approve the agreement. The government won the election. It all seems so straight–forward now but ratification was no sure thing in Canada. The attacks were vicious. Proponents of the free trade agreement were accused of selling our birthright, our sovereignty, our economic policy levers, our health care system, and our water. Senior citizens were told they would be turned out of their old age homes by the Americans coming across the border. This is a threat which, incidentally, prompted concerned calls from both my mother and the Prime Minister's mother. What are you doing? One of the more peculiar rumors was that we had struck a private deal, guaranteeing that the Canadian dollar, then trading at $.82 U.S., would move to par within the first few years. It baffled me then to explain how we were to fulfill that secret agreement. It baffled the Bank of Canada even more. As I exchanged my dollar for $.64 U.S. to make this trip, I secretly wished we had made that agreement. But at least we now have a name for our new two-dollar coin in Canada. It's called the American dollar. What is remarkable is that attacks of this kind did not succeed.

Let me tell you that we had many versions of Ross Perot in Canada before Ross himself got engaged down here. A family court judge in Alberta issued a 128-page tract denouncing the agreement. It sold like hotcakes and had many of the same ingredients. And she received the Order of Canada. The opposition in Parliament, though split internally, was fervently opposed in public. Nationalist crusades were launched, fueled by more media attention than any other single issue or single interest group. The government was really not ready for that kind of no-holds-barred debate, nor were the generally supportive business and academic communities. During the 1988 election campaign, the polls raced down and then up. The debate was anything but civil. Mike Wilson, who is with us tonight, denounced the liberal leader as a liar. Mike Wilson for goodness sakes, whose harshest words about any opponent, until that day, were terms like "misguided" or "ill-informed." Our election in 1988 was what they call in Newfoundland a doozie. And I don't think there was ever a real understanding in Washington of the political risk that this whole venture posed for Canada and for our Prime Minister in particular. I promise not to try to explain it again to our American colleagues. The issue of free trade was highly controversial and politically very divisive in Canada. And the angst it aroused went well beyond any rational explanation of trade provisions.

There were many colorful moments in the negotiations and not just between delegations, sometimes within each delegation. On occasion, Simon was amazed at all the help he had on the Canadian side. Virtually everyone had an opinion and was determined to express it. At one point I recall walking with him in Ottawa on the Sparks Street Mall and we approached two saffron-robed Hare Krishna disciples. Without missing a beat, Simon asked them, "And what's your view on U.S. countervail?" Surprisingly they had none.

Prime Minister Mulroney was firmly behind the negotiation all the way and I think deserves the full credit for its success on the Canadian side. It was a major part of his broader agenda to improve relations with the United States— a position much more advantageous to Canada than popular for him. But he never blinked. He had a basic question at each critical step in the process: Will we be better off with this agreement than without it? He accepted, without question, the judgment of his team when we suspended the negotiations. And he accepted, with enormous relief and satisfaction, the unanimous recommendation from his team on 4 October 1987, that we sign the agreed outline. I can only echo the point that Jim Baker made earlier today about the importance of leadership from the top in securing this agreement. The Prime Minister did stump me at one point during the October weekend just as I had reported to him by phone on the breakthrough which gave us an agreement. "How," he asked, "Derek, will it play in Drumheller?" I thought quickly about Alberta, red meat, oil and gas, the things that were relevant to Alberta, and replied tentatively, "Probably pretty well, Prime Minister." "That's great!" he said.

From October to December, the teams grappled with the "legal text." It was another very serious round of negotiation. Getting the devil out of the details. The showdown weekend for that episode was in December in Ottawa. This time Jim Baker sent his deputy, our host, Peter McPherson, to carry the flag. After all, it was winter. Peter was accompanied by Alan Holmer and many others from the USTR. We debated and negotiated everything from the content percentages of autos, to the simulcasting of cable television commercials. As well, the American team raised what seemed then to be arcane points of constitutional law. Ultimately these gave rise to the extraordinary "panel provisions," informally labeled "The Dead Judge's Provision," intended for political or constitutional cover, but not really for use.

Two years into implementation, however, the so-called extraordinary provisions were invoked by the United States, not once, but three times. I was only there for two of them. Carla Hills was not moved by our explanations regarding the original intent. After all, she had not been there. I can only hope that those provisions may help beat back the current constitutional attack on NAFTA. But back in December 1987, the tone was civil, and the intent was deliberate. Both teams knew they had a task to complete, and that's what was accomplished. Peter McPherson was then, and is now, a class act. And I'm delighted that our respect and friendship is intact to this day. Implementation was a challenge, not just because of "Dead Judges." Back in the 1980s it was a bit out of fashion to contemplate closer economic ties with the United States. We were accused of hitching our wagon to a falling star. In fact, one of my first assignments as Ambassador was to speak in early 1989 at a forum in Jasper, Alberta, on the decline of America, the rise of Japan and the Asia–Pacific economies. Very fashionable back then. Thanks to my in–house guru, Bill Dymond, I made a very factual case, highlighting the continuing significance to Canada of the U.S. economic engine. At the time, comments like that were almost heretical. Today they seem prescient. Frankly, my intent at the time was simply to be provocative. Anyway, some falling star.

Even after the election, and primarily because of the recession in 1990–1991, the FTA became the scapegoat for all that ailed Canada. And we were not helped by the many squabbles over bilateral trade, from lumber, to autos, to beer and wheat. The dispute settlement mechanisms were tested to the limit, including the never–to–be–used extraordinary panel provisions. Fortunately they withstood the test and in time the trade flows started to soar. So much so that many of those who opposed the agreement at its inception, namely many in our current government, are now among its staunchest defenders and are championing free trade initiatives virtually everywhere. The agreement survived two difficult years of recession and today it's fully and very successfully in effect. Two–way trade has more than doubled. More than a billion dollars per day are crossing our border.

Perhaps more importantly, the agreement became a catalyst for NAFTA and, I believe, for success in the Uruguay Round of multilateral negotiations. Notably, the dispute settlement provisions were replicated both in NAFTA and the WTO agreement. Obviously the success of the FTA and NAFTA is what is fueling talk now of a free trade agreement for the Americas, a concept which would have been unthinkable ten or even five years ago. Actually my son, Ian, is involved on the Canadian side in that concept. If nothing else it proves the old adage, the sins of the father are being visited on the sons. Unquestionably, too, success on free trade helped forge a closer and much more constructive political dialogue between our two governments, starting at the very top. I happen to believe it proved beneficial on bilateral issues such as acid rain, and then elevating Canada's voice in major global issues and events during the Bush Presidency. And you don't have to take my word for it. Jim Baker wrote in his memoirs: "Many times, Mulroney would play a critical role in shaping our thinking." He added that, "The U.S. was fortunate to have the Canadians as solid and supportive friends." It did not prove to be politically popular for our Prime Minister on the home front.

Canadians can be a bit tentative about the kind of relationship they want to have with the United States. They want it to be friendly but not too friendly. They want it to be cooperative but not too cooperative. They want Canada's role to be distinctive. And some seek differentiation— even disagreement— as the hallmark of distinction. That can be very tricky for diplomats as well as for political leaders. But more than anything, this ambivalence is a reflex of the power and balance between our two countries which, in turn, creates a disproportionate risk for Canadian leaders who initiate agreements of any kind with the United States.

I do think the agreement has helped temper many trade disputes. They were not eliminated and there's still a tendency to lapse into managed trade solutions, beneficial to neither side. But the threat of unilateral action has abated, with the notable exception of Helms–Burton. Efforts to establish common rules on countervail and antidumping have made very little headway, overwhelmed perhaps by the more politically resonant issues of labor and the environment. There's still too much hassle on border entry, both for people and for goods, although recent action by the U.S. Senate to block even further scrutiny of Canadians was a welcome relief here in Michigan, as well as in Canada. Some bureaucracies die hard. I recall being challenged at the main border on returning one summer to Washington and asked very pointedly, "Are you carrying any potatoes?" "Only in my stomach," I replied. Bureaucrats are not the only die hards. One of the contenders today for the leadership for the conservative party in Canada was and is one of the most rabid anti–free traders. And he has a one–issue platform, believe it or not— scrap the FTA.

The FTA did pave the way for an open skies agreement, which is paying real dividends to the airlines and to the passengers. Instead of 14 cross-border direct air links, there are now have more than 50. Bill Merkin is, to this day, regularly featured in the Canadian media whenever anything happens on the trade front.

There's talk in some quarters of the desirability of a common currency, since the secret deal Canadian critics warned about never really seemed to materialize. But I'm not sure how readily Americans would adjust to a 64-cent dollar. There are also calls to reduce Canadian tax rates to a more competitive level with the United States, thereby stimulating more employment as well as investment. All of this suggests that there remains much honest work for officials, provided there is the requisite political will to get something done. And that seems a bit elusive, on both sides of the border.

I have mixed views on Canada being side-tracked from the U.S.-European Union talks on transatlantic free trade. There may be political reasons for this, including some considerations regarding fish, but there's certainly no trade reasons for Canada's exclusion, no more than there were to exclude us initially from NAFTA. It makes no sense to contemplate separate tracks towards the same destination, unless the underlying objective is political, and not trade. At the same time, I recognize that Canadian involvement in such talks, particularly if they are largely political, might simply embroil us in U.S.-European affairs and distract us from the pursuit of our more pressing trade and economic issues with the United States. The FTA was, to put it mildly, highly politicized in Canada, unleashing anxieties and fears that, in many cases, defied rational explanation. It was a precursor to the fervor in the United States over NAFTA, and more recently, the backlash to globalization. Obviously the Administration's failure, or was it reluctance, to obtain fast-track negotiating authority on trade is the most recent manifestation of the same trend.

Trade policy initiatives and practitioners are accustomed to the specific demands of particular sectors and to the instinctive preference to protect and preserve, rather than expand. But when pseudo-nationalists, environmentalists, church groups, labor unions, and others join the debate, there are very few precedents and even fewer techniques to temper and contain those attacks. Not surprisingly, politicians tend to run for cover. After all, their first priority is to get elected and reelected. They look for issues which unite, not those which engender visceral divisions. The business community, normally the backroom champions of liberalized trade is even less inclined to counter the new trade gladiators. For one thing businesses are preoccupied with the unrelenting pace of change, technological, financial and human, affecting most of their business. The theories which have anchored trade policy initiatives in the past are no longer sacrosanct. The law of comparative advantage means very little to an unemployed mill worker. An increase in exports will not assuage those who are fighting for cleaner air or for cleaner water.

To be successful, future trade policy initiatives, whether hemispheric or global in scope, will need even firmer political resolve and broader techniques of dialogue and persuasion. It is, of course, unfair to saddle trade agreements with all of society's contemporary grievances. Yet our leaders have little option but to take account of those concerns to try to shape a healthy consensus on environmental, labor, and other contentious issues to parallel or complement objectives on trade. I don't envy them the task. Back in 1987, there was political will on both sides. We were determined to conclude a good agreement for our Prime Minister and for Canada. I know that Jim Baker and Clayton Yeutter wanted to get a good agreement for their President and their country. Their will ultimately coincided with that on the Canadian side, and is what, more than anything else, prompted the success of those negotiations. There were many players on both sides whose devotion and persistence made the agreement a reality, many are here tonight, and I'm just delighted to salute each of them. As I look back, it's hard to believe it was more than ten years ago. Many of us have gone on to other things. But for me, the memory of that weekend in Washington and the follow-up in Ottawa is still very vivid. And the success for both countries of what was negotiated is a continuing source of genuine pride.

THE NEGOTIATING PROCESS

A panel discussion led by Roger Porter

The following exchange of ideas and thoughts occurred at a roundtable discussion, which was part of Michigan State University's September 1998 Conference on the Canada–U.S. Free Trade Agreement. The conference served three functions: 1.) as a retrospective on negotiating the agreement; 2.) a discussion of what has happened in the ten years since the agreement; and 3.) what the future holds for U.S.–Canada bilateral relations and multilateral trade. The panel was moderated by Professor Roger Porter from the Kennedy School at Harvard. Panelists, all U.S. and Canadian negotiators, included Michael Hart, Konrad von Finckenstein, Simon Reisman, Michael Wilson, and Derek Burney from Canada; and Peter McPherson, Alan Holmer, Clayton Yeutter, William Merkin, Jean Anderson, and Charles Roh from the United States.

Roger Porter: It is a delight for me to be here and join such a distinguished group to discuss such a fascinating topic. I doubt that we will ever again have quite an array of people who were in at the start, forging this agreement, and I'm looking forward to the interaction between them. No negotiation takes place in a vacuum. There is always a context. And so I want to begin our discussion by posing to the panelists the question: What were the principle factors animating the circumstances in Canada, and what was going on in the United States at the time that the negotiations commenced. Derek, what was going on in Canada at this time?

Derek Burney: The genesis for the free trade initiative in Canada came from a combination of factors. We had a royal commission which had conducted a study of future economic prospects. It concluded that a free trade initiative with the United States would be a leap of faith but one worth taking. We had attempted a limited, sector by sector, expansion of our earlier agreement. That proved difficult because of a lack of balance within given sectors. The government had been reviewing our trade policy since the early 1980s and there was a strong sentiment that we had to get things right with the United States even though it was not clear how that should be defined. The Prime Minister and President Reagan had a number of meetings in which they explored ways of expanding trade between the two countries, culminating in the Quebec Summit in March of 1985. Canada's concern was that we're becoming more dependent on our trade relationship with the United States but that high exposure made us more vulnerable. To expand trade, and yet avoid excessive dependence, Canadians concluded that we needed a broad based agreement— an agreement which not only liberalized trade but also provided greater security for our access to the U.S. market

Roger Porter: Now, Clayton Yeutter was assuming his role as United States Trade Representative. President Reagan had completed his first term and was beginning his second term. He shifted Bill Brock, who had been the U.S. Trade Negotiator to the Department of Labor, and appointed Clayton. How did you view the setting in which this negotiation with Canada was taking place?

Clayton Yeutter: While Canada's relationship with the U.S. was primarily a bilateral one, the U.S. needed a more activist trade policy worldwide. When I became USTR in mid–1985, during confirmation meetings, everybody on the finance committee told me: "Your Administration is oblivious to what's going on in world trade." Nobody in the White House is paying attention. We have the largest trade deficit in the history of the country, and yet nobody seems to even have the word "trade" on their lips. Somebody needs to do something about this. So it became apparent when I moved in as USTR that we had to change that attitude. Jim Baker, who was chairing the Economic Policy Council, held the same view. And so we went about putting together a strategy that would make the U.S. much more activist. That involved a number of pieces of which an agreement with Canada was a major one. Another ingredient was to start using section 301, retaliatory authority, in a far more aggressive way than had ever been done before. And then there was the multilateral component of getting the Uruguay Round going. Further, on the bilateral side, was raising the level of aggressiveness in negotiations with Japan and the European Union. That was the overall picture at the time.

Roger Porter: Both countries had been through a recession. There was an enormous amount of protectionist sentiment in the U.S. Congress. Jean, you were dealing with anti–dumping and countervailing duty pieces.

Jean Anderson: Beginning about 1980, there had been a round of steel cases that tried to curb imports of steel from just about everywhere in the world, and also the first of a number of cases by the U.S. alleging subsidies on Canadian softwood lumber. Canada prevailed in that case. Then, in the mid 1980s there was a second softwood lumber case filed, which resulted in a preliminary determination of a 15 percent subsidy. While this number was not a result of full investigation, the issue was resolved in 1986 with a Memorandum of Understanding between Canada and the U.S. But the level of trade–remedy cases reflected the protectionist tenor of the times and was a cause for concern. Certainly within the Commerce Department there was great concern that protectionist forces were getting the upper hand and something constructive had to be done to arrest this trend.

Roger Porter: It appears that we had two elements at work here, both in Canada and in the United States. One was the concern that the situation could deteriorate and that steps needed to be taken to make sure that it did not. The other was the element of opportunity; that some real gains could be achieved if we entered into negotiations. Every negotiation needs to get organized. Let us first see how the Canadian side decided to organize itself. Simon, you were the chief negotiator.

Simon Reisman: Yes I was. But perhaps you ought to ask Mike Wilson because he was in the cabinet working with the Prime Minister, while I never knew what led him to do this wonderful thing. He belonged to the Tory Party in Canada and the Tories were always opposed to these talks. (Incidentally, I'm nonpartisan.) And suddenly they had a change of heart. I think there was an opinion poll that said the people thought free trade was a good thing. What actually happened, Mike?

Michael Wilson: Brian Mulroney and I, in the leadership campaign in 1983, had both come out against free trade. So that there was a change of heart on the road to Damascus, but it wasn't a result of a major debate. Rather it was more by osmosis that we came around to thinking that maybe this is something we should try. It was a gradual shift, until we suddenly saw that this is the way we have to go, especially in light of the protectionist pressures.

Roger Porter: Mr. Reisman how did you organize at the beginning?

Simon Reisman: One day I received a call from the Prime Minister, saying, "Will you put together quickly a paper telling me how I should initiate discussions, and what are the issues and the substance. What are the risks?" I took a half a day to write something, about 8 or 9 pages, which laid out a bit of a blueprint. Probably Derek was one of the first people to see it because when the Prime Minister got it he asked his trusted friend, "What about this?" And God bless him, he said, "That's pretty good stuff. This guy seems to know what he's doing." In addition to Derek's influence, something else was important. I had the good fortune to be Canada's lead negotiator when we negotiated the auto pact. George Ball was in the State Department. That was really the beginnings of the free trade approach. We got involved in that because there were deep troubles in that industry. We tried to reconcile a protectionist history with a need to trade, and developed an interesting device, which the Americans threatened to countervail. It resulted in consultation, negotiation, and a successful agreement. It was understood that Canada, as the smaller of the two countries, needed a bit of a transitional period to adjust. We insisted on certain things and George Ball went along. And the auto pact would eventually lead to a free trade agreement.

Roger Porter: Simon, what size staff did you have?

Simon Reisman: I ultimately had a staff of 110 people of which there may have been 40 professionals. The best in the land.

Roger Porter: Let's go over to the U.S. side.

Simon Reisman: On the U.S. side they didn't know what they were up against. Their team consisted of only a dozen people. They did not take this very seriously, the way we did.

Roger Porter: Clayton, you were the new USTR. In February of 1986 you appointed Peter Murphy and Peter's deputy, Bill Merkin, is with us. How did it look to you and Peter in February of 1986?

Clayton Yeutter: It's nice to have Simon answer for both sides. In terms of numbers, Canada always had more financial and human resources than the United States. Simon was giving us a little slack with the number 12. I think we were really more like 4 versus 400. But numbers aren't everything.

Roger Porter: Quality counts for something. Bill?

William Merkin: From the U.S. perspective, this set of negotiations was one of a series of international trade initiatives we were undertaking. We had many issues with Japan and Europe. We were trying to get the Uruguay Round started, so the USTR, which, in itself is a very lean and mean organization, did not have the resources to put a team of a hundred to this one set of negotiations. And so Peter Murphy was brought back from Geneva—he was our Ambassador to Geneva—to lead the team. In addition to him and myself we had one other full-time staffer, for a total of three full time people at USTR working on this. Consequently what we had to do was set up the team drawing on the resources of other government agencies, and we put together what was called a core group.

We had a representative from Commerce, State, Agriculture, Treasury, Labor, and from time to time Justice came in. Some of us remember our stimulating meetings, trying to sort through how to deal with Simon and his team.

Roger Porter: In short, the situation in the U.S. is that trade policy responsibilities are scattered all across the government and the role of USTR is to coordinate and bring them together.

Clayton Yeutter: That's correct. We should give great recognition to Peter Murphy for his role. As you know he's no longer with us. But Peter had the wonderful attribute of being calm and composed in the eye of a Reisman storm.

Simon Reisman: We all speak well of the dead.

Roger Porter: Another interesting thing in the U.S. context is that our Constitution gives Congress the responsibility in the area of trade. There are actually three provisions in the Constitution that were linked to trade: First, there can be no duties erected on goods passing across state borders. Second, Congress is prohibited from imposing duties on exports which had been one source of revenue under the Articles of Confederation. And third, Congress, rather than the executive branch, was given the authority to impose duties on imports. So Bill, before you and Peter could get rolling with these negotiations, you needed Congressional authorization. Tell us, Alan, how that happened.

Alan Holmer: An initial letter from Prime Minister Mulroney came in in the fall of 1985, and in November of '85 President Reagan notified the House Ways and Means Committee and the Senate Finance Committee that we wanted to proceed with the negotiations. That gave those committees 60 legislative days to disapprove the negotiations. Some bright staffer on the Senate Finance Committee said: "Let's have a hearing on the U.S.–Canada Free Trade Agreement." Clayton went up for a private meeting in an anteroom of the Senate Finance Committee. It was a firestorm, followed by a hearing, whereby of 20 members on the Finance Committee, 14 opposed the agreement. They were mad about our trade policies in general, and about the trade deficit in particular. They were upset about lumber, about Canadian subsidies, about textiles, and about the footwear decision that had occurred the prior fall. About 300 bills were introduced at that time proposing quotas on steel and other products. Senator Packwood, the Chairman of the Finance Committee, was committed to having a vote on whether or not the committee should disapprove the negotiations. And finally, by the skin of our teeth, we were able to get a vote not to disapprove the negotiations of ten to ten.

Roger Porter: You were up there, Clayton. Tell us about that meeting.

Clayton Yeutter: That was a dicey session. We felt that we had the votes to survive as the voting began, and then suddenly Senator Bill Armstrong of Colorado emerged as a "no" vote, which caused no end of consternation as there was no margin for error. At that point, one of the unsung heroes of this exercise was Senator Dave Boren of Oklahoma, who had the good judgment to call for a recess. That gave us a couple of hours to round up another vote, that of Senator Matsunaga of Hawaii to counter the loss of Armstrong. It resulted from a call from President Reagan to Senator Matsunaga saying, "Let's look at the broad national interests. I need your vote. You can vote down this agreement ultimately, but at least let us try to proceed with the negotiations." So in a statesmanlike act Senator Matsunaga changed his position and allowed the negotiations to proceed.

Roger Porter: Let's turn to the Canadians and discuss your principle objectives; and how did you see these negotiations starting? Simon?

Simon Reisman: I was appointed chief negotiator before we had a mandate. I didn't want a mandate too early because I wanted to participate in making up that mandate and keeping it pretty broad. I had a courtesy visit from Clayton Yeutter. He was new in the job, and he brought with him an old–timer named Mike Smith, who is in this room. I was alone, and we had a good talk about our objectives; what we wanted was to expand opportunities for trade on a secure basis. We didn't feel secure with U.S. trade remedies, countervail, antidump. Then I said to Clayton Yeutter: "We need an inspirational objective and an inspirational theme. Why don't we set as our goal to have broader free trade and investment so that by the year 2000 there is no border between our two countries for trade in goods and services." Investment came later. Clayton reacted very positively. He thought that was pretty good. At that point, a doubtful Mike Smith turned to me and said, "Have you ever heard of the Congress?" I had the good fortune of negotiating with the United States from 1946 through the 80's in GATT, about the Auto Pact and oil and petroleum, so I knew about the Congress. In contrast, the Americans never knew about the provinces, or of the general attitudes in Canada about trade with the Yankees; so I said to him, "You look after the Congress, I'll look after the provinces and the Canadian people." We thought we'd make a good start and leave some work for people coming after us. Clayton gave his position away when he said that they had a big worldview and Canada was only one country; a country which never gave them much trouble.

Roger Porter: There was someone on the U.S. side who had the responsibility of paying attention, and that's Bill Merkin. Bill, you and Peter were trying to figure out how to begin these negotiations. What was going through your mind at that time?

William Merkin: We didn't know what we were getting into with Simon or we might have prepared differently. From a negotiator's standpoint we had the difficult task of not getting too far ahead of the political process. It was great to talk about free trade with Canada and the grand vision, but we had political constraints in the United States. We did not want to appear too negative on the one hand, or get too far ahead of Congress on the other. We sought advice from the Agriculture Department on how to deal with the agriculture section. We looked to Commerce for advice in the area of subsidies and countervailing duties. We had the Energy Department help us in the energy area; and Treasury help us with investment and the financial services. Our piecemeal process was frustrating to Simon. He came in with "let's open up the border," which we knew we could not achieve.

Roger Porter: Mike?

Michael Wilson: We wanted to get assured access; and if not we had to have some mechanism to prevent Canada from being overwhelmed by a country ten–twelve times our size. About 75 percent of our exports are destined to the United States, up from two–thirds a few years ago. This is an enormous exposure. In the fall of 1985 I met with Robert Strauss, who warned me: "In trade matters, we can be sons of bitches. The only advice I'll give you is if you intend to go ahead, you better protect yourself."

Derek Burney: So we got the best son of a bitch we could find.

Roger Porter: Clear, but succinct. Peter?

Peter McPherson: In Canada, the free trade agreement issue had come to possess the public. Lots of media focused on it. Simon and Peter became some of the best-known personalities in the country.

Simon Reisman: In Canada, but not in the United States.

Peter McPherson: In the United States, there were numerous industrial interests which were pushing individual Senators, but there was almost *no* public knowledge. And that difference in the public interest and perception had a significant impact on how each side approached the negotiation. That fact permitted us to operate in a much more systematic, methodical way. We didn't feel the pressures that the Canadian side felt, because this was one of many things on our agenda, yet we considered it much more important than Simon thinks we did.

Derek Burney: The point here is that there were different perceptions on both sides about the goal. The U.S. came at it with a laundry list of irritants, wanting to get as much political cover as it could. We were coming at it from the top, saying, "let's not talk about irritants, let's blaze a new trail, new rules–broad-based negotiation." I think the lesson we learned was that, despite preliminary consultations about what the reciprocal objectives of each country were, there was a mismatch from the very beginning. Another lesson was that the scope of what you're trying to negotiate should be better understood at the beginning on both sides, particularly at the political level, so that there's no misunderstanding between the two sides as to what the combined objective is. One of the things that hamstrung this negotiation was this mismatch about the objective. And I'm not saying this was anybody's fault.

Peter McPherson: Often there's a question of the personalities involved, Peter versus Simon, but it's important to underline Derek's point that there were mismatches that were more fundamental than personalities.

Roger Porter: Now one of these issues, Konrad, was countervailing duty and anti-dumping suits that were going on in the U.S. How did you on the Canadian side, view the best way to deal with this irritant?

Konrad von Finckenstein: Our goal all along was to get a waiver from anti–dumping and countervailing action; agree with the Americans on legitimate and illegitimate subsidies; and have a dispute settlement mechanism. After two years, when Derek came into the negotiation, we realized that that was unachievable and the whole focus shifted to the dispute settlement mechanism, emphasized solely by the U.S. side, the result of which would be enforceable in the U.S. by U.S. courts. It would then be the U.S. judicial system constraining the U.S. government, because nobody else can economically constrain the U.S. government.

Roger Porter: Chip, how did this look to you on the U.S. side?

Charles Roh: While it was always thought that we had an irritant approach, I was struck, in our delegation meetings, that the U.S. side wanted a big agreement and that's what we ended up with. Our negotiating style tended to focus on irritants, which led to many an aimless debate, but in the end what we got was a big agreement. It also took care of some irritants. The dispute settlement issue was a bit of a shock to us because we had come out of the U.S.–Israel agreement— our lone experience with a bilateral free trade agreement— which had an extremely modest consultative dispute settlement. Hence it was a puzzlement to us, at first, to be asked for a binding dispute settlement. This awakened the usual U.S. negotiators' fears about how to handle the Congress.

Roger Porter: Sovereignty.

Charles Roh: It always amuses me that the United States of 250 million people and the world's largest economic power seems to be terrified of entering into agreements with small countries for fear that they steal its sovereignty. It's one of our national paradoxes.

Simon Reisman: That brings to mind a story about Bob Strauss, who was the first USTR under Carter. He was Chairman of the Democratic National Committee, and at the time was working as a lawyer with the Bank of Nova Scotia in Canada, that had an important issue on extraterritoriality. One day I was asked by Sid Ritchie, the chief executive officer of the Bank of Nova Scotia, to come to New York and participate in a big meeting with some of their principle clients. Also in attendance would be Bob Strauss and Robinson of American Express.

Before the meeting which I was supposed to address, Sid said, "Bob *Strauss* wants to speak to you privately before the meeting begins." He sat me down and very sternly said, "I understand you are having a very difficult time in the negotiations." I concurred, not knowing who sent him or what his power was. And he said, "The reason you're having difficulty is you're expecting things that are not available. You want a whole new regime with respect to subsidies and the provisions of anti-dump. Get rid of those two sets of provisions, have a new set of rules, and a dispute settlement arrangement to oversee that, otherwise you are asking the impossible. So I said, "We're in this because we want secure trade with you. Eighty percent of our trade is with you; we are not going to make a deal unless we get some security, and I don't know any other way of doing it, maybe you do. If you people cannot find some compromise, some way of meeting us on these issues, there won't be an agreement." He replied, "How can you say that," implying who are you to say there won't be an agreement? So I said, "Because of the press and public opinion, I have much negative power in the country now. And if the agreement is not good, I will oppose it. And if I oppose it, there never will be an agreement." He was startled, and became quite a different animal. The point had been reached that if the chief negotiator said "no dice," it would have fallen through.

He took the message back. We tried to get that message through to the President at summit meetings on five different occasions. There was never a meeting of our two delegations that we didn't say to them, "You've got to meet us somewhere on these matters, or there is no agreement." Peter and his associates kept working along, never saying no. Never saying "you can't have it." In the end, I had to walk away. And it wasn't until we walked away that the President brought Baker and Clayton in and said, "Go and make a deal with them." Your side never appreciated how vital this was until we pressed the point a minute to twelve.

Roger Porter: Let's let the U.S. side speak for themselves. Alan?

Alan Holmer: This whole circumstance shows what a brilliant negotiator Peter Murphy was. In a sense, he was in a conundrum. What Canada wanted was an exemption from the U.S. anti-dumping and countervailing duty laws. Peter knew if he said no to that, that might very well kill the negotiations on the Canadian side. Yet if he said yes that would kill the negotiations as far as the U.S. Congress was concerned. As Simon indicated, he danced for a while until ultimately we were able to get on the same wave–length as Canada. He also realized that at some appropriate time this was going to be kicked "upstairs" to Clayton Yeutter and Jim Baker. He didn't want to give things away at that stage because he knew, at the end of the day, somebody else will be at the negotiating table. So he kept those cards close to his chest. It was a brilliant negotiating strategy, and it succeeded.

Simon Reisman: That's just wrong. He is rewriting history. It's got nothing to do with what really happened. Peter could not reach the cabinet.

Clayton Yeutter: Simon, you can't speak for the U.S. modus operandi because you weren't there. And I don't try to speak for what your modus operandi was. The fact is that Peter was in continual contact with all key players through me, and there were no secrets with respect to how things were proceeding. My personal judgment is that the government of Canada maintained it's position on the subsidy, countervailing duty, and anti-dumping authority too long. We would have completed this agreement at an earlier date had the Canadian position been altered earlier.

Simon Reisman: If we had given you everything you wanted and asked for nothing, we could have completed it at any time. That's always easy.

Clayton Yeutter: That was my opinion, Simon. Its your privilege to have a different opinion. The fact is that in the end it turned out the way it should have. In any major negotiation, at some point it goes up to the highest levels of government, and whatever remains to be done is ironed out there. That was done in very good-faith by both sides, and we ended up with an agreement that has been very beneficial to both countries. But to suggest that the U.S. was not paying attention, Simon, is not right.

Roger Porter: Every negotiation has a period of ups and downs. And in this one, there was a clock ticking that was going to expire on 3 October.

Clayton Yeutter: At midnight.

Roger Porter: Because that was the final date on which the U.S. could transmit the agreement to the Congress and still meet the provisions under the fast-track negotiating authority. In the third week of September there was a pivotal meeting at the office of the U.S. Trade Representative where the Canadian side walked out. I would like to get both sides perception of this particular event. Simon, what was it that caused you to walk out?

Simon Reisman: After a score of attempts to engage the Americans in discussions on issues of concern to Canada, such as anti-dumping, the Americans never met us at the table. We wanted to put limitations on subsidies and other offending measures; introduce a set of rules to be followed by both countries that would make it unnecessary to use the old countervailing device. The notion that we desired a waiver to do what we pleased is nonsense. The most I could extract was an exemption on some quantitative amount, that was unsatisfactory. So we walked. The Americans were absolutely shocked because the clock was ticking. They figured that Canada wanted this agreement so badly that all they had to do is wait us out and wear us down, and we would take what we could get. It was not I alone who made the decision; it was all our negotiators.

Roger Porter: What did you expect by way of U.S. reaction to your decision to walk out.

Simon Reisman: After I walked, the U.S. side right up to the President, figured, this madman has gone off, but this doesn't really reflect his government's view. Then a call came in from the President's office to the P.M.'s office. That's when the U.S. got serious. That's when the President called Jim Baker and said, "Jim, we want the agreement. Go and get one." It was Jim Baker who was charged by the President with this task, and he said: "The Canadians walked; they walked reasonably."

I expected the Americans to come back, because they wanted an agreement with Canada. The President and Baker were wise; they eventually came back, and we got an agreement.

Roger Porter: Let us hear from the U.S. side. What was your reaction to this incident?

William Merkin: Despite what Simon thinks, Alan hit it dead on. I remember numerous discussions with Peter Murphy early on, when he expressed concern that at some stage the negotiations would have to be settled at a political level. So when the formal walk-out occurred in Washington in September, the event itself came as no surprise. That it happened that day was of concern because we had thought we expected to make more progress that day. But if you recall, Simon, you all came in that day having already gotten authority from the cabinet to walk out, or so I assume.

Simon Reisman: That's absolutely false. You don't know what we had in our hands.

Konrad von Finckenstein: I was there when the press release was typed. It was typed at the USTR office by my secretary.

William Merkin: While we tried to keep the discussions going that day, we went from room to room to determine whether there was a basis to continue discussions. The fact that you walked out on the negotiations while unfortunate, was not totally unexpected. We figured early on that the ultimate decision would rest at the political level.

Simon Reisman: That was your perception, but Peter was really surprised that we walked out. He was persuaded that if he waited this thing out, we'd cave in. And I think that was the advice he was giving Clayton. Peter was absolutely shocked as he said to me, "Do you realize what you've just done to me? You've probably ruined my career."

Before we decided to walk, I said privately to Peter, "Peter, all you have to do is tell me that there is no way in which you can meet Canada on any of these matters, and we'll shake hands and go home and say, 'we'll come back some other day. The Americans aren't ready to do business now.'" Peter never did that. He was shocked that I left; he thought that we would sit there and reach an agreement, which includes nothing on the matters that were important to us. We didn't have a press release in our pocket. I didn't want to walk away because once I did so, I was turning the whole thing over to somebody else. I didn't want to do that after the effort I had put into it.

Roger Porter: Derek, how did this look from the vantage point of the Prime Minister's office.

Derek Burney: Every step was being taken in close consultation with the cabinet. The cabinet was meeting while Simon was in session at the USTR. He indicated that he wanted to walk and the cabinet in Ottawa considered his arguments and directed him to suspend the negotiations. This was an agonizing moment for the Prime Minister. But he accepted without any equivocation the recommendation from the team that the negotiations be suspended, knowing that this was jeopardizing his re-election which was coming within a year. So, there was nothing tactical about the decision. It was a conscious decision based on the fact that we could not sell what we were seeing. It was not politically saleable in Canada, and I think Clayton will remember that this point was made at one of our first meetings. At that point Clayton and Jim said, "Why don't we just do a tariff deal?" to which we replied that a tariff deal by itself just won't fly.

Out of all of this came the weekend negotiation which did bring about an agreement. The important thing is that it worked, regardless of whether it went to the political level too early or too late. This was a pivotal decision for Canada, much more so than our American friends would acknowledge. Much more so than it was for the United States. This could have determined the fate of the Canadian government and that's why it was particularly courageous of our Prime Minister to give his negotiating team the full authority to walk, as well as the full authority to come back and renegotiate.

Clayton Yeutter: Let me add another U.S. dimension. Having people walk out of negotiations may have troubled Peter Murphy, but it didn't trouble me. People often walk out of negotiations. Mike Smith made a whole career of walking out of negotiations. It's a unique tactic. Obviously by walking out you're sending a pretty strong message to the other side, assuming that it's not done in a cavalier fashion. It was not intimidating as far as I was concerned. What it did do was to indicate clearly that it was time to raise this up to the highest levels of government and resolve it one way or another. That brought Derek into the picture in a major way on their side, and Derek's U.S. counterpart was Howard Baker. But Howard was not very familiar with trade. So that brought in Jim Baker, not only because he had been the White House Chief of Staff, but because he was involved in Treasury. He had been very much a part of the financial discussions with Michael, and he was also chairman of the Economic Policy Council. So it was logical to bring Jim in at that stage. Jim and I worked closely together then those few days, as was done by the group on the Canadian side. I suspect, that had we not raised it to the highest political level at that point, the negotiation would have failed.

Michael Hart: In the Spring of 1987, we were getting frustrated; things weren't happening, and I twice encouraged Jim to get involved directly in the negotiations. He said very wisely, "We in Washington work to deadlines. We have a deadline on October 3rd this year and if you fellows up in Canada will relax, you'll find that we will all be around that table and sometime just shortly before midnight on 3 October and are going to get a deal." He said that to me in June 1987.

Roger Porter: As the title of Michael Hart's book indicates, this was a decision taken at midnight. We did go right up to the wire and did produce an agreement. But now we've had 10 years to live with it and reflect on it. So, in rapid–fire fashion, please go down each side and share with us what you think are the single most powerful lessons learned from this remarkable saga, and let's start with you, Michael.

Michael Hart: I think the chemistry right here at the table was a microcosm of the chemistry of the negotiations, and is a microcosm of the chemistry of Canada–U.S. relations. Here was a relatively small country that shares a border with the United States. There are many Canadians who would be much happier not so close to the United States, but that's where God put us and it's always been very difficult for a small country. We are highly dependent on economic relations with the U.S. and must learn how to manage that relationship and how to get the best out of it. The United States has many issues, while Canada is just another pimple on the horizon, an irritant. So, they send people like Simon to negotiate.

What ultimately made the negotiations successful is that, by walking out, we changed the chemistry. Because all of the sudden, rather than Canada demanding an agreement, we were embarrassing the United States at the time that it was trying to negotiate a multilateral agreement. The message sent loud and clear to the Europeans, the Japanese, the Brazilians, and the Indians, was if the Americans can't even make a deal with Canada, who can they make a deal with? That changed the chemistry and gave us a kind of leverage which we had not had in the 18 previous months. It led to a good agreement, which did exactly what we wanted it to do. It created the circumstances in which Canadian industry could restructure and become more competitive, more outward looking, but with a lot of pain. The first five years of the agreement were an extremely painful period, made more painful, perhaps, by Mr. Kroes's obsession with zero inflation.

But out of that pain has come a much stronger economic structure in Canada— much more outward looking and trade oriented. This could not have been done without the agreement. So when you look back at it now the histrionics of the negotiations were fun, sometimes painful, but what counted is that at the end we got exactly the kind of agreement that Canada needed and wanted.

Roger Porter: Thank you. Chip Roh— 60 seconds. Biggest lesson you think we learned from this.

Charles Roh: I was struck by the fact that you go into these negotiations and you conclude a free trade agreement because it is such good economic policy. In between you negotiate like a bunch of mercantilists who hate each other. But having overcome these various political problems we finally reached an agreement that was overwhelming in its economic logic for both sides. It has proved to be everything we had hoped it would be.

Roger Porter: Thank you. Konrad.

Konrad von Finckenstein: We always looked at this from a vision, a conceptional view, while it appeared to us that the Americans looked at it purely as a solution to an irritant. It was only late in the negotiation that we realized that the irritants are of Congressional origin and they're something that the Americans have to deal with; otherwise you can't have an agreement. What we washed away as minor irritants in a big picture, were for them the context of the agreement.

Roger Porter: Jeanie?

Jean Anderson: A couple of things. First, I think that Canada is a lot more important to the United States than it thinks it is, as evident by the commitment at the highest political levels to get an agreement. Second, although the subsidy–countervail–dumping aspect was the crucial political issue at the time, what was really important about this agreement was all its other aspects— free trade, free investment, trade in services, energy and so forth. It's done a lot for both economies and so in a future negotiation, it's important to keep in perspective that what is a crucial political issue in one year, ten years later, although still important, may not have quite the same importance that it once did.

Roger Porter: Bill Merkin.

William Merkin: I've worked on U.S-Canada issues for a long time and if there's one major lesson to be learned it is that you can't forget how different our two political systems are. If the Canadian Cabinet makes a decision on a negotiating point, they can follow through on it because the government controls parliament. For the U.S. President to make a decision on a trade negotiating issue does not guarantee delivery, because we have to deal with the U.S. Congress. So, in many ways, you cannot count on us, as the Administration may not be able to deliver everything that you need in an agreement.

Roger Porter: Simon.

Simon Reisman: Well, we got a good agreement. What does the future hold? The United States does not have a fast–track arrangement so it is not equipped, today, to negotiate trade agreements. It is one of the periods when the protectionists in the U.S. win control and deny the executive the opportunity to proceed. I don't think that will change much. We left much work for the people who come after us. While they will be able to make progress, I don't think we'll make that 2000 date.

Clayton Yeutter: I think you're right.

Roger Porter: Clayton.

Clayton Yeutter: A couple of observations. In economic terms this was an overwhelming success story, as we all knew it would become. It was a hard sell, especially in Canada at that time. I can remember all those headlines in Canada saying what a god awful thing this was. You were selling the whole country off to the U.S. And every chance I got, I kept saying that Canada would be the greater beneficiary of the two, and that clearly turned out to be the case. But it was win–win for both sides and Simon, you're right, it's laid the groundwork for many other good things to happen. I would put that in a multilateral context too. One of the benefits that came out of this agreement was that many of its provisions are now incorporated in the World Trade Organization as a result of the Uruguay Round. Ours was really the precursor on services. The work on dispute settlement was of major benefit in the Uruguay Round, as was the work on rules of origin. Second, we did a good job of handling the political situation in the U.S. as it unfolded. It was a little easier for us than it was for you because things were so emotional on the Canadian side, but it wasn't easy for the U.S. either, as we faced pressures relating to the magnitude of the trade deficits. And yet we passed the U.S.–Canada Trade Agreement by a huge margin. Unfortunately, we didn't do nearly as well with NAFTA when the Mexico side of things came along and we're still paying the price politically.

Roger Porter: Michael Wilson.

Michael Wilson: I'll make two points. One is the need to engage potential support in the private sector, to make sure that they are outspoken supporters of the agreement, because the opponents will be very outspoken. I have some editorials going back to 1987–88, and will just read one quote here. It is from an organization called GATT–FLY, a church organization, saying: "From a Christian standpoint, free trade would require a number of human sacrifices on the altar of the almighty dollar." We had opposition leaders going into old age homes telling people who had reached the last residence of their lives that they will lose their old age security if they supported this agreement, that they might be out on the street when the Americans took over the old age home and ran them on a profit basis. If we hadn't had the support of potential beneficiaries, we might not have won that election. And then Canada would have gone down the other path, instead of the path of open markets, liberalization, greater rationalization, and competitiveness. It's frightening to think of where we might have been.

Secondly, it is important to have as broad an agenda as possible, and in a way, the irritants–based approach restricted that. The irritants that are causing difficulties between our two countries today, often are not part of the Free Trade Agreement. So to broaden it as much as possible is a very important lesson.

Roger Porter: Alan Holmer.

Alan Holmer: Four brief points. First is the tremendous importance of thinking long term as opposed to short term; thinking broad interest as opposed to narrow constituent parochial interests; and establishing a broad vision. I remember sitting in Jim Baker's office with Clayton and Jim, at about 11:00 on October third, with them saying, "This is in the economic interests of the U.S. Yes, there's a lot of opposition in Congress. We will set it up, and let's see if they'll turn it down." And we compelled them to look at the broad interest.

This brings me to the second point: managing expectations. The key is, what kind of question do you ask? If each provision of the agreement is to solve every political problem or every constituent problem that each senator had, can it occur tomorrow? If that was the question, the answer would have been no. Instead we changed the question to: will this agreement make the United States a better, more prosperous place to live in future years? Clearly the answer was "yes," and that's why Congress approved it.

Third, it is enormously important that the U.S. negotiators understand the political dynamic in Congress. I continue to be amazed at the extent to which negotiators often don't understand that political dynamic. It's equally important to focus on the political dynamic in the other country that you're dealing with.

Fourth, the key to being an effective negotiator is put yourself in the other guy's shoes. To try to see the world as he or she does.

Roger Porter: Derek Burney.

Derek Burney: The most important lesson is that the agreement has worked as well as it has. From both sides it more than lived up to expectations, and that relates not only to trade flows, but also to the way the mechanisms have worked. It did pay dividends in terms of other agreements that have been pursued since. Both the process and the substance of this negotiation paid dividends for NAFTA and the WTO. Next, you cannot succeed in negotiations without a political commitment from the very top.

Another point is that it has to be a pragmatic political framework for the negotiation; both sides must realize what each side can sell in their own country, recognizing the distinction in our two political systems. I hope our American colleagues recognize the huge risk for any Canadian Prime Minister to negotiate any kind of an agreement with the United States without being perceived as a guy who sold out the country. That came home to us time and again in this negotiation.

It may be that we need a different kind of negotiating apparatus to tackle agreements of this nature in the future. There are new interest groups that are raising their head in trade negotiations. And while we may think that their concerns have nothing to do with trade, we need to deal with them anyway. We may have to break new ground in terms of a negotiating apparatus if we hope to pick up on some of the things that were left over from this agreement. I don't have an answer as to how we do it, but the traditional negotiating approach may simply not be good enough to command the kind of political support to implement an agreement after the fact.

Roger Porter: We give the final word to our host and the man who brought us all together for this panel, Peter McPherson.

Peter McPherson: In many ways the chief lesson is that we were able to carry it out, and consequently we ought to look at how to do it again. There are many incomplete areas, such as the cross–border issues, service transactions, and agriculture. A whole range of things. They require a trade agreement II. It can't be done now without the fast–track, and in a depressed international economic situation, but there will be a day when we should look at doing it again in more than piecemeal fashion. For only a big deal can command the needed political support.

Roger Porter: Any good piece of work is inevitably the product of many hands. Ten years ago, these people put their shoulders to the wheel and produced an enormously successful agreement. They have reflected on that and have given us insights as to how it happened and what we are to learn from it.

Part Two

ECONOMIC ISSUES

THE CANADA-U.S. FREE TRADE AGREEMENT - AN OVERVIEW

Mordechai E. Kreinin[*]

At last count there were 80 regional economic blocks or preferential agreements in world trade. All but two major trading nations belong to at least one regional pact, the exception being Japan, and South Korea. Although they take several forms, two forms are the most common: Customs Unions (CU) and Free Trade Areas (FTA).

A CU is two or more countries which eliminate all restrictions on trade between themselves, and set up a common and uniform tariff to be levied on imports from outside countries (non-members). It is known as the common external tariff (CET). A prime example is the European Union (EU), which consists of 15 countries. By the mid-1990s, all restrictions on trade in goods and services within the EU were removed and a common tariff was instituted on imports from non-members. In fact the EU has gone well beyond the formation of a CU in its integration process. It introduced free mobility of capital and labor, and on July 1, 2002, eleven of its members will inaugurate a common currency called the Euro, to replace their national currencies.

An FTA involves two or more countries which eliminate all barriers to trade between themselves, but do *not* impose common restrictions on imports from non-members. As in the case of a CU, trade between members is free of tariffs and other restrictions, but unlike a CU there is no common external tariff. Rather each member country maintains its own tariff and other trade barriers against imports from the outside. The U.S.-Canada agreement is an FTA, and it is in the process of incorporating Mexico so as to create a three-country FTA known as the North American Free Trade Agreement, or NAFTA. Both the Canada-U.S. Free Trade Agreement (CUSTA) and NAFTA are much looser organizations than the EU. Should the U.S. and Canada desire to establish a common External Tariff to be levied on imports from third countries (except Mexico) and otherwise harmonize their commercial policies, they could become a

*Mordechai E. Kreinin is University Distinguished Professor of Economics at Michigan State University. He is past president of the International Trade and Finance Association and has been a consultant with the United Nations and the U.S. departments of State and Commerce.

customs union. There exists regional economic groupings in Central and South America, Central Europe, Asia, and Africa.

Both a CU and an FTA discriminate against non-members. In the case of a CU, members pay zero duty on imports from each other, while imports from the outside are charged the common external tariff (CET) so that the margin of preference in favor of members, or the margin of discrimination against non-members, is the CET. In case of an FTA, member countries pay zero duty on imports from one another, while each country levies its own national tariff rate on imports from outside the block. Hence in an FTA the margin of discrimination against outsiders is the national tariff and it varies from one member to another.

Members of most regional trade blocks also belong to an *international* trade organization known as the World Trade Organization or the WTO, which has about 130 member countries. And one cardinal rule of the WTO is a rule of non-discrimination in international trade, known as the Most Favored Nation principle, or MFN[1]. Countries are not allowed to discriminate between sources of supply; they must charge the same duty on a given product regardless of where it comes from. The two exceptions to this rule allowed under the WTO charter are CU and FTA; their members are allowed to discriminate against non-member countries. But regional groupings must meet certain criteria to qualify for a waiver from the MFN. The standards to be met are: *not* instituting a level of protection in the CET higher than the average of the constituent tariffs charged by members prior to regional integration (in case of a CU); and insuring that all or nearly all trade restrictions within the block are removed.

There is a debate in the economics profession whether the cause of trade liberalization throughout the world is better served by:

(a)   Multilateral , gradual, tariff reduction under the WTO (such as the Uruguay Round), which is a very laborious process but involves no discrimination, or

(b)   The regional approach manifested in the formation of CUs and FTAs, where each block may be capable of "deep" integration, but because of their discriminatory feature they distort global trade and investment, and each may affect adversely the interest of non-members that are being discriminated against. For example, Canadian exports to the U.S. may displace Asian exports because it enters the American market duty free, or Japanese investment in Asia

---

[1]   A country is not allowed to levy a tariff on imports from any trading partner higher than it imposes on imports from its most favored supplier.

> may be diverted to Canada because of free entry of the
> product of such investment to the U.S.

This can get increasingly complex if, as in the Americas, there are groupings with overlapping membership, with some countries belonging to more than one FTA— a situation that can be resolved by the proposed free trade of the Americas, or by otherwise merging two or more regional blocks.

However the debate is settled, the regional movement in the world is here to stay. So the role of the WTO is to minimize the discriminatory impact; make sure that blocks don't turn into inward looking fortresses.

CUSTA is an FTA. Formation of an FTA between the two largest trading partners in the world— the U.S. and Canada— was an idea bandied about for many years. The two countries share the longest unprotected border in the world. About three-fourths of Canada's exports are destined for the United States, and two-thirds of its imports originate in the U.S.; in turn, Canada accounts for about a fifth of U.S. exports and imports. The capital markets of the two countries are closely knit.

About 70 percent of U.S. imports from Canada were free of duty prior to 1989. Furthermore, since 1965 the two countries had a free trade agreement in automobiles and parts. It allows Canadian subsidiaries of the big–three U.S. automakers to rationalize production by specializing in a few models produced for the vast North American market, thereby exploiting economies of scale in production and distribution.

Yet there were continuous trade frictions between the two countries. American companies complained of restrictions on direct foreign investments imposed by Canada in the early 1980s (since abolished)and of the high Canadian tariff. Both Canada and the United States had "contingent protection" measures that were temporary and subject to proof of substantial injury to domestic industry. They included antidumping and countervailing duties, escape clauses, and safeguard measures that could take the form of a tariff or a quantitative restriction. Between 1980 and 1987 the U.S. took restrictive action on 19 cases against Canadian exports valued at $6.2 billion (much of which was accounted for by countervailing duties imposed in 1986 on Canadian exports of softwood lumber), while Canada took action on 26 cases against U.S. exports valued at $403 million. Such actions were an irritant to the relation between the two nations, as were the significant subsidies in the agricultural and energy sectors. Canadians complain that the U.S. procedures in investigating alleged unfair trading practices are "arbitrary and capricious." There were also disputes in the areas of service transactions, fisheries, and cultural exchange. Thus there was an impetus on both sides of the border to form an FTA. An FTA was negotiated between the two countries in 1985–1988 and it went into effect on 1 January 1989. The following is a list of its main provisions:

- Tariffs and quantitative restrictions between the countries were phased out gradually over a ten-year period, removed by 1998.
- Agricultural quotas restricting Canadian imports of U.S. vegetables, grain, poultry, and eggs were lifted, and Canadian subsidies of grain exported to the U.S. were ended.
- Provincial policies discriminating against U.S. liquor and wine were lifted; but the preferences for beer brewed within each province is retained.
- Canadian limits on energy exports to the U.S. ended, while the U.S. ban on exports of oil from Alaska no longer applies to Canada.
- The North American free trade agreement in automobiles and parts was left essentially intact.
- Both sides eliminated discrimination in services, each treating services originating in the partner country in the same way they treat their own ("national" treatment). Similarly the agreement ended most restrictions and provided for national treatment on cross–border investment.[2]
- Canada gives better protection to U.S. copyrights and patents, particularly those affecting broadcasting and pharmaceuticals.
- Both countries eliminated national preferences on federal government contracts in excess of $25,000.
- Each side excludes the other from trade actions taken against third countries or against the world. However, each country can specifically include the other in worldwide trade sanctions if its exports contribute substantially to the domestic problem that caused the action.

Although the two countries keep their existing laws against "unfair" foreign competition, such as antidumping and antisubsidy measures, sanctions under those laws may be appealed to a new bilateral dispute settlement tribunal. The tribunal replaced appeal to the national courts, but applies national laws and judicial standards. Its decisions are binding.

While both countries stand to benefit from the agreement, the gain in real income received by Canada (the smaller country) are far larger than

---

[2] National treatment means that each country (e.g.,U.S.) treats firms of the partner country (e.g. Canada) operating within it (in the U.S.) in no less favorable a way than it treats its own firms.

those accruing to the U.S. And that is for two reasons. First, being one-tenth the size of the United States, Canada gains more from economies of scale as its factories produce for a vastly larger market. For example, the Ontario furniture industry was able to specialize in specific lines, because it can now sell in the entire North American market. The U.S. realized smaller gains from integration because its market was vast to begin with. Second, when tariffs between a small and a large country are eliminated, the small country tends to gain disproportionately because its consumers and producers bore a disproportionate share of the tariff burden of both countries in the pre-free-trade situation (terms of trade effect of a tariff). Nevertheless both countries enjoy static welfare gain from the elimination of the deadweight losses of protection, gains from economies of scale, improvement in efficiency forced by increased foreign competition, and reduction inefficiencies caused by uncertainty over the introduction of new protective measures. Against these gains were transitional costs as companies in both countries adjusted to the new environment. But such costs are minimized to the extent that the new trade fostered by the agreement is the intra-industry[3] (rather than inter–industry)[4] variety, as was the case in the EU. At the same time, certain third countries— such as Australia, which exports products similar to those of Canada— may lose markets.

As had been foreseen, frictions persist even after the FTA. Only recently, controversies flared up in the areas of fishing rights, as well as the rights for magazine advertising in each other country. For that reason the two countries had agreed on a mechanism to resolve disputes between themselves, the nature of which will be discussed later. The WTO also contains such a dispute settlement mechanism on a global level.

Any FTA (or other preferential schemes) has "rules of origin", and CUSTA is no exception. Because members of an FTA charge different tariff rates on imports from outsiders, producers in a non–member country can ship their merchandise to the low duty member of the block, and from there the products proceed duty free to other members of the FTA. For that reason, an FTA needs to maintain border checkpoints between its members to insure that only goods produced within the FTA are accorded duty free entry. Certificates of origin presented at the border usually enforce this. (Such checkpoints are not necessary in the case of a CU, where the external tariff is uniform for all members).

---

[3] Exchange of similar products between the two countries.
[4] Exchange of totally different products.

But what does it mean to say that the good is produced within the FTA? Suppose all automobile components, which account for say 90 percent of the value of a car, are produced in Japan, and only the final assembly, accounting for only 10 percent of the car value, is performed in the U.S. Would it be considered a U.S.-made car, eligible to enter Canada duty free, or is it essentially an automobile made in Japan, and therefore would have to pay the Canadian duty even though it is shipped from the U.S.? "Rules of Origin" specify the minimum proportion of the product that must be manufactured within the FTA in order for it to be accorded duty–free passage from one member of an FTA to another. The minimum proportion differs from one FTA to another (depending on the agreement), and within an FTA they may vary between products.

In the case of the CUSTA, the rules of origin were superceded by those of NAFTA, which includes the U.S., Canada, and Mexico. Hence, the following rules apply now:

To acquire duty–free status, a good must be produced entirely in the territory of one or more of the three integrating countries. If materials or goods originating outside of North America are used in production of the final product, such goods must undergo sufficient change inside the FTA that would convert them from one tariff classification to another. As an alternative to the transformation requirement, the materials originating outside of North America may not constitute more than 50 percent of the value of the final product. In other words, half the value of the product must be produced within North America.

In the case of automotive goods different rules of origin apply. Vehicles that transport 15 or fewer persons must have a minimum of 56 percent North American content (maximum of 44 percent materials and parts originating elsewhere), rising to 62.5 percent after January 1, 2002. For vehicles transporting 16 or more people, the respective minimum North America content requirements are 55 and 60 percent.

These and other issues of regional integration, as applied to CUSTA, will be discussed by world renowned experts assembled here, each in his/her area of specialty. Apart from accounts by negotiators, there will be three types of panels: (a) One devoted to thematic subjects, as they apply to CUSTA; (b) Analysis of problems within CUSTA of certain critical industries; (c) and going beyond CUSTA, what does the future hold for the expansion of free trade in the Americas and elsewhere.

ECONOMIC CONSEQUENCES OF FREE TRADE: A CANADIAN VIEWPOINT

Richard G. Lipsey[*]

To discuss the Canadian point of view on the consequences of the Canada–U.S. Free Trade Agreement we begin with the Canadian government's original objectives. We then see what was achieved in the actual negotiations and follow this with a study of what actually happened, setting this in contrast to some of the Canadian fears about what might happen. These fears were articulated in the great Canadian debate that began with the negotiations and carried on after the signing, during the free trade election, and right up to the election in 1993 of a Liberal government one of whose main planks was to radically amend or even cancel the agreement. This debate finally ended for all practical purposes when faced with the reality that the new government decided to leave the agreement in place.[1]

℘

In the course of debates and election campaigns the objectives of free trade with the U.S. became exaggerated by many supporters—just as the detractors exaggerated the possible losses. In fact, the gains, as seen by

---

*Richard Lipsey is Professor Emeritus of Economics at Simon Fraser University and a Fellow of the Canadian Institute for Advanced Research. From 1983 to 1989 he was Senior Economic Advisor for the C. D. Howe Institute.

[1] In October 1985, the two governments agreed to enter negotiations. The negotiations began under a Canadian Conservative government in the spring of 1986. A framework agreement was reached in October 1987 and the full text was agreed in December 1987. When the Liberal dominated Canadian Senate refused to ratify the agreement, an election occurred in November 1988 largely on the issue of free trade with the U.S. The Conservatives won the election and the agreement was duly ratified by the Canadian and the U.S. legislatures. The next election in October 1993 was won by the Liberals whose election platform included an anti-free trade plank. The Liberals soon abandoned their promise of either renegotiating or abrogating the FTA.

policy analysts and as set out by the government, were not unreasonable expectations.[2]

Two main objectives were paramount. First, on the positive side, the elimination of tariffs on Canadian–U.S. trade would leave 75–80 percent of total Canadian trade tariff free and would constitute a major move in the direction of free trade. It would come close to completing a process that Canada had begun with two bilateral trade liberalizing agreements with the U.S. in the 1930s and continued when Canada became a charter member of the GATT in 1947. In spite of moving towards freer trade, Canada had done so less rapidly than the U.S. When the FTA negotiations began, Canadian tariffs were substantially higher than U.S. tariffs on almost all major groups— an average of about 10 percent for Canada and less than 5 percent for the U.S.

Canada had built up industries under heavy tariff protection in the early stages of its industrial development (as had the U.S.). Subsequently, Canadian manufacturing had performed well under some significant tariff reductions during the Kennedy and Tokyo rounds of GATT tariff cuts. Many economists now felt that the infant industry phase was over for Canada and the time had come to remove its remaining tariffs. If this were done in the context of a bilateral agreement, Canada would obtain tariff-free access to the U.S. market. This was the goal of "increased access."

The anticipated gains from achieving increased access were to have Canadian resources allocated according to Canadian comparative advantage. The gains would be measured in better, more productive jobs paying higher wages on average than could be paid by inefficient protected industries. Estimates suggested modest, but not insignificant, gains from this more efficient use of resources in the range of 2 to 6 percent of GDP. More uncertain, but potentially more powerful, were dynamic growth effects. If Canadian firms became more innovative when fully exposed to competition from dynamic U.S. firms, growth rates could favourably be affected. As is well known, even modest changes in growth rates in the order of ½ to 1 percent cumulate over a generation to large increases in national income and living standards.[3]

The second Canadian objective was to defend itself from what was seen as a rising tide of U.S. protectionism. Canadians feared an increasing use of U.S. trade remedy laws, particularly anti-dump, countervail, escape clause, and section 301 measures as tools of what they called U.S. "contingent protection," and Americans called "trade remedy laws." The

---

[2]   See Kelleher, Lipsey, and Smith.
[3]   For further discussion of possible dynamic effects, see R.G. Lipsey 1989.

free trade negotiations were seen by Canadians as providing a change to bring these measures under some control at least making them more predictable and possibly eliminating them completely. This was the goal of "security of access."

The anticipated gains from achieving the security of access objective were reduced uncertainty in cross–border trade. Why this goal was far more important to Canada than to the U.S. can be seen by considering a firm intending to serve the two countries' combined market from a location in one or the other. The proportion of the firm's output that will have to cross the Canada–U.S. border would be about 90 percent if it locates in Canada and only 10 percent if it locates in the U.S. The insecurity of access caused by unpredictable application of both country's trade remedy laws is thus vastly more serious if the firm locates in Canada rather than in the U.S. Eliminating all trade remedy laws on Canada–U.S. trade and substituting domestic laws against predatory pricing and dumping would give firms serving the combined market the same treatment no matter in which country they were located. Without going this far, uncertainty would be significantly reduced if the application of these laws could only be made less capricious and the amount of political pressure to which they were sometimes subjected could be reduced.

During the course of the intense debate that took place in Canada, while the agreement was being negotiated, and then after it was signed but before it was ratified, other objectives and fears were formulated. Exuberant politicians could not be stopped from making all sorts of unreasonable claims such as Canadian prime minister Mulroney's boast that the agreement would provide "Jobs, Jobs, Jobs," while his opponent, Liberal leader John Turner, claimed that the agreement would be the end of Canada as a sovereign nation.

∅

When the text of the agreement was finally presented, Canadians counted many successes, and one major and several minor failures. Of course, trade is mutually advantageous so a liberalizing measure that constitutes a bargaining success for one country is likely to be a success for the other as well. But there were differences of objectives, particularly when exceptions to the free trade principle were being negotiated. In these cases, one country's success in protecting some sector or activity is likely to be correctly seen as the other country's failure in not being able to open it up to full international competition.

The major Canadian failure was in not achieving its goal of complete exemption from U.S. anti–dumping laws— the most extreme form of the security of access objective. The Canadian negotiators had tried for this, although many outside observers thought that it was a vain attempt. For example, writing in 1985 and in a monograph that circulated widely in Ottawa before negotiations began, Lipsey and Smith (1985: 182) stated:

> ". . . . it is doubtful that the U.S. Congress would agree to exempt Canada from its countervail laws. . . . Therefore, we do not consider this possibility further."

Against this failure, there were some significant security of access successes. Canadian access to the U.S. market (and U.S. access to the Canadian market) was made more secure in a number of specific ways.[4]

- The Agreement removed the threat of quantitative restrictions and the U.S.'s ability of use them to force Canada to adopt VERs[5] (407 in combination with 1101 and 1102).

- Canadian energy products, especially oil, gas, electricity, and uranium, were given increased security of access to the U.S. market. (902 and 905).

- The use of national security claims to restrict access of one country's energy products to the other's market was severely restricted. (907).

- The auto pact was incorporated into the agreement so that the ability to abrogate it was removed and it can only be eliminated by abrogating the entire FTA.

- Canada will not be unintentionally sideswiped by U.S. global safeguard action aimed at others, as has happened several times in the past (since it must be named specifically to be affected) (1102).

- The agreement severely constrains the circumstances under which safeguard action can be undertaken and the severity of the permitted measures.[6] This contains a measure used earlier to keep Canadian shakes and shingles out of the U.S. market (1102).

- Both countries promise that any future liberalization of rules and regulations applying to domestic financial services will be automatically applied to the other country by virtue of national treatment in services (1907).

---

4   The list comes from Lipsey and York pp 16–17. Numbers in parentheses refer to the article of the Agreement.

5   A VER is a Voluntary Export Agreement whereby one country agrees to limit its exports to a second country, usually to avoid some trade restrictions on the part of the importing country that would be more harmful to the exporting country than its VER.

6   A "safegard" is a temporary import restriction designed to curb a large surge in the import of some commodity.

As well as all these specific provisions, an eleventh hour agreement, made at the ministerial level after the Canadian delegation had walked out of the talks, instituted a bi-national dispute settlement mechanism to oversee the application of each country's trade remedy laws. Although many Canadian critics dismissed this as inconsequential, it was path breaking and a major U.S. concession— although one that a free trader would see as a win-win situation from both nations' points of view. According to the agreement, a dispute settlement panel made up of citizens from both countries is empowered to make binding decisions concerning the fairness with which each country has applied its own laws. This was a major concession of U.S. (and Canadian) sovereignty to an international body. It is perhaps fortunate that the critics missed this completely and that the supporters did not trumpet it loudly. Excessive boasting about the concession on either side might have aroused Congressional concerns over the acceptability of the entire package— which was all that either legislature was empowered to judge under U.S. fast track and Canadian constitutional procedures.

፠

Virtually all tariffs were removed on one of three time paths, immediately, or over five or ten years. (This means that they are now all gone, making Canada–U.S. free trade a reality in almost all goods and many services.) In addition many other measures, ranging from trivial to quite important increased access across the border. Lipsey and York (pp. 14–15) listed 17 of these.

There were, however, some minor setbacks on the access front. First, the domestic content provision of the auto section gave substantial protection to domestic parts manufacturers over parts manufactured outside the FTA. Second, transplant auto factories were left out of the agreement placing them at a significant disadvantage compared to the big three domestic auto companies. Third, substantial trade restrictions remained on textiles. Fourth, government procurement was only marginally opened. Fifth, a few goods were exempted from the articles affecting trade in goods. These were:

- Controls by either country on the export of raw logs.
- Controls by Canada of the export of unprocessed Atlantic fish.
- Measures related to the domestic sale and distribution of beer.

On the services front, the right of establishment[7] and national treatment[8] were substantial gains for all future service establishments. No longer could domestic measures for such ostensible purposes as environmental or quality control be used as concealed barriers to trade by applying them differentially to foreign and to domestic firms.

Two strong special interest groups won out over free trade in sugar and shipping. The U.S. refused to make significant changes in its sugar restrictions except to permit unlimited entry of Canadian food products containing up to 10 percent sugar. Nor would it make any change to the Jones Act. This act was grandfathered, leaving shipping between domestic ports outside of the agreement.

Canada managed to grandfather all of its import quotas that protect its supply managed dairy and feather industries. The U.S. may not have pushed this further since it knew that the then–current Uruguay round of GATT negotiations was likely to force the "tariffication" of all quota schemes—presumably as a prelude to bringing the tariffs down in subsequent rounds of negotiations.[9] This tariffication was adopted when the Uruguay round was finally completed several years later.

Against stiff U.S. opposition, Canada managed to gain an exemption from all of the aspects of the treaty for its cultural industries which are broadly defined to include not only performing artists, writers, and painters, but magazine and book publishing.

✠

Two years into the FTA,[10] Canadian employment was up 200,000 (not due to the FTA), restructuring was going according to plan and foreign investment seemed to be responding favourably.[11] Then the country entered, as did the rest of the industrialized world, the most severe

---

[7]   Right of establishment means that any Canadian or American company selling services in its home territory has the right to establish outlets in the other country subject only to the rules and regulations applying to domestic firms in the country.

[8]   National treatment, which prevents countries from treating foreign firms differently from domestic firms, is discussed in more detail in a later section.

[9]   Tariffication refers to the replacement of import quotas by tariffs which have the same restrictive effect.

[10]   The argument in this section is based on Lipsey (1993).

[11]   These were the conclusions of the United Nations survey. See UN (1990).

recession since the Great Depression of the 1930s. Opponents blamed the resulting job losses on the FTA.[12]

Although no one could be sure how much of the job loss was due to the restructuring brought about by the FTA, it was clear that Canada in general, and Ontario in particular, was very badly hit by a serious, world-wide recession. Indeed the nation-wide job losses had a number of causes:

- First and foremost, was the cyclical loss.

- Second, was the restructuring of the older industries under the impact of a changing and globalizing world economy. Much of that restructuring took place in the U.S. in the previous recession of the early 1980s. There, the old smoke stack industries gave way to the "rust belt" as widespread readjustment occurred. At that time Ontario and Quebec were shielded by a severely undervalued dollar (due to capital movements). As a result, the readjustments did not occur then, nor did they occur during the prolonged recovery that brought prosperity to efficient and inefficient firms alike during the mid and late 1980s. Then came the recession of the early 1990s, which coincided this time with an overvalued Canadian dollar, all of the structural readjustment that had taken place over 10 years in the U.S. border states took place in Canada over one recession.

- Third, there was a world-wide readjustment of the location of manufacturing industries, particularly those that use mainly unskilled labour, due to the globalizing of the economy.

- Fourth, the Bank of Canada undertook to drive the inflation rate to zero just as the adjustment to the FTA was taking place. This drove both the absolute level of interest rates, and the spread against the U.S. rates to high levels.

- Fifth, partly as a result of high interest rates, and partly as a result of the budget deficit that sucked foreign funds into Canada, the C$ was overvalued throughout the recession.

---

[12] It should not go unnoted that business commentators often perpetrated the same exaggerations as did the critics of the FTA. The financial press of the time contained numerous articles criticizing the Bank of Canada for its zero-inflation policy. These articles typically blamed all of the recession-induced unemployment on the Bank— with no acknowledgement that the recession was worldwide and would undoubtedly have severely hit Canada whatever the Bank's monetary policy. (No doubt the Bank had some marginal effect in increasing the severity of the recession, but quantifying that effect is close to impossible over so short a time period.)

These general arguments were given strong support with the publication of the best attempt to make a preliminary judgement of the effects of the FTA. The C. D. Howe Institute's detailed study of the trade statistics for 1988–1991 (Schwanen 1992) showed:

> ". . . .that, in fact, Canada's exports to the United States over the FTA's first three full years of operation performed the strongest in those sectors that were liberalised by the agreement— particularly nonresource-based manufacturing. In contrast, Canada's exports to other countries and in sectors not opened by the FTA languished. These developments belie expectations by opponents of the deal that the FTA would make Canada more dependent on exports of natural resources, or that freer trade with a slow growth economy like that of the United States would reduce Canada's potential for growth."

These big gains in the U.S. market had occurred in spite of the overvalued Canadian dollar and sluggish overall growth in the U.S. economy. Furthermore, the gains in exports were concentrated in high-value-added manufactured goods rather than in resource industries. Also, many of those services for which trade was liberalized by the FTA had shown impressive increases in U.S. sales at the time in which sales of Canadian services were falling in other markets.

℘

A recent evaluation by the CD Howe Institute (Schwanen 1997) shows continued gains from the FTA. Below is a summary of their findings.

Merchandise Trade. Canada and the U.S. are each other's best customers. Each trades more with the other than with any other country. The total of Canadian exports to and imports from the U.S. was C$673 billion in 1997. This is the largest bilateral trade flow of the world and it exceeds the GDPs of most of the world's countries. Since the FTA was formed, Canadian exports have increased from about 25 percent to about 35 percent of Canadian GDP and about 80 percent of these exports now go to the U.S.

During the first eight years of the FTA, which takes us just before the Asian meltdown, the U.S. economy grew at about the same rate as did Japan and Europe and less slowly than the emerging Asian nations. Yet Canadian exports to the U.S. grew significantly faster than did Canadian exports to the rest of the world. The same is true when Canadian imports from the U.S. are compared with those from the rest of the world. Imports from the U.S. did not, however, grow quite as fast as exports, so that the typical Canadian surplus on the merchandise account widened considerably.[13]

The importance of the FTA is shown by the fact that Canadian exports to, and imports from, the U.S. grew faster in the group of commodities where trade was liberalized than the group where tariffs were already zero or insignificant. They also grew faster than exports to and imports from the rest of the world.

As with previous tariff cuts, there were many broad product categories where there was significant growth in both imports from and exports to the U.S. This suggests that the rationalization of product lines that had been going on through all previous tariff cuts still had some way to go.[14] In those categories where both countries still had significant tariff cuts to make under the FTA, this two-way expansion was particularly noticeable in the categories of meat and dairy products, chemicals, industrial machinery and office telecommunications, and precision equipment.

To try to isolate changes due to the FTA, Schwanen examined trends in the trade statistics. All exports have been growing over the years but they found that exports of the goods that were liberalized grew much faster after the FTA than before it while for other exports— to the U.S. in non-liberalized categories and to other countries in all categories— the rate of growth only accelerated slightly.

Schwanen also made calculations of revealed comparative advantage (RCA). The RCA for some Canadian export expresses the percentage of total U.S. imports of that good coming from Canadian sources as a ratio of the percentage of total U.S. imports coming from Canada.[15]

Of the 16 categories of Canadian exports where U.S. tariffs fell significantly, 12 showed an increase in Canada's RCA, while only 7 did so in the 8 years before the FTA (a period over which tariffs were relatively stable). On the import side, of 18 product groups where Canadian tariffs were significantly reduced, the U.S.'s RCA rose in 15, whereas in the period prior to the FTA only 4 groups saw such an increase. The U.S. gains in RCA came in several areas where prior econometric models had

---

[13]   In trade with the U.S., Canada usually has a surplus on the merchandise account and a deficit on the services account.

[14]   Writing about this before the FTA began, Lipsey and Smith (1985: 109) had this to say about past tariff cuts: "... as trade barriers have been reduced, both our exports and our imports have increased in virtually all sectors. This supports the "niche" concept. Whole industries have not disappeared in either country. Instead, each industry has specialized in particular niches so that trade had increased in each direction, in each industry."

[15]   So, for example, if 25 percent of U.S. imports of *commodity* X come from Canada, while only 18 percent of *all* U.S. imports do so, Canada's RCA for product X is 1.39.

predicted that Canadian firms would loose out to U.S. competition, in textiles, steel, clothing, and furniture and furnishings (although within these broad categories Canadian exports of some product lines did expand substantially).

Wine: a success story. Before the agreement was signed, great fears were expressed over the Canadian wine industry, located mainly in Ontario and British Columbia. It was heavily tariff protected and, with a few notable exceptions, concentrated mainly on cheap low-quality products. Contrary to most people's expectations, rather than being decimated, the industry has moved strongly up market and now produces a wide variety of lower to upper medium range products, some of which have won international competitions in Europe!

Why did this surprising result occur? The high Canadian tariff was levied on a per unit rather than on an ad valorem basis. Charging a tariff by the gallon gave most protection to the low quality wines with low value per gallon. The higher the per-gallon value of the wine, the lower the percentage tariff protection. Responding to these incentives, the Canadian industry concentrated on low quality wines. Their market for these wines was protected by the nearly prohibitive tariffs on competing low quality imports and the high prices charged by higher quality imports. These prices had to cover the tariff and the hidden charges that provincial wines monopolies levied in order to protect local producers. When the tariff was removed, the incentives were to move up market producing much more value per acre of land. Within a very few years Canadian wines were competing effectively with imported products in the medium quality range because the Canadian wine growing land was suited to good quality wines. British Columbia and Ontario wines do not yet reach the quality of major French wines in the $30–$50 range but they compete very effectively in quality with wines in the $10–$20 range and sometimes even higher up the quality scale. The success of the wine industry is a fine example of how tariffs can distort incentives and push an industry into a structure that makes it dependent on the tariff. Looking at the pre-FTA industry, very few suspected that it would be able to survive let alone become a world-class competitor.

Trade in services. Canada's trade in services to most parts of the world has been expanding, making it difficult to separate the effects caused by a general worldwide liberalization from liberalization coming specifically from the FTA. In any case, the FTA's effects were expected to be marginal since the provisions of right of establishment and national treatment would have noticeable effects mainly on new service establishments. The Howe Institute's study could go no further than concluding that the data was not inconsistent with the FTA having had some influence in increasing Canadian service exports in communications, architecture, engineering and other technical services, and service imports in management and advertising.

Long-Run Competitive Ability. During the debate preceding the agreement Canadian critics argued that the Canadian firms would not be able to hold their own in open competition with the more advanced U.S. economy. This claim simply does not stand up to scrutiny. After all, Canadian exports had risen every time tariffs had been cut following the successive rounds of GATT negotiations and there was no reason to believe that the reactions to the current round of tariff cuts would be any different.

The pessimism misses the role of the exchange rate as an equilibrating mechanism. Poor, intermediate, and advanced nations trade successfully with each other the world over. Each nation's living standards depend mainly on its own productivity. But the ability to trade depends only on being able to produce something that is wanted, while the exchange rate ensures that exports can be sold. This was David Ricardo's message in the early 19th century and it is as important, and as little understood, today as it was in Ricardo's time.

Today, 10 years after the FTA went into effect and within a year of the final elimination of all tariffs, the Canadian economy is performing satisfactorily. Furthermore, the country's main troubles were of its own making and unrelated to the FTA: a high debt/GDP ratio as a result of massive budget deficits now happily in the past, some insecurity among foreign investors as a result of endemic fears that the country will break up under the impact of Quebec separation, and weaknesses in world markets for many primary goods in which Canada still has comparative advantages.

Employment and Productivity. In spite of much hyperbole on both sides about massive favorable or unfavorable effects of the FTA on employment, discernable effects on overall rates are hard to locate. This is exactly as it should be. Trade theory predicts that trade liberalization does not destroy jobs in the aggregate any more than trade restrictions can create them. Tariffs affect the allocation of resources among alternative uses not the total amount of resource use. So trade liberalization is about eliminating low-productivity, low-wage, tariff-protected jobs and substituting high-productivity, high-wage, non-protected jobs. Trade liberalization creates winners and losers on jobs. It should, however, raise the average levels of wages and efficiency by reallocating output from product lines where a country is an inefficient producer to product lines where it is efficient.

With these predictions in mind, what do we actually see on the employment front after 8 years of the FTA? First, the long-term decline in total employment accounted for by manufacturing employment that has been observed in most developed countries continued for a while after the FTA, then stabilized. The percentage of the labour force employed in manufacturing fell steadily from 22 percent to 17 percent in 1988, the year that tariff cuts began. The rate of decrease then accelerated to reach 14.5 percent in 1993, but after that the proportion rose gradually, reaching 15.5 in 1997. Second, manufacturing wages continued their long term relation of being higher than the average wage in all industries. Having remained constant at about 118 percent of the national average from 1985 through the first recession years of the FTA, they began to rise after 1991 and reached 121 percent of the average all-industry wage by 1995.

In an attempt to see if the influence of the FTA could be isolated, Schwanen divided 81 Canadian manufacturing industries into two groups, FTA-sensitive and FTA-non-sensitive. These were after-the-fact groupings to see if those industries observed to be more affected performed differently than those observed to be less affected. The FTA-sensitive industries were divided into those whose exports expanded rapidly, those whose imports expanded rapidly, and those in which both imports and exports expanded rapidly. The FTA-non-sensitive industries were subdivided into those that were already largely tariff free, those few that retained protection, and those that were liberalized but had slow trade growth.

In terms of share of total manufacturing employment and weekly wage as a percentage of the average manufacturing wage, these industries showed remarkably small differences. The main contrast was between two sub groups within the non-FTA sensitive group. Those industries that were already essentially tariff free, mainly automobiles, pulp, paper, and aerospace had the largest increases in employment and wages relative to the average for all manufacturing. Those that had been liberalized but had slow growth in trade had the largest decreases. The difference in performance between the whole group of sensitive and whole group of non-sensitive industries was too small to be regarded as significant.

Although the small differences in these industries relative performances may seem surprising, they do suggest that the detractors were wrong in suggesting that the FTA would have strong negative effects on manufacturing industries. The similarity in the performance of relative employment and relative wages between the FTA-sensitive and the FTA

Control Over Environmental and Social Policies. Many critics argued that Canada gave up control over environmental and social policies through the FTA. For example, famous Canadian author Margaret Atwood argued before a Senate Committee that the Agreement would force Canada to adopt U.S. gun laws and hospital administration practices. (See Lipsey and York 1988: 123–4) No horror story seemed too extreme.

Most of these criticisms were based on a misunderstanding of the doctrine of national treatment. This is the fundamental principle that guides the FTA (and the NAFTA). It leaves countries free to establish any laws whatsoever, and allows them to differ as much as desired among member countries, with the sole proviso that these laws must not discriminate on the basis of nationality. So Canada can have any tough environmental laws that it wishes, or standards for particular goods, but it must enforce these equally on Canadian and U.S.-owned firms, and on domestically produced and imported goods. The idea of national treatment is to allow a *maximum* of policy independence while preventing national policies from being misused as concealed barriers to trade and investment. Thus there is nothing in either agreement that gives the U.S. any say over any non-discriminatory Canadian policy, and vice versa.

So neither Canada nor the U.S. has lost control over its economic and social policies. What each has given up in the FTA, and along with most of the other nations of the NAFTA and the WTO, is the ability to use social and environmental policies as a covert way of discriminating between domestic and foreign goods, services and investment.

✵

Opinion surveys show that Canadians identify themselves with their country's natural resources. The possibility of a sellout of these resources thus touches a raw nerve in the Canadian psyche. This was exploited unscrupulously by the FTA's detractors.

Water. No amount of debunking seemed able to stop the preposterous allegations that the deal involved a sellout of control over Canadian water to the U.S. The agreement says nothing about water in rivers, lakes and oceans. (Bottled mineral water is mentioned because it is a simple traded commodity.) Nor does any other trade liberalizing agreement, including the European community and the GATT on which much of the FTA was modeled, give members any rights over other members' natural water supplies. Since the FTA was signed, several provinces have taken decisions about supplying water to the U.S. without the slightest suggestion from U.S. sources that the FTA gave them a say in the Canadian decision.

Oil. Petroleum provided another Canadian sensitivity which the opponents exploited. Basically the agreement on all energy, including petroleum, was in two parts: the U.S. agrees to be a good customer by not shutting off its demand on grounds of national defense (as it had done in the past); Canada agrees to be a reliable supplier by not shutting off its supply on grounds of a self–declared shortage. On Canada's side the details are that, in the event of a national emergency sufficient to cause the government to override commercial agreements for the supply of oil, the Canadian government will make it available on the open market, where the U.S. can buy it, a proportion of the diminished supply no smaller than the proportion the U.S. was buying previously. This caused a storm among the FTA's critics, and to this day it is misunderstood even among neutral observers on both sides of the border.

In fact the provision is relatively innocuous. First, it is a restatement, with some ambiguities removed, of the International Energy Agreement that Canada signed with 21 countries after the first OPEC oil crisis, and which remains in force today. Second, the sharing provisions come into force only when there is an emergency of sufficient magnitude that the government intervenes to override commercial agreements. It therefore deals with what is expected to be a rare event, such as a nuclear disaster which interrupts normal electricity supplies. In the first 10 years of the agreement no one has even publicly discussed invoking this provision.

℘

Mel Hurtig, Canadian publisher and strong anti–free trade advocate, argued in his best seller *The Betrayal of Canada* that the FTA would destroy Canada's very nationhood. Such hyperbole would not be worth mentioning were it not so widely circulated. Here is a sample of his prose:

> "The single most important overall impact of the Free Trade Agreement is already clear—a big decline in the standard of living of Canadians. And the future will be much worse. The less obvious result is as certain as the fact that you are now reading these words—the destruction and disappearance of our country."

Ten years after the Agreement was signed, Canada is a strongly independent nation still able to take policy lines that disagree with the U.S. as when, for example, it continued to trade with Cuba in spite of strong U.S. disapproval. Ten years after the FTA, the Canadian economy is strong and vibrant. Growth in output and employment continues and, although unemployment is higher than Canadians would like it to be, that is an endemic problem that no one has succeeded in blaming on free trade.

Far from being the cause of Canada's problems, the FTA (and the NAFTA) are one small part of the structural solution. Rationalizing production on the basis of one North American market is not the most important thing that is happening to Canada, but it is one important step in helping Canada to deal with the modern globalizing, and fiercely competitive, world.

Bibliography

Hurtig, M. (1991), *The Betrayal of Canada*, (Toronto: Stoddart).

Kelleher, Hon. James (1985), *Report by the Minister for International Trade to the Rt. Hon. Brian Mulroney, Prime Minister of Canada, Ottawa, September 25, 1985*. (The text of the quote is taken from the press release that accompanied Kelleher's report.)

Lipsey, R.G. (1989), "Unsettled Issues in the Great Free Trade Debate," *Canadian Journal of Economics*, February, *22 (No 1)*, 1–21.

_____(1985), "Reflections on Canadian Regional Policy: Canada and The United States North America and the Western Hemisphere," The George Van Roggen Memorial Lecture (Vancouver: Business Council of National Issues) March 1993. Later published as "The Case for the FTA and NAFTA," *Canadian Business Economics*, Winter 1995, Vol.3, No.2, 23–39.

_____ and M. Smith (1985), *Taking the Initiative: Canada's Trade Options in a Turbulent World*, (Toronto: C.D. Howe Institute).

_____ and Robert C. York (1988), *Evaluating The Free Trade Deal: A Guided Tour Through The Canada–U.S. Agreement*, (Toronto: C.D. Howe Institute).

Schwanen, Daniel (1992), "Were the Optimists Wrong on Free Trade?" *C. D. Howe Institute Commentary*. No 37, October.

_____ (1997), "Trading Up: The Impact of Increased Continental Integration of Trade, Investment and Jobs in Canada," *C. D. Howe Commentary* 89, (Toronto: C.D. Howe Institute).

Trefler, Daniel (1999), "The Long and the Short of the Canada–U.S. Free Trade Agreement, Paper prepared for the Micro–economic Policy Analysis Division, Industry Canada, manuscript.

UN Center on Transnational Corporations, Regional Economic Integration and Transnational Corporations in the 1990s: Europe 1992, North America and Developing Countries, (New York: United Nations) 1990.

THE CANADA-U.S. FREE TRADE AGREEMENT: THE ISSUE OF ASSURED ACCESS

Paul Wonnacott[*]

The history of U.S.-Canadian economic relations is a story of success. The border between the two countries is one of the most open in the world— in spite of difficulties which people are having getting across the border. Each country is the other's best trading partner— about one fifth of U.S. merchandise trade is with Canada, and about four fifths of Canadian merchandise trade is with the United States. In each country, exports to its North American partner have followed a long-run upward trend as a percentage of GDP. The upward trend has been marked by a reduction of tariffs, with the Free Trade Agreement a decade ago being the logical capstone of that process.

These well know facts— clichés, if you like— are worth repeating and reemphasizing, because in talking about relations between the two countries, there is a natural tendency to focus on problems, on points of disagreement— such as the anti-dumping duties (ADD), and, even more important, countervailing duties (CVD) aimed at offsetting government-provided subsidies. I will be playing the bad cop to Richard Lipsey's good cop. He will talk about the impressive accomplishments of the FTA; I will speak of some of the frictions between the two countries. Before addressing the problems, I want to reemphasize the main point: most trade between the two countries is quiet, uncontroversial and beneficial; and it was to increase these benefits that the two countries entered the Free-Trade Agreement. For the United States, the FTA held out several promises:

---

*Paul Wonnacott is Alan R. Holmes Professor Emeritus at Middlebury College and was a member of the President's Council of Economic Advisors from 1991 to 1993. He has taught at Columbia and the University of Maryland and has held positions with the U. S. Department of State, the Board of Governors of the U. S. Federal Reserve System, and the Canadian Royal Commission of Banking and Finance.

- The FTA was a way of gaining assurance that Canada would not repeat policies which the United States found objectionable— notably, screening of international investment and the national energy policy. Incidentally, the Conservative government of Prime Minister Mulroney also wanted to make it more difficult for Canada to backslide, and an international agreement would do just that.
- American firms would gain freer access to the Canadian market, and free trade would help international firms— with plants in both countries— to rationalize their operations.
- Some saw the FTA as the beginning of a move toward hemispheric free trade.

But Canada had far more at stake than the United States, largely because of the huge difference in size of the two countries. In terms of population and GDP, Canada is roughly one tenth the size of the United States. Furthermore, most of the Canadian population is strung out in a long, narrow band within 100 miles of the U.S. border. And Canada lives with the problem of the missing middle. In the 1,000-plus miles from Toronto to Winnipeg, population is sparse. The vast Northern Ontario shield is utterly inhospitable to agriculture. There are small towns with colorful names: Nipigon, Kapuskasing, and Killaloe, and a few small to mid-sized mining and port cities— Sudbury, Sault Ste. Marie, and Thunder Bay— but otherwise, people are few and far between. To get from the population center of southwest Ontario to the Canadian West, the best and easiest way to drive is through Michigan and other American states. The missing middle aggravates the strong regional differences in Canada. Of the five political parties in the Canadian Parliament, only one— the ruling Liberal Party— can currently be spoken of as a national party. The other party that has historically enjoyed national support— the Conservative Party of Prime Minister Brian Mulroney who negotiated the Free-Trade Agreement with the United States— was almost eliminated from the House of Commons in the last election. The other parties— most obviously the Bloc Quebecois, and, less conspicuously, Reform with its base in the West— are primarily regional parties. The missing middle increases the natural focus of Canadians on their relations with their neighbors to the south.

Much of Canadian history has been the effort by the Canadian government to forge east-west ties to counterbalance the two main facts of Canadian economic and political life— the centrifugal forces within the Canadian federation, and the natural ties of Canadians to the south, to the United States. As a youngster growing up in Ontario, I have strong memories of only two political events during the last year of the Second World War. One was the zombie issue— whether soldiers drafted for home defense would be sent overseas against their will to fight against Hitler's legions. The passion of that event is hard for Americans to understand. Our family was visited by a relative— an Army officer— whose diatribes against Prime Minister MacKenzie King left my young mind confused about whose side Mr. King was really on. The other political event that stuck in my memory was an election— not a Canadian election, but the final presidential campaign of Franklin Roosevelt. I was left with the impression that U.S. elections were more important for Canada than were Canadian elections. Perhaps that impression was correct. Perhaps it still is?

The difference in size between the two countries has a number of important implications for bilateral trade:

1. Canada has much more at stake in U.S.–Canadian trade than does the United States. Bilateral trade between the two countries is one of the top 100 issues of importance for the American economy. For Canadians, it is one of the top two or three. This means that bilateral trade issues are followed much more closely by senior Canadian politicians— including the Prime Minister— than by their American counterparts, and bilateral trade issues are likewise followed much more closely in the Canadian than in the American press. During the free trade negotiations, a knot of reporters would congregate outside the USTR building on 17th Street. They were almost all from the Canadian media. In Canada, Simon Reisman was a celebrity— except to the *Toronto Star*, for whom he played the role of Darth Vader. In the United States, his counterpart was Peter Murphy. He was much better known to the Canadian than to the U.S. public.

   This first point— that Canada has more at stake from the bilateral arrangement— is more or less obvious; it follows directly from the difference in size. If ten Americans send a total of $100 worth of goods to Canada, and a single Canadian sends $100 in goods back, the importance of that transaction— and the gains from it— will be greater for the Canadian than for each of the 10 Americans.

2. What is not so obvious is that Canada gets more of the gain, not only per person, but also in total. That is, in our example, the gain to the single Canadian is greater than the sum of the gains to the 10 Americans. Why is this so?

One answer is that the gains from trade depend on the diversification of an economy. The American economy, with its large population and variety of climatic zones, is more diversified than the Canadian; Americans need international trade less than do Canadians— although care should be taken not to overstate this case; trade is important for the United States, too.

The second answer lies in economies of scale. The Canadian economy is just too small to produce many goods at an efficient scale for domestic consumption. To gain economies of scale, Canada needs to specialize in a limited number of goods, producing them at a large scale for the export market as well as for the domestic market, and import many other products. Even in the United States— where economies of scale have been downplayed by international economists until the past 10 or 15 years— economies of scale can be important; witness Boeing. But what is true of relatively few industries in the United States— aircraft, computers and software, pharmaceuticals— is true of many, many industries in Canada. Exports hold the key to their gaining efficient volumes of production.

For Canada as a whole, economies of scale represent an important gain from international trade. Prior to the 1960s, when economists generally focused on the traditional triangular gains from a reduction in existing tariffs, it was hard for economists to see how a reduction of trade barriers could raise Canadian GDP by more than one-quarter or, at the most, one-half-of-one percent. But once economies of scale were taken into account, gains from the complete elimination of trade barriers might rise to the range of 5 to 10 percent of GDP. Such gains would, however, depend heavily on market access to foreign countries. In other words, the reciprocal reduction of barriers became a matter of prime importance— either multilateral reductions through GATT, or bilateral reductions with the United States.

The importance of international trade as a way to gather economies of scale came to the fore in the middle 1960s, as Canada and the United States engaged in talks leading to the Autopact of 1965, which provided duty–free passage of automobiles and original equipment parts between the two countries, and which acted as a precursor for the broad

Canada–U.S. Free Trade Agreement of a decade ago. Canada wanted to move beyond the branch plant system— with many models of cars built in each plant at a low, inefficient scale— to have efficient, specialized auto plants. The United States likewise had an interest in increasing efficiency in the subsidiaries of its automobile companies in Canada. And both countries saw the Autopact as a way of dealing with instability in existing arrangements, specifically, the possibility of a U.S. countervailing duty in response to the Canadian duty remission program.

3. Although the smaller countries gain more from free international trade than do large countries, this is not unfair. It is not unfair for Canada to get more than half the gains from bilateral trade; that's the way markets work. To see why this is so, consider a hypothetical, purely domestic American example. Suppose that, for some reason, Michigan seceded or was expelled from the United States, with trade barriers thereupon being erected between Michigan and the remaining 49 states. Who would be hurt the most? Rather clearly, Michigan. In other words, Michigan gets most of the gain from free trade between Michigan and the other 49 states. But this is in no way unfair. The statements about Michigan would also apply to every one of the other 49 states if it alone were expelled from the union. It's obvious that each of the 50 states cannot gain an unfair advantage at the expense of all the other 49.

4. Because of the difference in size between the two countries, it was important that the initiative for the negotiations come from the Canadian side— as, in fact, it did. If the United States had taken the lead, there would quite possibly been a cry of American economic imperialism from Canada. It was important for the American side to take a relatively light touch in its negotiations. This morning, we have heard a lively exchange by the participants in the negotiations. In this negotiation, Simon Reisman obviously played an important and constructive role. If, however, Simon had been representing the U.S. rather than the Canadian side, we might wonder whether the negotiations would have broken down within the first week.

5. Where economies of scale are important— where domestic industry reorganizes and specializes to reap the gains from open international trade— then the industry becomes very vulnerable to an increase in foreign tariffs or other trade barriers. Particularly for the smaller country, it is essential that

foreign trade barriers not only be reduced, but that guarantees be provided against the reintroduction of barriers. Thus, *assured access* to American markets was the central objective of the Canadian government in the free-trade negotiations of a decade ago.

As seen from the Canadian side, the problem of assured access was even more important in the general free-trade negotiations than it had been in the Autopact. After all, most Canadian automobile production was carried on by Canadian subsidiaries of General Motors, Ford, and Chrysler. The Big Three have an interest in stable policies toward Canada; they don't want changes that will inflict costs on their Canadian subsidiaries. But many Canadian firms in other industries lack an American associate which takes its interests into account.

In passing, however, I might note that, even in the case of the Autopact, there has not been entirely smooth sailing. During the early part of 1971, the American government was concerned that a large fraction of the domestically-generated increase in aggregate demand was being siphoned off into imports. This, of course, led to President Nixon's decision to upset the Bretton Woods apple cart of pegged exchange rates. As a related matter, some American officials believed that the Canadian government was not acting in good faith on the Autopact; Canada was making it clear that it intended to extend transitional safeguards indefinitely. As a result, a decision to repudiate the Autopact— presumably as a prelude to renegotiation— was included in the preliminary version of the press release announcing the New Economic Policy of August 1971. When a State Department official saw the preliminary press release, he almost went into cardiac arrest. He quickly persuaded his Treasury colleague that it really wasn't the thing to do, to announce such a bombshell without at least having discussions with Canada first. What followed was a Keystone Cops routine. Fortunately, the renunciation decision was printed separately on the last page of the press release. The reporters were kept waiting while the last page of each copy of the prepared press release was ripped off.

The Canadian desire to achieve assured access to the American market not only shaped the Canadian negotiating strategy in the free-trade negotiations; it was also the precipitating factor inducing Canada to make the initial overture for those negotiations. There was a growing view in Canada that bilateral free trade could hold major gains. But Canadians were driven to the table less by hope than by fear. They were fearful of what they saw as rising American protectionism, which had been aggravated by macroeconomic policies in the United States, a very high exchange value of the U.S. dollar in the mid 1980s, and rising U.S. trade deficits. (Is there a danger that this scenario will be repeated in the near future?)

And so, Canada invited the United States to bilateral talks. In a shmaltzy, sentimental "Shamrock Summit" between Prime Minister Mulroney and President Reagan, the two leaders committed themselves to free-trade negotiations. In proposing the negotiations, Prime Minister Mulroney hoped that the negotiations would not only sweep away barriers on both sides of the border. He also hoped that, in the process, the growing interprovincial barriers to trade would also be brought down. In other words, he saw U.S.-Canadian negotiations as a way of easing the difficult regional problems within Canada. Without mentioning a brand label, Mr. Mulroney said that he hoped that, as a result of free trade, he would be able to buy Moosehead beer in Ottawa, without having to wait for his next trip to Washington. This may seem puzzling to an American audience, but Moosehead beer, brewed in the Canadian Maritimes, could be bought in Washington but not Ottawa. The reason? U.S. barriers to beer imports were less rigid than barriers *between* the Canadian provinces.

Because of the importance of assured access, Canadians were determined that the negotiations must be about much more than an elimination of tariffs. Two objectives were at the top of Canada's list:

1. A disputes settlements mechanism, which would curb what Canada saw as the arbitrary and politically-motivated application of countervailing duties by the United States, with the CVD on lumber being the prime example.

2. More broadly, the negotiation of special arrangements between two countries that would greatly limit or even eliminate CVDs and ADDs on trade between the two countries.

To make a long story short, after extended negotiations, Canada felt increasing frustration; on the American side, concessions on these two points— and particularly the second— were seen as possible barriers to Congressional ratification. But without progress on these two points, an agreement was unacceptable to Canada. Their only way out, as they saw it, was to suspend negotiations, to create a crisis atmosphere which would push the decisions up to a more senior level. In the crisis negotiations— in which Peter McPherson,[1] played an important role as Deputy Secretary of

---

[1] See, Michael Hart, *Decision at Midnight* (Vancouver: University of British Columbia Press, 1994), pp. 329, 333, 355, 357–61.

the Treasury— there was an agreement on a disputes settlements mechanism, and an agreement to continue negotiations on CVD and ADD.

I have already suggested that the world can look quite different from Washington and Ottawa. Decades ago, when I was working on the automobile industry, I was periodically surprised, appalled, and amused at how differently the Autopact was described on the two sides of the border. Perhaps, as George Bernard Shaw observed in speaking of the United States and Britain, we are two nations separated by a common language.

Nowhere, perhaps, is this more true than with respect to ADD and especially Countervailing Duty Laws, which for most of the 20th century have been significant elements of trade law. On our side of the border, we usually speak of them as "fair trade laws"— laws aimed at "leveling the playing field," so to speak. Canadian negotiator Rodney Grey coined a much more colorful and critical term— he referred to CVD and ADD laws, at least in their U.S. versions— as "contingent protection." As seen from Canada, the U.S. laws were intended to give U.S. businesses shelter from legitimate foreign competition. The term "fair trade laws" on one side of the border; the term "contingent protection" on the other. It may, of course, not be a matter of language at all. Perhaps we have an illustration of a simple fact: What is "fair" depends so much on your viewpoint.

Anti–Dumping Duties

Dumping has traditionally been defined as selling at a lower price in a foreign market than at home. The reason for ADD is to offset and give domestic producers protection from these lower prices. Traditionally, since Jacob Viner's early work in the 1920s, economists have been skeptical of ADD, except where dumping is used in a predatory manner to drive out domestic competition. If countries want to sell us goods consistently at a low price, is it not in our interest to buy them? From a free–trade viewpoint, does it matter whether we can buy bananas cheaply because foreign countries have a particularly good climate for banana–growing, or because they are willing to sell us bananas more cheaply than they sell them at home?[2] The world is, of course, more complicated than this simple question suggests. If a manufacturer can cover fixed costs by selling in a

---

[2]   There is a substantial literature critical of anti–dumping duties. See, for example, Robert Litan and Richard Boltuck, eds., *Down in the Dumps* (Washington: Brookings, 1991), and Michael Finger, *Antidumping: How it Works and Who Gets Hurt* (Ann Arbor: University ofMichigan Press, 1993). For the opposing view, see Greg Mastel, *Antidumping Laws and the U.S. Economy* (Armonk: M.E. Sharpe, 1998).

protected home market and dumping extra output on the world market, there may not only be an international misallocation of resources, but also the loss of high incomes that can arise in industries with major economies of scale. In economists' jargon, there may be a loss of quasirents.

Where free trade is reciprocal— where the exporting country can't use a protected base to cover its fixed costs— the case for ADD is severely weakened. Thus, the question arises as to whether U.S. and Canadian ADD should be eliminated within the free-trade agreement as it has been within the European Union, and perhaps replaced with general rules of competition. For the long run, this strikes me as a very good question. For the short run, I doubt that a major revision of the ADD is worth the political chips that would have to be expended; there are more important causes for free traders to promote, with greater chances of success.

I come to this conclusion even though U.S. ADD law has gone beyond its original design, to become something of a dog's breakfast. Dumping now includes not only sales below the home price, but also sales below the constructed price as calculated by the U.S. government— a price that includes a normal profit. It's not hard to see how such a provision could be enacted; some goods are exported to the United States without exactly the same model being sold in the home country, so there is no firm basis for a calculation in the traditional manner. But, from an economic viewpoint, this way of calculating a dumping duty doesn't make much sense— a company in a toughly competitive market may be selling at very little profit or loss in all markets, without discriminating between domestic sales and imports. The major redeeming feature of this law is that its application is limited; those who petition for ADDs need to show that the dumped goods damage domestic competitors.

At any rate, anti-dumping cases have not been the most important source of friction between Canada and the United States.

Countervailing Duties

That distinction, rather, falls to countervailing duties, where frictions are partly due to differences in attitudes towards government in the two countries. The United States has a greater commitment to free markets, although perhaps not so much as we sometimes like to think. In Canada, there has— certainly until recently— been a stronger belief in a benign government, and a greater taste for large government programs. One of the principal U.S. negotiators of recent decades, who has extensive experience in both Japan and Canada and has warm relations with both countries, has told me that he thinks Canada has just as much tendency to tinker with the market as do the Japanese. With the wide difference of opinion between the two countries, it is not surprising that government subsidies and countervailing duties are major bones of contention. Nor is it altogether surprising that accusations of bad faith have been made in each country against the other over subsidies and countervailing duties— some Americans believing that Canada has not acted in good faith on the Autopact, and Canadians complaining of U.S. bad faith in our application of CVDs to lumber.

Perhaps, while I'm washing dirty linen, I might as well do it all. Negotiators on both sides of the border sometimes liken their counterparts across the border to officials from the Third World. As the free-trade negotiations wound up, Simon Reisman modestly allowed that he had outmaneuvered the Americans, who, he said, had "negotiated like a Third World Country." His Deputy, Gordon Ritchie, was taken aback by this breech of diplomatic etiquette. Simon, I'm afraid, could be a bit outspoken in his boisterous youth. At any rate, Ritchie's attempt to dump cold water on his boss came to naught when the Prime Minister's wife, Mila, called Simon to cheer him for his "Third World" dig at the Americans.[3] On the American side, trade negotiators have sometimes complained to me that dealing with Canadians is just like dealing with a third world country. On the U.S. side of the border, such comments have been kept quiet within the government, out of the public eye. In the light of the differences in size and priorities between the two countries, it's doubtful that any American newspaper would have the slightest interest in such complaints. I'm sure that they never attracted the attention of Mila Mulroney's U.S. counterpart, Nancy Reagan.

Let me turn to two cases in which the U.S. countervailing duty has been important— automobiles and lumber.

Automobiles

The Autopact of 1965 grew out of a difficulty raised by the Canadian Duty Remission schemes introduced several years before. Under those schemes, Canadian auto producers could earn duty-free imports of selected parts (transmissions and engines) if they exported equivalent amounts of parts and met other conditions. This duty remission could reasonably be

---

[3]   Gordon Ritchie, *Wrestling with the Elephant: The Inside Story of the Canada–U.S. Trade Wars* (Toronto: Macfarlane Walter & Ross, 1997), p. 136.

considered an export subsidy, countervailable under the U.S. trade law of 1930. It was not particularly objectionable to the U.S. big-three auto producers, because their subsidiaries in Canada stood to gain from the Canadian program. But an independent U.S. parts maker sued to force the Treasury to impose countervailing duties. The plaintiff was expected to win, and something had to be done. In this case, the threat of CVDs led to a constructive outcome: the Autopact that provided duty-free passage of new parts and equipment.

As Japanese automobile sales became more important in North America, Canada was anxious to attract Japanese plants. To do so, the Canadian Government made secret agreements with Japanese firms providing for duty drawbacks as a reward for exports. When news of these drawbacks leaked out, there was a negative reaction in Washington; the United States thought that such export incentives were to be eliminated as part of the Autopact of 1965. This problem, and the knotty questions which arose when the U.S. Treasury ruled that Canadian-built Hondas would be subject to duties because they did not contain specified levels of North American content, were diffused by the free trade agreement— although this issue has not entirely disappeared. The Japanese government has recently launched a WTO complaint against Canada, on the ground that the Autopact discriminates against Japanese firms who continue to pay duties on exports to Canada.

Softwood Lumber

If Canadian automobile policies— most notably the secret duty drawbacks— raised doubts among American trade specialists regarding Canadian good faith, the lumber case led to well-publicized Canadian charges of appallingly bad faith on the part of the United States.[4] In fact, softwood lumber has been the *most* important trade irritant between the two countries; Daniel Schwanen of the C. D. Howe Institute found that this dispute, in terms of the value of trade, dwarfed all other bilateral disputes.

In the early 1980s, the U.S. lumber industry was under pressure, in part because they had overbid for stumpage fees— the rights to cut lumber— during the inflationary spree of the late 1970s. They were also under pressure from imports from Canada, and observed that Canadian provincial stumpage fees were substantially lower than theirs. Could they

---

4   Ritchie, p. 196, in a chapter colorfully entitled "Thugs and Bullies."

use the lower Canadian stumpage fees to argue that the "playing field" was unlevel? Were the lower Canadian stumpage fees an unfair subsidy?

Under U.S. law, such complaints go before the Commerce Department and the International Trade Commission in a quasi–judicial procedure. In 1983, Commerce rejected the claim for a countervailing duty. Under U.S. law, foreign subsidies are deemed to be distorting and therefore countervailable if, among other things, they are directed toward a single industry— such as cars or steel. Generally available subsidies— most obviously, subsidies for the college education of engineers, or government expenditures for general road construction— are not countervailable because their benefits are generally available to many industries, and do not distort competition.

In the 1983 decision, the Commerce Department concluded that Canadian stumpage fees were not countervailable because, among other things, they were "generally available" to a number of industries— lumber and wood products, pulp and paper, and furniture.

But the decision was not taken as final; the lumber industry pressed its case once more, with powerful political support. This time the Commerce Department found that the low provincial stumpage fees did represent a government subsidy. Two justifications were given for the switch in position. A court decision in the Mexican Carbon Black case narrowed the definition of generally available, and there were fewer actual users of stumpage in Canada than found in the 1983 decision. Specifically, furniture manufacturers, who were included among the 1983 users, were now found to own "negligible" stumpage rights.[5] The United States announced a 15 percent CVD on softwood lumber imports from the four major Canadian provinces (British Columbia, Alberta, Ontario, and Quebec).

Needless to say, many Canadians were enraged by what they saw as a political manipulation of what was supposed to be a quasi–judicial procedure, resulting particularly from the pressures of Senators Baucus and Packwood.[6] As a result of the uproar in Canada, the two countries reached a "Memorandum of Understanding" (MOU) in 1986, under which the Canadian provinces, rather than the U.S. Treasury, got the 15 percent levy. It would be collected by the Canadian government and distributed to the four provinces, provided they did not pass the money back to the lumber producers.

---

[5]   U.S. Department of Commerce. Preliminary Affirmative Countervailing Duty Determination: Certain Softwood Lumber Products from Canada, October 1986, p.17.

[6]   Ritchie, p. 198.

During the free trade negotiations, one question was what would be done about the MOU. Would the barrier to Canadian lumber exports be eliminated, or would the MOU be grandfathered, like the Autopact? The language of the FTA said that the agreement "does not impair or prejudice the exercise of any rights or enforcement measures" arising out of the MOU. On the American side, some interpreted this as a grandfathering of the MOU; on the Canadian side, it was deemed to be "deliberately ambiguous."[7] The stage was set for another round of disputes.

It came in early September 1991, when the Canadian Government repudiated the MOU. To make a long story short, the outcome of the ensuing negotiation was that specified quantities of Canadian lumber would be permitted into the U.S. market free of special charges; exports in excess of those levels would be subject to levies.

What do we make of this whole business, from an economic and political viewpoint?

1. Although the exemption of "generally available subsidies" from countervailing duties makes sense— it would be idiotic to impose CVDs for general education expenditures— the line between specific and generally available subsidies can be very hard to draw in practice, and may not make economic sense. In its 1986 decision, the Commerce Department recognized that this was "one of the more controversial aspects" of the CVD Law. The CVD law, like the ADD law, is flawed. The problem, from a political view, is what can be done about the two trade remedy laws.

2. In passing, I would like to raise doubts about the wisdom of including codes on CVD and ADD in the GATT during the Tokyo Round. There was a benefit— in requiring countries to apply damage tests before imposing such duties. But there was also a cost. The codes suggested that every self-respecting country needed CVD and ADD laws, and therefore encouraged the spread of such laws. Worldwide, the number of anti-

---

[7] Ritchie, p. 201. If, as Ritchie says, the words were deliberately ambiguous, an American might object to Ritchie's conclusion that the U.S. view was "demonstrably false," that the Canadian repudiation of the MOU (mentioned in my next paragraph) was a breach of the understanding at the time of the free-trade agreement.

dumping duties in force more than doubled between 1990 and 1997.[8]

3. Domestic economic pressures or mistakes can slop over to the international arena. One of the precipitating factors in the lumber case was the pressures faced by U.S. firms that had overbid for stumpage rights at home. Similarly, the rise of domestic steel minimills in the United States has encouraged big steel to press for actions against imports.

4. Quite apart from the generally available criterion, "subsidies" may be hard to identify, particularly those associated with natural resources. Clearly, the United States and Canada both have a comparative advantage in wheat on world markets, based on the vast fertile middle of our continent. It would be absurd to argue that we have an unfair advantage in wheat. To do so would be to undercut the whole idea of mutually beneficial trade. On the other hand, one cannot arbitrarily rule that it is impossible to subsidize the use of natural resources. Take electricity, for example. If Canada were to sell electricity more cheaply to the United States than at home, U.S. electric producers might have a legitimate dumping complaint. On the other hand, if the provincial governments set regulations requiring lower electric costs at home than for the export market, there would be a case that heavy Canadian energy users were being subsidized. The obvious solution is for Canada to export electricity at the domestic price (plus transmission costs), neither higher nor lower.

5. This suggests one way that the stumpage problem might have been solved: by allowing exports of Canadian logs to the United States. For a variety of reasons, however, this solution was ruled out by both countries. The FTA provides specific exceptions to the rules against export controls in the case both of Canadian logs and U.S. logs. Having ruled out the one simple solution, we may have been condemned to the messy but not altogether unsatisfactory outcome we have reached.

---

8   Thomas Klitgaard and Karen Schiele, "Free versus Fair Trade: The Dumping Issue," Federal Reserve Bank of New York, *Current Issues in Economics and Finance*, August 1998, pp. 1 and 3.

6. Specific trade frictions may drag on and on. The lumber case may seem like a shaggy dog story. But, in the overall picture, it is not so bad. When I was with the Council of Economic Advisers in the late 1960s, there was a running dispute with the European Community over their barriers to U.S. oilseeds (mainly soy beans). When I came back to the Council in the early 1990s, this dispute was still going on and on. I'm just glad I missed the intervening 20 years of that controversy. It was essentially intractable: the European Common Agriculture Policy created fundamental problems in European trade policy.

Fortunately, some problems do get solved if they are worked on long enough. When I was at the Council, I was pessimistic that Ontario's barriers to U.S. beer would ever come down, in spite of our high punitive duties on Ontario beer. Even though Canada exported much more beer to the United States than it imported, it seemed to me that the Canadian beer industry had an incentive to press for continued barriers to U.S. beer; it was worth risking their export market in order to continue their cushy, profitable markets at home. On this, however, my prediction was overly pessimistic: U.S. beer is now readily available in Ontario stores. And interprovincial barriers have also come down— not so surprising, as they were nuisances for the Canadian beer industry. Mr. Mulroney, in his enforced retirement from the Prime Ministry, may sip his Moosehead Beer without traveling either to the Maritimes or to Washington.

Part Three

ISSUES IN THE NEGOTIATIONS

AGRICULTURAL ISSUES IN THE CANADA-U. S. FREE TRADE AGREEMENT

David B. Schweikhardt[*]

As negotiations began on a free trade agreement between the United States and Canada, world agricultural trade had reached a state of disarray that demanded the attention of policy makers. Agricultural trade policy, exempt from many of the multilateral provisions contained in the General Agreement on Tariffs and Trade, was a complex set of policies that incurred rising costs on consumers and taxpayers. These trade policies, combined with the often contradictory domestic agricultural policies pursued by many nations, led to an increasing number of trade disputes on agricultural issues.

The agricultural trade relationship between the United States and Canada in the 1980s reflected this growing disarray in world agricultural trade policy. During the decade preceding the negotiations, an increasing number of trade policy disputes arose on agricultural products, and agricultural trade between the two nations was marked by an increasingly complicated set of trade policies that sought to accomplish a variety of conflicting objectives. It is within this context that the impact of the Canada-U. S. Free Trade Agreement on agricultural trade must be judged.

United States-Canadian Agricultural Trade Relations: Entering the Negotiations

Agricultural trade between the United States and Canada experienced significant growth in the decade prior to the negotiation of the Canada-U. S. Free Trade Agreement. U.S. agricultural exports to Canada averaged

* David B. Schweikhardt is an Associate Professor in the Department of Agricultural Economics at Michigan State University. He specializes in agricultural and trade policy. His recent research has focused on the impact of the FTA and GATT on Michigan and U.S. agriculture. The research for this article has been partially funded by the Elton R. Smith Endowment in Food and Agriculture Policy.

$1.8 billion during the period from 1981 to 1985, an increase of 13 percent over the average exports from 1976 to 1980. Canadian agricultural exports to the United States averaged $1.5 billion during 1981 to 1985, compared to $800 million in 1976 to 1980 (table 1).[1] U.S. agricultural exports to Canada were diversified across a wide range of products. Fruits and vegetables represented the largest share of U.S. exports to Canada, but animal products, grains, and oilseeds each contributed a major share of shipments (table 2). U.S. imports from Canada were somewhat more specialized, with livestock products and grains comprising the largest share of Canadian shipments to the United States. Canadian exports of fruit, vegetable and oilseed products to the United States were quite modest throughout this period.

Table 1. U.S.-Canadian Agricultural Trade, 1976-1985.						
Average(billions of U.S. dollars)	1976-80	1981	1982	1983	1984	1985
U.S. Exports to Canada	1.63	1.99	1.82	1.84	1.96	1.62
U.S. Imports from Canada	0.80	1.15	1.40	1.50	1.85	1.89
U.S. exports to Canada as percent of total U.S. exports	5.4	4.6	5.0	5.1	5.2	5.6
U.S. imports from Canada as percent of total U.S. imports	4.9	6.9	9.1	9.1	9.6	9.5
Canadian exports to U.S. as percent of total Canadian exports	15.5	14.3	17.3	18.3	21.7	27.3
Canadian imports from U.S. as percent of total Canadian imports	57.4	58.2	60.5	60.1	59.1	57.0

The importance of this trade relationship, and thus of a potential trade agreement, was borne out by the shares of each country's total agricultural trade that took place with the other country. As was true for non-agricultural trade, Canada was increasingly dependent upon the United States as both a market for exports and a source of imports (table 2). The U.S. share of its total agricultural exports that were shipped to Canada was

---

[1]   All data are expressed in U.S. dollars and are based on U.S. sources of trade data. There were discrepancies between these data sources. For example, Canadian trade statistics reported that U.S. exports to Canada averaged $2.1 billion in 1976 to 1980 and $2.6 billion (U.S.) in 1981 to 1986 (Blandford and Sorenson, p. 2).

rather small (an average of 5.4 percent during 1976 to 1980 and ranging from 4.6 to 5.6 percent from 1981 to 1985). Canada was more dependent on the U.S. as an export market, shipping an average of 15.5 percent of its total agricultural exports to the United States during 1976 to 1981. This share increased during the 1980s, reaching 27 percent in 1985. At the same time, the United States supplied a significant source of Canada's agricultural imports. Imports from the United States represented 57 percent of total Canadian agricultural imports from 1976 to 1981 and ranged from 57 to 60 percent during the first half of the 1980s.

Table 2a. U.S. Agricultural Trade with Canada by Product Category, 1980-1996 (millions of U.S. Dollars)

U.S. IMPORTS FROM CANADA

Year	Total	Animal	Dairy	Grains	Fruits	Vegetable	Oil seeds
1980	1061	556	5	125	31	47	237
1981	1150	550	5	132	37	13	209
1982	1395	728	14	221	42	20	199
1983	1504	729	35	239	39	90	211
1984	1851	771	57	262	42	100	264
1985	1894	986	67	257	46	94	185
1986	2018	949	72	294	57	104	210
1987	2214	1051	63	332	65	123	243
1988	2443	1137	59	425	115	141	263
1989	2915	1232	33	558	60	207	262
1990	3152	1485	21	539	62	212	289
1991	3306	1494	15	566	67	237	301
1992	4102	1853	17	778	70	249	286
1993	4621	2003	40	945	75	304	369
1994	5231	1932	40	1276	98	337	328
1995	5631	2140	68	1298	95	439	357
1996	6794	2628	82	1541	108	568	459

Agricultural and Trade Policy Setting: Entering the Negotiations

By the mid 1980s, world agricultural trade policy could be characterized as being in a state of disarray. Rising levels of export subsidies, widespread use of import quotas, tariffs at prohibitive levels, and increasing levels of government spending for domestic agricultural subsidies led to calls for "mutual disarmament" in agricultural trade policy (National Center for Food and Agricultural Policy). This state of disarray in agricultural trade policy was marked by an escalation of the costs of these policies to taxpayers and consumers. From 1979 to 1981, these policies were estimated to have cost taxpayers and consumers $100 billion. For 1984 to 1986, the cost of these policies had reached $220 billion for taxpayers and consumers (Allen, *et al.*). The distortions created by these policies, combined with their escalating costs, led to calls for reform of agricultural trade policy and made agricultural trade issues a centerpiece of the Uruguay Round of GATT negotiations that opened in 1986 (Hathaway).

Table 2b. U.S. Agricultural Trade with Canada by Product Category, 1980-1996 (Millions of U.S. Dollars)

U.S. EXPORTS TO CANADA

Year	Total	Animal	Dairy	Grains	Fruits	Vegetables	Oil seeds
1980	1852	278	10	166	398	260	237
1981	1989	333	12	172	436	334	209
1982	1820	228	12	209	333	326	199
1983	1844	288	13	201	319	323	211
1984	1963	338	10	226	300	327	264
1985	1622	283	10	201	247	252	185
1986	1542	295	10	183	250	244	210
1987	1809	382	13	181	270	298	243
1988	2019	390	18	262	318	318	263
1989	2221	424	15	312	330	364	262
1990	4197	802	27	559	702	785	289
1991	4554	877	32	615	689	1032	301
1992	4902	892	44	770	708	1133	286
1993	5271	943	47	803	728	1227	369
1994	5504	1026	48	1305	686	1344	328
1995	5812	1053	84	1032	709	1231	357
1996	6146	1089	111	1130	714	1237	459

Source: U.S. Department of Agriculture, Foreign Agricultural Trade of the United States, various issues.

This international setting provided the context within which agricultural trade issues were negotiated in the Canada–U.S. Free Trade Agreement. Each country used a complex set of trade barriers and domestic subsidies to support their agricultural sectors. This complex web of subsidies complicated the negotiations, yet provided a major reason why trade liberalization between the countries was viewed as necessary to relieve some trade tensions. Agricultural trade policy between the United States and Canada reflected the broader problem in international agricultural markets during the 1980s: Tariffs on agricultural products posed a barrier between the two nations, import quotas were used to protect domestic markets and defend domestic agricultural subsidies, and a variety of agricultural subsidies led to trade disputes between the two nations[2] (table 4).

Table 3. Trade shares of U.S. Canadian Agricultural Products, 1985.

	Canada's share of total U.S. exports in category	Canada's share of total U.S. imports in category	U.S share of total Can. exports in category	U.S. share of total Can. Exports in category
Grains and feeds feeds	1.7	41.2	7.7	80.2
Oilseeds and & products	3.2	11.2	10.1	81.3
Meat and live animals	6.4	28.5	81.3	50.2
Poultry and eggs	15.3	26.0	67.5	98.7
Dairy products	2.3	8.8	6.8	14.3
Other animal products	6.5	16.4	27.1	63.3
Fruit and nuts	20.6	2.8	73.8	55.0
Vegetables	27.1	6.8	44.5	76.6
Tobacco	0.3	3.1	33.6	79.0
Fibers	3.4	0.0	98.4	84.6
Other products	0.4	3.9	89.1	37.0
Total	5.6	9.5	27.3	57.0

---

[2] Between 1879 and 1986, the United States filed trade complaints against Canadian exports of wine, onions, potatoes, raspberries, sugar, live cattle, hogs, and fresh-cut flowers. During the same period, Canada filed trade complaints against U. S. exports of potatoes, onions, sugar, livestock, and corn.

Trade Barriers on Agricultural Products

As the two countries entered the negotiations on the Free Trade Agreement, tariffs on agricultural products were a significant barrier for some commodities. In addition, agricultural trade had been exempted from the provisions of GATT restricting the use of quantitative trade barriers. Consequently, as the negotiations opened on a U.S.–Canadian agreement, both countries relied on tariffs and non–tariff barriers to protect agricultural markets and support their domestic agricultural policy objectives.

**Table 4. Agricultural trade disputes between
the United States and Canada, 1979 - 1986**

United States complaints against Canada	Canadian complaints against United States
Wine	Potatoes
Onions	Onions
Potatoes	Sugar
Raspberries	Livestock
Sugar	Corn
Live cattle	
Hogs	
Fresh-cut flowers	

At the opening of the negotiations, nearly 50 percent of agricultural trade between the two countries was duty free, and tariffs on the remaining products averaged 6 percent on both sides of the border (Gifford, p. 10). U.S. tariffs on agricultural products were lowest on grains, livestock products, and a variety of fresh fruits (table 3). Tariffs were higher on vegetables, cheese, wine, and soybean oil. Tariffs on vegetables also varied during the year, with higher tariffs being imposed during those seasons of the year in which U.S. products were being delivered to the market. In addition to these tariffs, the United States also imposed import quotas on dairy products, wheat, corn, barley, sugar, peanuts and tobacco. These "Section 22" quotas were designed to permit the operation of U.S. domestic price support programs by limiting imports and reducing the government's cost of supporting the prices of these products.[3]

---

[3]   These "Section 22" quotas were established by Section 22 of the Agricultural Adjustment Act of 1933 as amended in 1935 (Tweeten, p. 253).

Canada's tariffs schedule on agricultural products was similar to the United States' tariff structure on agricultural products, but tended to have higher tariffs on many fruits and vegetables (table 4). Soybeans, corn, hogs and pork, and cattle and beef were duty free or had minimal tariffs at the time of the negotiations. Canada also used import quotas and licenses to enforce domestic agricultural policies. Import licenses were required for wheat and barley to protect the Canadian Wheat Board's monopoly buying status. Import licenses and quotas were used to restrict imports and enforce Canada's domestic supply management policies for dairy products, eggs, and poultry meat.[4]

Domestic Agricultural Subsidies

In addition to trade barriers, government support for agriculture in the United States during the 1980s included direct payments (target prices), price supports (loan rates), production controls (acreage controls), export subsidies and import restrictions (tariffs on a wide variety of products and import quotas used to maintain price supports on a more limited range of commodities). Canadian support for agriculure included a combined price support and domestic production quota control system for dairy and poultry, direct payments on dairy, transportation subsidies on grain, and state monopoly trading of wheat, barley and oats (Goodloe).

Comparing this complex set of policies requires a common measure of the level of government support provided across countries and across industries. The simplest measure of the degree of trade protection is provided by a comparison of domestic prices with world prices. Figure 1 compares these estimated producer-to-border-price ratios for wheat, rice, ruminant meat, dairy, and sugar for United States and Canada. In those sectors in which there was little or no border protection (rice and ruminant meat for Canada, and ruminant meat for the United States), the ratio of producer to border prices was close to 1.0 in the 1980s. In other sectors—particularly dairy, in which the producer to border price ratio was nearly 2.0 for both countries—the degree of border protection was much greater.

While producer-to-border price ratios provide a measure of the import protection provided to an industry by border protection policies, such measures do not reflect other forms of government support provided to the agricultural sector that may affect trade patterns or that may arise in

---

4   Both countries' use of quantitative import restrictions to support their domestic agricultural policies was permitted under GATT prior to the Uruguay Round Agreement (Hathaway, pp. 108-109).

trade negotiations. During the 1980s a broader measure of government support for agriculture was developed to provide a common comparison of the wide variety of policies used to support agriculture (primarily as a tool for use in the GATT negotiations). This measure, the Producer Subsidy Equivalent (PSE) was designed to measure the total transfers to an agricultural sector arising from government policies. The policy transfers in this measure include:

- Income support, including direct or indirect cash transfers between the government and producers.

- Price intervention, including various forms of government intervention that alter prices at one or more links in the marketing chain.

- Border policies, including tariffs, import quotas, and other import barriers that transfer income to producers.

- Input assistance, including implicit or explicit taxes or subsidies on the use variable inputs used in agricultural production.

- Marketing assistance, including programs that affect processing and marketing costs in the agricultural and food industries.

- Infrastructure support, including policies that affect farm structure, producer knowledge and productivity, and other forms of agricultural infrastructure.

- Regional support, including regional, state, or provincial transfers to agricultural producers.

- Economy–wide policies, including but not exclusive to agriculture, that provide support to agriculture, including exchange rate policies, general transportation policies, and general tax policies (USDA, 1994, pp. 1–9).

Though PSEs can be measured in a variety of forms (total transfers, total transfers per unit of production) the most common measure is to express the value of transfers to an agricultural sector as a percentage of the total value of production in that sector. Figure 2 shows the aggregate PSE for 13 commodities in Canada and 12 commodities in the United States for the 1982 to 1992 production years.[5] In both countries, transfers

---

5   The commodities included in the Canadian PSE measure include barley, beef and veal, corn, flaxseed, dairy, oats, pork, poultry, rapeseed, rye, soybeans, sugarbeets, and wheat.

to agricultural producers peaked in 1986 and 1987, just as negotiations on the Canada–U. S. Free Trade Agreement were unfolding and the worldwide agricultural depression of the 1980s reached its depth. By 1992, the U.S. transfers had declined to their levels of the early 1980s, while Canadian transfers remained at somewhat higher levels.

Comparisons of the PSEs for individual commodities indicate those commodities in which transfers to agricultural producers are largest. The dairy industry had the largest policy transfers to producers, with the remainder of the livestock industry showing relatively low levels of policy transfers. Among crop producers, sugar had the largest PSE ratio in the United States, with both countries having relatively large PSE ratios for wheat. The heavy reliance on policy transfers by many of these industries during the 1980s, and the trade conflicts created by these transfers, foreshadowed many of the policy disputes that would arise during the negotiations and during the subsequent implementation period.

Agricultural Provisions of the Canada–U.S. Free Trade Agreement

The Canada–U.S. Free Trade Agreement sought to address many of the major trade barriers and domestic agricultural policies affecting agricultural trade between the two countries. The major provisions of the agreement affecting agriculture included:

- Tariffs on agricultural products were scheduled to be eliminated within ten years. Fruits and vegetables were included in the 10–year tariff elimination.

- A temporary tariff would be permitted on fruits and vegetables for 20 years as a means of achieving relief from import damage if two conditions were met—if import prices of a product are below 90 percent of the average monthly import price over the preceding 5 years (excluding the highest and lowest years) for 5 working days and if planted acreage of the product is not higher than the 5–year average (excluding the higher and lowest years). This temporary duty

---

The commodities included in the United States PSE measure include barley, beef and veal, corn, dairy, oats, pork, poultry, rice, sorghum, soybeans, sugar, and wheat. Dairy products (with a PSE of 59 and 74 percent in the United States and Canada, respectively), sugar (73 and 38 percent), wheat (42 and 40 percent), and corn (28 and 13 percent) had the highest average PSEs from 1984 to 1986. Beef, pork, and poultry each had an average PSE of less than 12 percent in both countries.

may not be higher that the lowest duty that would have been in place and may not be applied more than once in a 12-month period.

- The U.S. would not place quantitative restrictions on imports of Canadian products containing less 10 percent sugar.

- Canada would eliminate import licenses for U.S. wheat, barley, oats and their products when support levels in the countries were equal.

- Canada would eliminate transportation subsidies for grain shipped through western ports to U.S. markets.

- Canada would increase import quotas for poultry, poultry products, and eggs but would not eliminate these import quotas.

- Each country would be exempt from the other's meat import laws.

- Neither country would use export subsidies on agricultural products shipped to the other country (Normile and Goodloe, pp. 42–43).

Changes in Agricultural Trade Patterns Under the Canada–U.S. Free Trade Agreement

The period since the implementation of the Canada–U.S. Free Trade Agreement has been marked by continued rapid growth in agricultural trade between the two nations (table 2). U.S. agricultural exports to Canada were $1.8 billion in 1987, the year before implementation began, and reached $7.0 billion in 1998 (USDA, 1999, p. 9). U.S. exports of vegetables to Canada increased from $300 million in 1987 to $1.2 billion in 1996, replacing grains and animal products as the leading U.S. export category (figure 5). Fruit exports increased from $269 million to $700 million during the same time period. Animal, grain, and oilseed exports also increased, with animal products reaching $1.0 billion in 1996 (compared to $382 million in 1987), grain products reaching $1.1 billion in 1996 (compared to $180 million in 1987) and oilseeds reaching $450 million in 1996 (compared to $300 million in 1987).

Canadian agricultural exports to the United States showed a similar aggregate growth during this period. As was true prior to the agreement, the pattern of Canadian exports to the United States differed from that of U.S. exports to Canada. Canadian exports of animal products increased from $1.0 billion in 1987 to $2.6 billion in 1996, representing the largest category of product shipments to the United States. Grain exports from Canada to the United States increased from $300 million in 1987 to $1.5 billion in 1996. Vegetable product exports from Canada to the United

States increased from $120 million in 1987 to nearly $600 million in 1996. Nearly all of this increase was in shipments of frozen potato products.

Given the tariff structures in place prior to the agreement and the comparative advantage that each country might be expected to hold, these changes in trade patterns are consistent with the expectations of analysts at the conclusion of the negotiations (Normile and Goodloe, pp. 44–51).

Continuing Issues in United States–Canadian Agricultural Trade

Though the Canada–U.S. Free Trade Agreement made substantial progress in removing agricultural trade barriers between the two countries, the period since the completion of negotiations has been marked by a series of disputes that continue to affect agricultural trade between the two nations. Despite the significant growth in agricultural trade under the agreement, disputes continue to arise about the impact of domestic agricultural policies on trade between the nations, the impact of non–tariff barriers, the remaining trade barriers that were not included in the agreement, potential dumping of products in exports markets, and impact of exchange rates on trade between the nations. A brief review of some of these issues can provide an outline of the trade policy agenda that continues to face policy makers in the two countries.

Wheat. The agreement eliminated tariffs on wheat and wheat products. The agreement also eliminated the threat of the imposition of U.S. Section 22 import quotas on wheat and eliminated the use of Canadian rail subsidies for grain shipment to western ports. In subsequent years, Canada unilaterally eliminated its remaining rail subsidies on eastern grain shipments. In the late 1980s, U.S. imports of durum wheat increased significantly, eventually triggering an investigation by the U.S. International Trade Commission.

Despite a finding by the USITC that the increased imports had been caused by drought conditions in the United States rather than any form of dumping, a formal complaint was filed by the United States alleging that the Canadian Wheat Board was selling grain in the United States at less than its acquisition price paid to Canadian farmers and that the remaining Canadian rail subsidies were distorting trade between the two countries. A binational panel ruled that there was no compelling evidence that Canadian wheat was being sold in the United States below the Board's acquisition cost (Carter, pp. 136–140).

Soon after that ruling in 1992, the U.S. threatened the imposition of new tariffs on milling wheat. This decision was based on an investigation by the U.S. International Trade Commission that concluded that increased Canadian wheat exports to the United States were causing an increase in the cost of the U.S. wheat program. Subsequent negotiations on this issue resulted in an agreement that imposed new tariff rate quotas on Canadian durum and milling wheat exports to the United States; the establishment of a bilateral commission to examine the impact of both countries domestic policies on grain trade; and a "peace clause" that prohibited any further actions by either country on grain trade that were inconsistent their obligations under GATT or the free trade agreement.

Despite the unilateral elimination of Canadian rail subsidies, the decoupling of U.S. wheat payments to farmers under the Federal Agricultural Improvement and Reform Act of 1996 and, in recent years, the unilateral decision by the United States not to exercise its right to use export subsidies on wheat as permitted under the Uruguay Round Agreement of GATT, grain trade between the two nations remains a highly contentious issue. In December 1998, negotiators again were forced to deal with a variety of grain trade issues, including transshipment of U.S. grain through Canada and phytosanitary issues affecting wheat, barley, and oats (U.S. Trade Representative). Some of these issues arose as part of U.S. farmers' objections to increased imports of wheat from Canada and continued allegations of Canadian dumping of grain in the United States.

In addition to these issues, domestic agricultural policies in each country continue to affect trade relations in the grain sector. The presence of the Canadian Wheat Board, and the questions raised about its monopoly buying and exporting status, continue to plague U.S.–Canadian relations. Questions about the transparency of the Board's pricing practices and whether those practices constitute dumping of grain into the U.S. market continue to be raised on the American side of the border. It is anticipated that the United States will make state trading monopolies a high priority in any future round of negotiations under the World Trade Organization. Despite U.S. claims that the Board may be distorting grain trade between the two countries, some evidence suggests that the elimination of the Board's monopoly exporter status would actually increase U.S. imports of grain from Canada.[6]

Dairy and Poultry Products. The Canada–U.S. Free Trade Agreement permitted both countries to continue their use of import quotas on dairy

---

[6]   For example, Carter (pp. 139-140) contends that Canadian exports of barley to the United States would increase if the Canadian Wheat Board lost its monopoly exporter status.

products. In addition, Canada was permitted continue its use of import quotas on poultry meat and eggs. These import quotas permitted the United States to operate a price support program for milk, while Canada used its import quotas to operate its supply management policies for dairy and poultry.

Under the terms of the Uruguay Round Agreement of GATT, all countries were required to convert their quantitative import barriers into tariffs. To comply with this requirement, the United States and Canada converted their dairy import quotas on butter, cheese and dry milk into tariff rate quotas (Canada also did so for its import quotas on poultry and eggs). These tariffs were to be reduced under the terms of the Uruguay Round Agreement, but would remain prohibitive at the completion of that transition period.[7]

Following the completion of the Uruguay Round negotiations and the conversion of these import quotas into tariffs, the United States claimed that the Canada–U.S. Free Trade Agreement required the elimination of all such tariffs. The central issue was whether the tariffs created under GATT fell under the jurisdiction of the Canada–U.S. agreement. A NAFTA dispute settlement panel, hearing the first dispute to be lodged under Chapter 20 of that agreement, ruled that such tariffs did not fall under the provisions of the Canada–U.S. Free Trade Agreement and could be retained (Barichello and Romain, pp. 163–64). As a result, trade in these industries remains largely unchanged by the Canada–U. S. agreement and the issue remains a point of contention for the U.S. dairy industry.[8]

Potatoes and Beef. In addition to disputes about the alleged dumping of grain, other U.S. producers have alleged that Canadian exports have been dumped in the United States. In response to complaints by U.S. potato producers, the U.S. International Trade Commission investigated the impact of Canadian potato products to the United States. Canadian potato acreage increased by 20 percent between 1992 and 1996, and U.S. imports

---

[7]   Both countries created tariff rate quotas on these products. At the end of the implementation period, the U.S. tariff will be $1.227/kg on cheddar cheese, $1.541/kg on butter, and $0.86/kg to $1.556/kg on dry milk. Canadian tariffs will be 245.6 percent on cheddar cheese, 298.7 percent on butter, and 243.4 percent on dry milk. Canadian tariffs on poultry meat and eggs would also be prohibitive after the Uruguay Round Agreement is fully implemented.

[8]   An exception to this conclusion is that the U.S.-Canadian agreement did include provisions to increase Canada's global import quotas on poultry products. Since the United States supplies virtually all of Canada's poultry imports, this translated into an increase in U.S. exports to Canada. The remaining tariffs beyond this quota remain prohibitive.

of fresh and frozen potatoes from Canada increased by 150 percent and 130 percent, respectively, during that same period. At the same time, U.S. exports to Canada were hampered by Canadian packaging regulations.

This investigation concluded that U.S. imports from Canada had not had a significant impact on U.S. prices or production nationally, but that Canadian exports had displaced U.S. fresh potatoes in the Northeastern region of the United States (U.S. International Trade Commission). Since the outcome of U.S. dumping cases is determined by the impact of imports on the national market, the success of a dumping case in the potato industry appears problematic. Nevertheless, the U.S. industry continues to express concerns about the impact of Canadian exports and of further expansion of the Canadian potato industry on U.S. producers.

In recent months, a dumping case has also been initiated by U.S. cattle producers seeking relief from imports of live cattle from Canada. This case claims, in part, that the Canadian Wheat Board's pricing practices for feed barley provide an implicit subsidy to Canadian cattle producers. This investigation is in the early stages and the outlook for such a case is unclear.

Technical Barriers to Trade. In addition to a variety of dumping issues, the greatest number of trade issues between the United States and Canada is in the realm of technical trade barriers. A variety of issues, such as frozen potato package sizes, wheat disease infestations, pest control regulations in fresh produce, and differences in phytosanitary barriers on several products have all come to the fore in recent years. These barriers remain the most important source of trade frictions that require the attention of policy makers. In December of 1998, for example, United States and Canadian negotiators reached agreement on an 18-point agreement of understanding on agricultural trade issues. Aside from a few points on grain shipping regulations, the remainder of these points dealt with technical barriers to trade (U.S. Trade Representative). With the removal of tariffs on most agricultural products, an increasing number of trade disputes in the future can be expected to center on technical barriers to trade.

Conclusions

The Canada–U.S. Free Trade Agreement can be considered a success in achieving many of its objectives in liberalizing bilateral agricultural trade. The agreement's primary objective in agriculture—the removal of most import tariffs and quotas—has contributed to the growth in agricultural trade witnessed during the past decade. Despite frequent criticism of the agreement in the United States, Canada remains the United States' largest bilateral trading partner in agricultural trade, with Canada serving as the second largest market for U.S. agricultural exports (second only to Japan) and as the largest source of agricultural imports entering the United States. Given the disparities in population in the two countries, the relatively balanced flow of trade between the two countries is remarkable: In 1996 the average Canadian consumed nearly nine times as much in U.S. food products as the average American consumed of Canadian food products.

The remaining issues in agricultural trade policy are likely to be some of the most vexing problems faced by negotiators. In the grain and dairy sectors, domestic agricultural policies will continue to create trade frictions as domestic policy objectives conflict with trade policy objectives. In other sectors, dumping issues and technical barriers will continue to arise. Changes in exchange rates will also continue to have a major impact on agricultural trade.

All of these issues suggest that the policy agenda will be a lengthy one for future agricultural trade negotiations. Whether these negotiations take place on an ad hoc basis, or whether they are incorporated into some broader framework of negotiations between the two countries–perhaps a second Canada— U.S. agreement that deals with a wide range of trade problems across industries— agricultural issues will remain a central part of the U.S.–Canadian policy agenda well into the future.

Bibliography

Allen, Kristen, Barbara Elliot, Tim T. Phipps, G.E. Rossmiller, and M. Ann Tutwiler. *Agriculture in the Uruguay Round of GATT.* Washington, D.C.: National Center for Food and Agricultural Policy, August 1988.

Barichello, Richard and Robert Romain. "Prospects for the Canadian Dairy Sector Following the Upcoming NAFTA Panel Ruling." In *Understanding Canada/United States Dairy Disputes*, edited by R.M.A. Loyns, Karl Meilke, and Ronald D. Knutson. Winnipeg: University of Manitoba, 1996.

Blandford, David and Vernon L. Sorenson. "An Overview of U.S.-Canadian Trade Liberalization." In *Agricultural Trade Between the United States and Canada*, Department of Agricultural Economics report number AE 4633, University of Illinois at Urbana-Champaign, September 1987, pp. 1–8.

Carter, Colin A. "Understanding the Canadian/United States Grains Dispute: Factors and Impacts." In *Understanding Canada/United States Grain Disputes*, edited by R.M.A. Loyns, Ronald D. Knutson, and Karl Meilke. Winnipeg: University of Manitoba, 1995.

Gifford, Michael. "A Briefing by the Canadian Agricultural Negotiator." In *U.S.-Canadian Agricultural Trade Challenges: Developing Common Approaches*, edited by Kristen Allen and Katie Macmillan. Washington, D.C.: National Center for Food and Agricultural Policy, 1988, pp. 9–13.

Goodloe, Carol A. *Government Intervention in Canadian Agriculture.* U.S. Department of Agriculture. Economic Research Service, Agriculture and Trade Analysis Division, January 1988.

Hathaway, Dale E. *Agriculture and GATT: Rewriting the Rules.* Washington, D.C.: Institute for International Economics, September 1987.

National Center for Food and Agricultural Policy. Mutual Disarmament in World Agriculture: A Declaration on Agricultural Trade. May 1988.

Normile, Mary Anne and Carol A. Goodloe. *U.S.-Canadian Agricultural Trade Issues: Implications for the Bilateral Trade Agreement.* U.S. Department of Agriculture, Economic Research Service,

Agriculture and Trade Analysis Division, Staff Report Number AGES880209, March 1988.

Tweeten, Luther G. *Agricultural Trade: Principles and Policies.* Boulder, Colorado: Westview Press, 1992.

U.S. Department of Agriculture. *Estimates of Producer and Consumer Subsidy Equivalents: Government Intervention in Agriculture, 1982–1992.* Economic Research Service Statisical Bulletin Number 913, December 1994.

U.S. International Trade Commission. *Fresh and Processed Potatoes: Competitive Conditions Affecting U.S. and Canadian Issue.* Investigation 332–378. USITC Publication 3050, July 1997.

U.S. Trade Representative. Record of Understanding Between the Governments of the United States of America and Canada Regarding Areas of Agricultural Trade. 4 December 1998, 7.

DISPUTE SETTLEMENT UNDER THE FREE TRADE AGREEMENT

Konrad von Finckenstein[*]

The FTA has two principle dispute settlement provisions, chapter 18 dealing with disputes under any aspect of the agreement, and chapter 19 dealing with disputes arising under the application of anti-dumping and countervailing duty laws.

First some background: Canada's key goal from the outset was to gain secure access to the U.S. market. To obtain this, Canada began by demanding:

1. Secure access by way of an exemption from anti-dumping countervailing duties, and replacement thereof by new rules to govern subsidies in Canada and the U.S., rules that would describe permissible and illegal subsidies; and

2. A binding dispute settlement mechanism to determine whether a subsidy was permissible or illegal.

As it turned out, it was impossible to obtain the exemption and a new set of rules through the negotiations, and at the end of the day the only concession that Canada could obtain was a binding dispute settlement regarding the application of antidumping and countervailing duty laws. This was, in effect the half loaf that we took home, no new rules, but a binding dispute settlement process on the application of the existing rules. This allowed us to argue with conviction that we had secured guaranteed access to the U.S. market. This was the origin of chapter 19 dispute settlement.

Chapter 18 process has quite a different origin. It grew out of both parties' frustration with the GATT process. We found that the GATT dispute settlement was:

*Konrad von Finckenstein is Commissioner of Competition for Industry Canada's Competition Bureau. At the time the Canada-U.S. Free Trade Agreement was negotiated, he was Senior General Counsel for the Trade Negotiations Office.

- too lengthy, had too many delays built in;
- involved panellists from other countries not necessarily having the expertise in the issue before them;
- did not provide for automatic adoption of panel reports; and
- was uncertain about how an award would be implemented.

Chapter 18 was meant to be a device to overcome all of these issues. We provided for specific time periods, a standing roster of panelists and a host of fail safe provisions should a party attempt to stop or delay the process. Basically, if one party wanted to persue a dispute to the bitter end it could drive the process all the way from consultations, to commission meetings, to panels and finally to a panel report. This was a considerable improvement over the GATT process. However, in fairness, the process did have some short comings:

1. The decision as to whether a panel report would be binding or non-binding was left up to the parties. Unless the parties agreed in advance that a decision would be binding, the report would only be advisory. As could be expected, the parties never elected that a panel should render a nonbinding decision.

2. Advisory opinions of the panel had the down side that the losing party did not have to adopt the panel recommendation if it did not agree with it. The winning side could then suspend benefits, but unfortunately, if the losing side disagreed with such action it could counter suspend. This never happened but the agreement left open such a possibility and such action was at times threatened.

This very unsatisfactory state of affairs was later corrected in chapter 20 of NAFTA, which did away with the distinction between binding and non-binding reports. Chapter 20 also made it quite clear that there could be no counter retaliation by the losing party.

Chapter 18 also allowed parties to choose to use either the GATT process or the chapter 18 process to resolve a dispute. Once having chosen either route, the party was precluded from changing its choice of forum. The same provision can be found in chapter 20 of NAFTA. Since the negotiation of chapter 18 the Uruguay round has been completed and the WTO has been created. The WTO has put in place a dispute resolution process similar to chapter 18 of the FTA and chapter 20 of NAFTA. Obviously the WTO process is more attractive, as a complaining nation can attract other intervening nations and a panel judgement carries with it the weight of all the WTO members. As a result, I believe that in the future the chapter 20 process (i.e. the improved chapter 18 process) will only be used in those cases where there is an obligation under the FTA/NAFTA that does not have a parallel in the WTO. All other disputes will be taken to the WTO.

On the whole, chapter 18 was a limited success. It had some mistakes, but it set the pattern that was to be followed and perfected, first in NAFTA and then in the WTO.

Chapter 19 is quite different. Strictly speaking the heart of chapter 19, namely Article 1904, is not a dispute settlement process but a binational judicial review. However it is judicial review with a difference.

As a result of the negotiations:
- this judicial review would be as broad as possible;
- the record is as extensive as possible,
- the jurisprudence to be applied encompasses any pronouncement in the country regarding antidumping or countervailing duty; and
- the reviewers are not only lawyers but include non–lawyers as well, so as to bring to the table the broadest perspective possible.

In the negotiations for chapter 19, Canada demanded that a permanent tribunal be set up and that decisions of the panel be given precedence. Although neither of these demands became part of chapter 19, as a compromise the parties agreed to the panelists being selected from a standing roster of experts.

Let's recall that this whole dispute settlement debate was really played out against the background of the Softwood Lumber II dispute which resulted in the infamous Memorandum of Understanding. This dispute was very much in our minds when we negotiated this chapter, and with every single provision we asked ourselves "how would this play if we have Softwood Lumber III before us?" As it turned out we were wise to do so, as Softwood Lumber III did come along and every single provision of the process was invoked, tested, and to our great relief, turned out to work exactly as planned. Softwood Lumber III in my view proved that the chapter 19 process to review antidumping and countervailing decisions (negotiated and drafted in 24 hours) works and disciplines the protectionist excesses of the agencies that administer AD/CVD laws.

We were so concerned about getting this process right that the negotiators drafted in detail the specific provisions of chapter 19. All other FTA provisions were originally only set out in point form in the so called "Articles of Agreement" on 3 October. They were then fleshed out in detail following the 3 October deadline. This detailed drafting, given the terrific time pressure, underlines the importance attached by both sides to chapter 19.

The provisions regarding the Extraordinary Challenge Procedure were added to chapter 19 post-3 October. The rationale for adding this procedure was different for the two nations. We were concerned that the process could give rise to constitutional challenges. Particularly, we were concerned that if a panel made a grave error, such an error could constitute a denial of fundamental procedural safeguards, which could lead to an appeal to the Canadian Courts under the Charter of Rights. Our worst fear was that in such a case the Canadian courts would feel compelled to step in and assert jurisdiction. The Americans did not share our fears however, they were worried that a panel could apply new law, make errors of a jurisdictional nature or make rulings that would be totally inconsistent with U.S. procedural law, and as a result tempt American courts to intervene and assert jurisdiction.

Both sides driven by divergent reasons saw a need to prevent domestic courts from reviewing panel procedures. They therefore agreed to establish the Extraordinary Panel Procedure. The barrier to invocation was raised as high as possible. The agreement provides that the process can only be invoked "if the integrity of the binational panel process is threatened." While we, as negotiators, assumed this would be a near insurmountable threshold, experience has shown that it was not. In none of the three cases where the procedure was invoked can a case be made that the integrity of the process was threatened. The extraordinary challenge procedure which was instituted as a fail-safe measure for panels that behave totally arbitrarily, instead seems to have become a routine additional step in controversial countervailing duties cases.

One can assume that this panel procedure, set up to correct totally unacceptable panel findings, may well have been the germ of the idea that led the WTO to establish its Appeal Process. While the WTO process is quite different in procedure and outcome, both processes were borne by the perceived need to restrain panels or reverse panel decisions that were beyond legally acceptable limits.

Interestingly enough, one of the aspects of the chapter 19 process, which was debated at great length and which was fundamental to the Canadian, side was article 1903; an article that has received very little critical attention.

This article actually represents a dispute settlement process by itself on a very narrow issue. It sets out a procedure to ensure that neither legislature could amend its laws to make existing antidumping and countervailing duty laws more protectionist or to overturn an adverse panel decision. The Canadian side wanted an absolute freeze on antidumping and countervailing duties laws as they stood in 1983. This was impossible for the U.S. to grant as the Administration cannot bind Congress (parenthetically the Canadian government could not have bound Parliament either). In the end, both sides settled for the process set out in article 1903. This article allows a party to request a panel to review legislation to ascertain whether amending legislation overturns panel rulings or whether the legislation violates the GATT or the object and purposes of this FTA and of Chapter 19. The effect is a de facto freeze. The compromise on article 1903, from my perspective, was the single most difficult point to settle and certainly the one that was most bitterly fought over. However it seems to have achieved its objective; as to my knowledge its provisions have never been invoked.

In summary, let me say that as negotiators we can justifiably be proud of chapter 19. It is a totally new procedure, it has no analogue in international or domestic law. It served the purpose for which it was designed, i.e to take the over-protectionist aspect out of AD/CVD application. It ensures that AD/CVD laws when applied against the other country are applied objectively respecting the parameters of the legislation and that the calculations of duty and the findings of injuries are justified by the facts. Additionally, article 1903 ensures that legislatives do not multiply chapter 19 proceedings. While it has not eliminated disputes regarding the application of AD/CVD laws it provides a framework in which they can be resolved.

&

Additional comments about dispute settlement and the Canada–U.S. Free Trade Agreement by former Canadian Minister of Finance, Michael Wilson; Charles E. Roh, Jr., former Deputy Chief Negotiator of the North American Free Trade Agreement for the United States; Sylvia Ostry, Distinguished Research Fellow at the Centre for International Studies at the University of Toronto; and Konrad von Finkenstein

Michael Wilson: There were some very contentious parts of the agreement. Each was a significant part or non–part of the negotiations. While in Canada, we said "culture is not on the table," it was very much a part of the negotiations, and its management was critical. When asked what culture meant, Simon Reisman replied, "culture is culture, it's agriculture, it's aquaculture, and it's sylvaculture." Of these, agriculture and culture are represented on the programs, but we may hit the other two cultures in the dispute settlement part. I would like to divide this session into four sections of 20 minutes each: dispute settlement, selected legal issues, autos, and culture. Let me start with Chip Roh, who was the Chief Legal Counsel for the U.S. delegation, to be followed by Konrad Von Finckenstein. Jon Fried was called away on short notice so Konrad has kindly agreed to pinch hit.

Charles Roh: I shall outline the two dispute settlement mechanisms that were agreed upon and our motivations for incorporating them in the F.T.A. Peter Murphy approached me in late 1986 and said, "Why don't you chair the dispute settlement negotiating group for the U.S.?" I said, "I've got a million disputes on my table; what are you talking about?" To which he replied, "Oh, you know, slap something together some rainy afternoon and it'll be okay." Then I had my first meeting with Konrad Von Finckenstein of Canada; he turned out to be the biggest trade negotiator I have ever met, yet he could not get my name straight. I became "Cliff Blipton," practically everything but Chip. He wanted a "binding dispute settlement." When I asked what he meant by that, his reply was: "this is to be revealed." The most important part of the binding dispute settlement centered around countervailing duty decisions. What eventually became Chapter 19 of the Agreement was a compromise. Canada wanted to replace the countervailing duty and dumping laws with a system on the use of subsidies, and wanted those rules to be enforced by binding dispute settlement decisions, binding in the sense that they had to be automatically carried out. The United States didn't want this. It was a difficult subject because the countervailing duty law was part of the U. S. culture. Most U.S. negotiators would have loved to get rid of it, but the agreement would have been dead on arrival at the U.S. Congress.

The compromise on this issue, worked out on 3 October, had actually been proposed internally in May by Congressman Gibbons. It was very strange by international law standards. What Canada would get was a binding dispute settlement, where the decisions of bi-national dispute settlement panels had to be enforced. Instead of having international rules, each country would keep its own national laws, and what the panels would review is whether the administering authorities of each country had abided by their own national law. I doubt that any analogues for such a scheme existed before we incorporated it in the Canada–U.S. FTA. This curious deal was concluded at the highest level and it worked out well. There have been a few highly visible disputes that created great anxiety on the part of the country that lost the dispute. But for the most part the system has worked successfully. There is a large lobby in the United States that would like to get rid of the system, representing those industries that are most inclined to file cases against foreign products, but there is no serious thought of abandoning it.

On Chapter 18, which contains the more traditional dispute settlement provisions, the United States and Canada shared an interest in making sure that this agreement would be enforceable. Trade agreements have an advantage over most international agreements in that there exists an alternative to shooting each other when it comes to enforcement. One can use trade retaliation instead. What we did was borrow the GATT system, where we would consult to resolve disputes, but if that failed, we would put it to a panel of experts. Our problem remained what do you do with a panel decision , because governments, even the complaining one, don't always like the these decisions. So we introduced a fairly ingenious device: Let the parties resolve the dispute. I am pleased to say the United States and Canada have normally resolved these disputes roughly in accordance with what the panels had concluded, or something even more sensible. One of the blessings in the 1980s was that the U.S. Congress was under the illusion that the U.S. always abided by its agreements and that this procedure was going to keep those unruly foreigners in line. It was only later that we discovered that the U.S. was also in occasional violation of agreements. Our provision worked fairly well and it indeed inspired the system of NAFTA.

Sylvia Ostry: The appellate body can only review the legal aspect of the panel decision, and not the administrative procedure, the procedural fairness, or the due process of the domestic agency. This body is introduced at the end because of the fundamental skepticism by the Americans about the legal capability of the dispute process. Is there a relationship between Chapter 19 and the radical addition of an appellate body in the WTO?

Von Finckenstein: In fact it is mainly Chapter 18 that became the dispute settlement under the WTO. Several aspects of Chapter 19, such as procedural fairness, are included as well.

Charles Roh: Unlike the WTO, the FTA has an appeal process which can be used as a matter of right. There is a permanent reviewing group, removed from all political pressures. They have a way of deciding issues that you and I might think are legal and actually are factual. In the WTO, every single case but one has been appealed; not so under Chapter 19.

There, private parties initiate disputes, not governments, but only governments can appeal. Consequently, there have been only few appeals.

Under Chapter 18 you can dispute any issue, as to whether the behavior of the government is in accordance with the Free Trade Agreement. Under 19 you can only deal with anti–dumping and countervailing duty.

It is a misnomer to call Chapter 19 dispute settlement. It sometimes makes U.S.–Canada relations appear very contentious because, in fact, the disputes are initiated by private parties and hence are not inter-governmental in nature.

AUTOMOTIVE

Mustafa Mohatarem[*]

It is not surprising that this conference contained much discussion of autos. They account for about a quarter of the trade between the U.S. and Canada. General Motors alone accounts for about 10 percent. The auto discussion was very contentious within the context of the U.S.-Canada negotiations. Much of the Canada–U.S. trade in 1987–1988 was already duty free. Companies that met the Autopact safeguards could trade duty free across the border and Chrysler had pretty much integrated its U.S. and Canadian operations so that in fact we operated almost as borderless companies. Indeed, the Autopact was always cited as a great success that encouraged the two countries to proceed to a broader agreement. Yet, autos proved to be one of the most contentious issues, and the final decisions in autos were not made until Monday night at 2:00 a.m.

There were four reasons for this contentiousness. First, the auto industry in both countries in the early 1980s was hit hard by increased imports from Asia, so political sensitivity to any freeing of trade was high. Second, the United Auto Workers (UAW) and the Canadian Auto Workers (CAW), the two unions, had split recently, and both chose to oppose the agreement on grounds that it would damage employment in the respective country. I'm not sure how that was possible. But that was a key issue, because the UAW is an important political force in the U. S. and the CAW is a political force in Ontario. Third, many of the U.S. negotiators believed that the safeguard provisions of the Autopact were transitional, and so the auto manufacturers themselves were not unhappy to leave the safeguards alone. While they were irrelevant to our business, for U.S. negotiators they constituted an important issue. Fourth, and most importantly, was the fact that the Japanese manufacturers had begun to establish auto plants in the U.S. and Canada. And much of the debate was about how to accommodate this entry into auto manufacturing in the U.S. of non–Autopact participants. Since much of the Japanese investment was coming into the U.S., Canada responded by resuscitating the duty remission programs that

---

[*]Mustafa Mohatarem is Chief Economist for General Motors.

it had agreed to eliminate as part of the Autopact. In fact, the State of Michigan filed a 301 complaint regarding those duty remission programs. The consensus view was that the U.S. would decide that they were violating Canada's agreement with the U.S., and there was a likelihood of retaliatory actions by the U.S.

Much of this debate could have been avoided, because Canada offered the Japanese auto companies an opportunity to accept the Autopact provisions. But that would have required significant investment in North America, and the Japanese were not willing to commit to that. That lack of commitment left them vulnerable to the rule of origin issue. It took on a life of its own because Congress did not understand the difference between the "rule of origin" and "local content requirement." With the U.S. tariff on cars at less than 2.5 percent and 3 percent on components, rule of origin was not important to anybody's decision making. Yet because Congress, and to some extent the UAW, confused the rule of origin with a local content requirement, they insisted on having the highest possible rule of origin. Fortunately, the Canadian side resisted and we ended up with a 50 percent rule of origin. While I think this was too high, nonetheless that was as low as you could get the U.S. Congress to approve.

A number of presenters have implied that the FTA essentially resolved the auto issue in the U.S.; it did not. And that because the Japanese manufacturers continued to pursue Autopact benefits, without being willing to make the commitments to the type of investment that Autopact members have made. There has been a constant pressure on the Canadian government to offer the same terms to the Japanese manufacturers as is given to Autopact participants, and to some extent Canada has given in to that pressure. It eliminated its tariff on auto components. And now the Japanese have launched a challenge in the WTO to the Autopact itself. This is probably the first time that a country which has almost total access to another country's market has challenged that country's trade policy. Japanese exports to Canada in 1997 were up 100 percent, and they are up 70 percent in 1998; yet they are challenging Canada's trade policies in the WTO. I am not sure I understand the full logic of that.

What has the FTA–NAFTA Autopact meant? It means that we pretty much operate as an integrated industry, definitely between the U.S. and Canada, and increasingly between the U.S., Mexico, and Canada. In making planned location decisions in GM, we no longer consider the border as relevant.

In the U. S. there were concerns about Canada's attempts to entice Japanese production into Canada, while we did not want any measures to be taken that would curb our ability to trade across the border. In that we were successful, and both countries benefited. One only has to drive on the "Queen's Highway" from Toronto on down, almost as far as Tennessee, and see all the auto and auto component plants along what we call the I–75 belt, to illustrate the point.

Dumping and countervailing laws have been problematic for us on both sides of the border and we were fairly strong supporters of having common laws. In case of an integrated industry, when each country attempts to judge the impact of dumping on the country's operations alone, problems arise. Let me cite a specific example. A south Korean company was dumping autos in Canada. Canadian government Internal Revenue agreed that they were dumping, yet because the displacement was of U.S. production, they ruled that there was no injury in Canada. Similarly in steel, when U.S. and Canadian steel industries file anti–dumping complaints against each other, it disrupts a company like GM that prefers to buy in a single steel market. So we have lobbied on both sides of the border for a common set of rules.

Question: *Can you please spell out the difference between rule of origin and local content requirement?*

Answer: A rule of origin specifies the level of content you need to qualify for tariff removal. A local content requirement states that you can't participate in a market without achieving some level of local content. A country can have a 100 percent rule of origin, but if it had an open external border, a foreign company would have the opportunity to participate in its market either through local production in or through exports. The rule of origin is not necessarily exclusionary. A local content requirement always is.

Question: *A contentious issue during the U.S.–Canada negotiations was the Japanese auto plants being built in both countries. Did the same issue carry over into NAFTA?*

Answer: Very much so. When Mexico entered the GATT, it had received an explicit exemption for its restrictive auto decree which stated that you can only participate in the Mexican market if you produce there. That was not true in either the U.S. or Canada. This clause in the NAFTA negotiations was grandfathered, or at least grandfathered for ten years. It will be phased out over a ten year transitional period. So Mexico retains all the elements of the auto decree, even though BMW and other companies are producing in Mexico without complying with the strict terms of the decree.

Question: *By way of clarification, when (in response to the previous question) you talked about local content, it was actually a value added requirement.*

Answer: You are right; One can achieve the Canadian value added requirement without purchasing any inputs in Canada; namely, by assembling enough vehicles, and exporting them out of Canada. The only thing that's left under the original Autopact is the privilege of the bonafide manufacturers, essentially the big three, to import free from all sources because of the level of content they achieve. The Japanese don't have that privilege, even though they are achieving a value added in Canada, very much equivalent to what the output would be under the Autopact. This I think is what generates their complaints. The Japanese started and now the Europeans have followed. Such a continued discrimination against third countries will not be easy to defend.

James Blanchard has outlined a number of interesting statistics about trade between the two countries, and of course autos are important to him. I want to give you one statistic about the Autopact and its impact on trade. Canada sells more cars, trucks, and parts to the U.S. than all the goods and services it sells to every other country in the world combined. The Autopact was indeed one of the most successful trade agreements ever. And we believe that the treatment of third world countries is defensible and indeed that Canada is out to defend it.

CULTURAL ISSUES

William A. Dymond*

It is not unusual to find a paradox in trade policy. One of the most enduring paradoxes in the public mind and frequently in the media is that exports are good and imports are bad. So a sharp rise in imports is often regarded as evidence of declining fortunes, even when the opposite is the case. As trade negotiators we contribute to this when we measure success by "who got the most concessions in return for the fewest concessions." Yet we all know that the concessions we give bring far greater benefit to our own economy than the concessions we get. We add to the confusion by using language in negotiation that is different from language we use when explaining the results to our cabinet or to the public. How often in negotiation were we presented an offer only for us to trash it as utterly worthless. But then we go back to our ministers to say we've really given away nothing, and bought back "a horn of plenty," to borrow from Shakespeare.

So it would be surprising if the cultural trade issue were not rich in paradoxes. The central paradox is that Canadians expect the government to protect Canada's cultural industries, and, at the same time maintain an open market. Not that Canadians buy much of the products or services of their industry; but they want them to be produced and available. The policy mix deployed traditionally in Canada to capture this paradox is a combination of subsidy, investment controls, and content requirements, all designed to leave some space in the Canadian market for the Canadian industry. This paradox has been at the heart of cultural issues in our bilateral trade relationship for over a generation. We first encountered it in the tax measures taken in the 1960s and the 1970s dealing with magazines and border broadcasting. The objective was not to keep such products or

---

*Ambassador William A. Dymond is Director of the Policy Planning Secretariat for Canada's Department of Foreign Affairs and International Trade. During the Canada-U.S. Free Trade Agreement negotiations he was Minister Counsellor (Commercial) at the Canadian Embassy in Washington. From 1986 to 1987 he served as Senior Advisor to the Trade Negotiations Office in Ottawa.

services out of the market, but to save some advertising revenue for Canadian magazines and broadcasters. This was repeated in the 1980s, and it was understood that unless we took culture out of the agreement there would be no agreement. Canadians would be prepared to forego the benefits of an FTA if there were not an exception for Canadian culture. And we carried forward this cultural exception into our free trade agreements with Chile. It is this paradox which explains why cultural issues are governed by emotion and sentiment more than any other bilateral trade dispute.

While wheat or softwood lumber disputes are generally confined to their constituencies, cultural issues generate waves of national feeling, which make them especially tricky to handle. We have great difficulty in persuading the United States of these points. The Americans don't get the point that our measures, modest as they are, to defend Canadian cultural industries are the necessary price for Canadian participation in trade agreements. Short shift is given to the perception of Canadians that very large issues are at stake, which exceed the boundaries of economic interest. This is paradoxical because the U.S. appears to believe that a little dose of protection is good for you. We have heard over the course of the last day about the initiatives that were needed in the mid 1980s to reassure Congress that the U.S. administration had a viable trade policy. And part of this viable trade policy was provision 301, provoking hostility not only in Canada but in other countries as well. And yet it was argued, and I accept the argument, that this was the necessary pre-condition to allow the U.S. to move ahead in the Free Trade Agreement and the Uruaguay Round. The paradox is that it doesn't appear to work the other way. Canadian cultural industries argue that it is not possible to treat things like books, films, and music as pork bellies. Yet they exort the government to deploy precisely the same type of measures as the producers of pork bellies would have us use to defend their interest.

In the future cultural issues will become harder rather than easier to solve, and that for a couple of reasons. First, the rapid growth in market size will produce rapid growth of controversy and disputes. Second, rapidly changing technology will bring new issues to the dispute table. Already in Canada there is a raging debate on convergence. Should broadcasting or telecommunication laws govern in the future? The major problem is the absence of an agreed set of trade and investment rules in the sector. In cases such as softwood lumber or wheat, there exists a body of rules that governs the behavior of participants in a particular issue. In cultural trade issues we are not so fortunate. In the past decade Canada has argued effectively that there are no rules and there ought not be any. The

U.S. for its part must rely upon the provisions of the GATT/WTO, and reliance upon a 50-year-old instrument constructed in a different time and circumstances must be of limited effectiveness.

The idea of a separate set of rules for a particular product category or sector is not heretical in itself. They existed in textiles and clothing, in softwood lumber, or in steel. But in Canada the cultural issue is an emotional one. There is no evidence of a change in Canadian policy towards culture nor in the U.S. policy of attempting to persuade the rest of the world that normal trade rules can apply to cultural sectors. But one factor will remain constant in Canada, and that is the paradox of a cultural trade policy which combines free trade with protectionism. In my view we will defend the paradox and we will pay the price for defending it. So, my message to the Americans is "leave us some space." Refrain from pressing us too hard. And if I may quote from an Irish poet, "Tread softly because you tread upon their dreams."

ৰ

Additional comments about cultural issues and the Canada–U.S. Free Trade Agreement by Sylvia Ostry, Distinguished Research Fellow at the Centre for International Studies at the University of Toronto; and William Dymond

Sylvia Ostry: I don't know another country in the world that believes that culture is a commodity or a service. Canada is unique in this regard, for a variety of historical reasons. So the notion that we would serve as an example does not strike me as credible, at least not till China gets into the WTO. Next, if biodiversity remains to be defined, then cultural diversity is, by definition, a good thing. A level playing field on a global landscape would be very boring indeed. Culture may be more analogous to R&D or intangibles.

William Dymond: The messages coming out of English Canada and French Canada on the matter of a cultural exception are basically the same. At one point, I was told in Paris: "Oh yes, Dymond, we understand you've got a French speaking minority in Canada; you've got to protect that." My answer was: you totally misunderstand. Our cultural policy is designed to protect the French speaking minority in Canada and the English speakers in North America. On the diversity point you are absolutely right, the French have a text on the table which talks about a cultural exception to promote cultural diversity. So what we really need to apply in the sector is Mr. Axworthy's landmine treaties, because the place is full of landmines. You trip over words and people get red in the face.

Part Four

CANADA-U. S. FREE TRADE
AND THE FUTURE

AN AMBASSADORIAL VIEW

James Blanchard[*]

I wish to offer some reflections on the overall U.S.-Canadian relationship. But first a couple of flashbacks. Back in 1988, I proposed that the State of Michigan open up a trade office in Toronto in addition to the offices we had in Brussels and Tokyo. Initially they laughed in Lansing and Detroit, including staff members on a number of knowledgeable, pro-free-enterprise newspapers. They maintained that everything we will ever do with Canada has already been developed. Our response was that we should have offices on the soil of our number one trading partner, because the Michigan-Ontario relationship is bigger than most national relationships. Also, we believed there was room for the relationship to grow. Since then, trade has more than doubled between our two countries, and even more so between Michigan and Canada. This year alone, a hundred billion dollars of trade will go back and forth across the Ambassador Bridge in Detroit. While that happens to be the busiest intersection, there is also the Detroit-Windsor Tunnel and the bridges at Port Huron, Buffalo, and Sault Ste. Marie. And since NAFTA, merchandise trade has gone up about 60 percent.

Politicians always like to talk about jobs and that was my slogan for two campaigns. It worked. When I didn't use it, I lost an election. I think there are other reasons to support trade than jobs, but jobs is certainly one of them. A strong case could be made that the trade between our two countries supports somewhere between five and six million jobs. But there

---

*James J. Blanchard was U.S. Ambassador to Canada from 1993 to 1996. He served as Michigan's Governor from 1983 to 1991. Governor Blanchard is the author of the recently published work Behind the Embassy Door: Canada, Clinton and Quebec.

is still a great potential, even after the Free Trade Agreement which, in turn, laid the foundation for NAFTA. That potential lies with medium and small businesses and where there remains a great deal of ignorance about the most important relationship our two countries have.

In 1998 the firm Epic/MRA conducted a poll on trade, examining attitudes about NAFTA as a foundation for the future of fast-track and the Free Trade Agreement of the Americas. That nationwide poll asked the respondents what country they believe the United States imports the most products from? Fifty percent said Japan. Twenty one percent said China. Seven percent said Taiwan. Six percent said Mexico, and five percent said Canada. Most likely you'd get a different answer in Canada. On the second question we get a lot better. Where is the top destination for United States exports? Twenty two percent said Japan. Thirteen percent said Canada, and thirteen percent said Mexico. Better, but obviously we have a lot of work to do on the public information front. And that's one reason why, I wrote *Behind the Embassy Door: Canada, Clinton and Quebec*, which came out at the end of 1998. It's about this fascinating, interesting, important, often-times humorous, and obviously very serious relationship we have with Canada.

That relationship embraces almost any issue that we're working on cooperatively with Canada: From Haiti to Bosnia, to NAFTA, to Great Lakes water quality, to tracking the Russian Mafia on the West Coast, and the organized criminal elements. It is by far the most multi-faceted relationship of any two countries on the face of the earth. Historically, we were allies in World War I, World War II, Korea, the Persian Gulf; and founders of the UN, NATO, and NORAD; and partners in various organizations like the G7, the OECD, and the OAS. We are each other's largest trading partner. The United States does more trade with Canada than with all the European nations combined. Ninety-five percent of that trade goes smoothly. But in Canada, we always read about the things that don't, although you don't necessarily read about them in the U.S.

I have some observations about that. First, most of the disputes involve agriculture, where there's too much supply, or fishing where there's too little. Too many boats, too much technology, chasing too few fish. There is a third area, culture, in which there are differences in the way we view that sensitive issue. It involves sovereignty. It involves nationhood. But it also involves some people hiding behind these reasons attempting to steal markets. It's a tough one. My conclusion is that we need to vigorously negotiate and work through these things and never take them for granted, because little differences can become big arguments very quickly. It is absolutely no win for the U.S. and Canada to have a high profile, well publicized trade dispute. Disputes need to be resolved professionally and quietly. And I say that because, once a trade issue surfaces in the Canadian press, everything becomes a war: beer war, lumber war, fish war. Once a trade issue surfaces, the poor Canadian negotiators can never win because even if you skin us alive, Simon, your press will say you got bullied by the American group. Whenever a tough issue comes up, we compromise, we work it out, but when the Canadian negotiators go back to Ottawa they get accused of selling out to the U.S. The reverse is true here. If it becomes high-profile, the Americans are usually accused by the general public of being morally deficient: if you can't get along with the Canadians, who might you get along with?

Second, I travel around Canada, and we traveled in every province, our friends would bemoan the fact that they are taken for granted by the U.S. So I say to you policy makers from Canada: do you really want more attention from us? Such attention doesn't always arrive wisely, justly, or at a moment in time when you need it. There is some advantage to being the quieter side of the partnership. Obviously, we can always improve the relationship. Indeed we must either work to improve it, or it will fall back. It does not stand still, and you don't want it to stagnate. But you must have an agenda to work on.

I worked on finalizing NAFTA and it is because of your work that NAFTA occurred. I also worked on the national unity issue from the U.S. point of view, and we're very proud of our strong support of a strongly united Canada. The third issue we worked on was open skies; and I am very proud that we got that done. It's because of the momentum and the confidence developed at the free trade agreement and NAFTA that we were able to get it. Earlier negotiators went through thirteen rounds of negotiations over twenty years and couldn't achieve success. Then both President Clinton and Prime Minister Chretien gave us their personal support at the right time to get it done. Three years later there are three million additional passenger seats per year going back and forth. The airlines are doing very well, but most importantly, the people, the consumers, and the communities are far better off. That is another legacy of your work and of the whole free trade movement between our two nations.

Of course, our relationship does go beyond trade. We have the world's largest energy relationship. The United States receives more energy from Canada than from any other nation. We had the first environmental relationship of any two countries. In 1909, we signed the Boundary Waters Treaty, negotiated by Sir Wilfred Laurier and Theodore Roosevelt. It's the first international environmental agreement, designed not only to protect boundary waters, but to prevent pollution therein. And that has led to everything from our Great Lakes Water Quality Agreement to the Acid Rain Accord, as well as another thing that Ambassador Burney and many of you were involved with—National security. We're proud of the peace process in Northern Ireland. George Mitchell is my law partner. So is Bob Dole, by the way. But Mitchell was greatly assisted in the Northern Ireland negotiations by two people, one of them a Canadian. Canadians are helping police the streets of Haiti—still a difficult situation. They are peacekeeping in Bosnia, in what was a forerunner to our effort to try to end that genocide. And there are 100 Canadians working inside Cheyenne Mountain in Colorado Springs alongside Americans, monitoring the skies for the launch of any foreign object. The list goes on and on.

It's not only a remarkable partnership, but it is remarkable that two large countries that live next to each other would get along so well. I don't think there's anything in the scriptures that ordains that two nations with a 4,000 mile border need to get along so well. The opposite is usually the case. But ignorance and lack of information does lead to problems. An example is the section 110 dispute. Congress passed a law saying you have to produce written documents when you go back and forth between Canada and the U.S. It is not only absurd, it is stupid. They will repeal it, but what scares me is how they didn't even notice what they were doing. You can see that I'm a statesman now that I'm out of office.

There are enormous differences between our two countries and they do affect our business, legal, and political strategies. The differences between our two cultures and countries are greater than we realize. That became very clear to me after three years in Ottawa. The best thing you can say to an American is the worst thing you can say to a Canadian, which is "You are just like us." That's a killer statement, and God help anyone who gets appointed to a diplomatic post and makes the mistake of saying it when they go north of the border. But it doesn't matter down here.

Our political systems are totally different. Yet our people were always projecting our own system onto theirs. You have the parliamentary system in Canada, and we have a representative democracy. Your system was set up to be efficient. Ours was set up to thwart the consolidation of power, thwart the king, and not to work. So I laugh at the pundits on the Sunday television talk shows in the U.S. complaining about how awful gridlock is. But Canadians have no excuse. They have one house, all the power, it almost all resides in the cabinet and the prime minister. The prime minister can do whatever he or she wishes. By nature Canadians want to consult their country for a hundred years before they do anything, but technically they can move that stuff pretty fast. Americans cannot. Every time some jackass introduces a bill in Congress, and most bills will never have a hearing or see the light of day, you might get a story in the *Ottawa Citizen* or the *Vancouver Sun* that so and so is going to do something terrible to Canada. It was hard to explain to callers on the phone that just because someone puts a bill in the House, doesn't mean it is serious. And the Canadians would say to me "Mr. Ambassador, you're supposed to know—how could the U.S. Congress and the president shut your government and not function?" I said well, we have checks and balances and that's the way it is. Well can't you just fire these people? Throw 'em out of this caucus? I said no. By the same token we don't understand why you let Quebec vote over and over to leave the country.

We are different societies and we look at the world differently. Jake Warren used to say when Americans get up in the morning, if they look at the rest of the world which is rare, they might look east to Europe, or even to Africa, to their roots, or west to Asia, to the booming economies. Maybe south once in a while. But always Americans assume that their friends to the north are doing OK and are just like them. When Canadians get up in the morning, they look east and west for the same reasons, but there's always one eye on the south to see whether people in the U.S. know what they are doing and how it is going to affect Canada, domestically or internationally. We look at history differently, too! Consider the War of 1812. American children are taught that it was a war against Britain to secure the Revolution. Canadians believe they beat the U.S. in that war. And U.S troops burned Toronto and York, Canadians went up the Potomac—and to prove a point, they burned the Congress and the White House. It's a war both sides won but you can't tell anyone in Canada that.

The political community in Canada is more internationalist and more free trade, even considering the difficult battle about the Free Trade Agreement in national elections between Mr. Mulroney and Mr. Turner. Partly, it is because Canada is a smaller nation; Canadians need to be more sensitive to the world. Compared only to the United States do they look small; in fact, Canada is not. Canadians are more sensitive to the world of economics, but that is serving them well, even allowing them to play very good "catch up ball" in Latin America. When President Kennedy went to Ottawa in 1961 and urged Canada to join the OAS, Diefenbaker was determined never to join. But Brian Mulroney did lead Canada into the OAS, and the country is reaping enormous benefits as a result. Canadians are quintessential multilateralists, while Americans are unilateralists. You fancy yourselves as the peacekeepers, while considering us the gunslingers. We do not want to be the world's policemen, but if our allies want us to and we think the cause is right, we will send in the Marines, and we don't care what the UN says. However, we do want our allies to support us.

Our styles are different, and this is a sensitive matter here. You're negotiators by nature. We are more deal makers. We like to cut deals. My sense is we like to cut deals and we may even break them if we don't like them later. You guys like to negotiate forever. And you are still negotiating the relationship of Quebec to the rest of the country. I do not mean that as a criticism; it is just that they are different cultures. Yours is slower and more deliberate—you could say thoughtful. We're fast, abrupt, we move along. You're more orderly. We're more into change. You're negotiators, and we are litigators. When someone in Canada has a problem, they document it, they go to the government, ask for an inquiry or a committee. Then it is studied for a long time and at the end there will be some sort of negotiated compensation. In the U.S., if you have a problem, you sue, whether there's any justification or not. I hate to say that as a lawyer, but that's what it is. Any given day, General Motors faces 4,000 product liability lawsuits in the United States. That same day, they'll face an average of 12 in Canada.

Our cultures are different. You are more orderly and civilized. We are certainly more aggressive and oftentimes more violent, which is tragic, although you are more violent on the hockey rink than we are. But even there, Canadians blame U.S. TV for the increased violence in hockey, and there may be some truth to it, I hate to say. It's slower there, it is faster here. There are some tremendous benefits to being slower, including more deliberate decision making. People have time for each other and they really have time for relationships. Being a politician in Ottawa is like being a pig in the mud, but we loved it; whereas Washington, as much as we like Washington, is a town of drive-by friendships. Everybody is so busy, unless of course the President calls you for a movie. Other than that, nobody is willing to change their schedules for anybody. In Canada, weekends are for families, and families appear to be considerably stronger. In America, weekends are for babysitters. Canada is more bureaucratic, it used to drive me crazy, while we're more entrepreneurial. Bureaucrats are highly regarded in Canada, but universally detested in the U.S. You'd never find a U.S. Cabinet member carrying the water of a bureaucrat who had caused a problem 10 years before, and getting on TV apologizing. Heads will roll here. But the respect accorded to institutions in Canada causes a kind of continuity. You're more pro-government, while we're fundamentally anti-government.

And the tastes: everywhere we went in Canada, they served salmon. No wonder we have a salmon shortage. Salmon is on every menu. In the U.S. it is steak or chicken. Canadians eat salmon, Americans eat steak. And then having a good cup of tea is a major experience in Canada. That's of course more British, but it is important to take the time. It is properly prepared. Here if you order tea, they give you hot water and throw a bag on the table. It's tough to get ice in glasses in Canada, while we are the only culture in the world that likes to eat ice.

Then there are the differences in phraseology. At first I had to get used to the fact that every time they use the phrase "to table," in the United States that means you get rid of it. You shelve it. In Canada it means you present it. If Canadians say "you went to college," they usually are talking about high school or trade school; in the United States it usually means attending a university. I have never met anybody in Canada who took a vacation--it is holiday. Americans say holiday for days like Christmas or Easter. Then there is Canadian bacon that you can get here in Kellogg Center, but it is not on any menu there— it is back bacon. Then there is the word scrum. I guess it comes from rugby— that's press or news availability. That's what Americans call it.

There are differences in attitudes. Americans are fundamentally an optimistic culture. Canadians are somewhat less so, or maybe even pessimistic. Perhaps it is the weather. Canadians are also world-champion nit-pickers. They nit-pick everything all the time, including yourselves, despite the fact that they live in one of the greatest nations on earth. Americans, on the other hand, are the world's biggest braggers. Everything has to be the greatest. For instance, when I talk about my alma mater, Michigan State University, people notice that I say that it is the greatest campus in North America. Perhaps I should say the world.

Finally, on a serious note, Canadians have, in most respects, a stronger sense of community, of interconnectedness, of taking care of each other, of taking time to worry about each other than Americans do. Although in our small towns we still retain that quality. Americans, on the other hand, have a stronger sense of nationhood, of a belief that our best days are ahead, that our history is glorious, that there are values that bind us together, and there's a story about our country we all believe in and are proud of. You'd never hear a governor of Michigan say I'm a Michigander first and an American second; he or she would be thrown in the Detroit River. So I think between community and nation, Americans and Canadians can learn much from each other. You have cultivated that relationship. The most special relationship between any two countries in the world. Thank you.

DISARMING THE "UNDEFENDED BORDER": REFLECTIONS ON THE RATIONALE FOR A CANADA–U.S. CUSTOMS UNION

Michael Hart*

Natural frontiers exist between nations, but the border between Canada and the United States is not one of them. Birds fly over it, fish swim through it, ore bodies lie under it, stands of timber straddle it, rivers traverse it. As in the movement of trade, so in the disposition of resources. The continent is an economic unit. Its bisection is political, not geographic. What nature has joined together, Canadians have sought to sunder.

James Eayres, Sharing a Continent *(1964)*

That eloquent phrasemaker, Sir Winston Churchill, once referred to the Canada–United States frontier as "guarded only by neighbourly respect and honorable obligations." Perhaps, but he would have a hard time today bringing a box of his famous Havana cigars from Canada to the United States. He would be equally hard-pressed to explain the red tape involved in importing a car into Canada from the United States—including one made in Canada. Even now, after a decade of "free trade, the Canada–United States border continues to bristle with uniformed and armed officers determined to ensure that trade between Canadians and Americans complies with an astonishing array of restrictions, prohibitions, and regulations. 1 January 1998 may have been a red-letter day in Canada–U.S. relations, the first day in history on which not a single tariff was levied on two-way trade in Canadian and American goods, but the job of disarming the border remains unfinished.

* *Michael Hart is Simon Reisman Professor of Trade Policy, The Norman Paterson School of International Affairs, Carleton University. He was a member of the task force that prepared for Canada's participation in the negotiations with the United States and was a senior member of the Canadian Free Trade Agreement negotiating team.*

today than they did then. Firms and individuals on both sides of the border have benefited enormously from this gain, but there remain barriers in place that suggest that the forces of protectionism and nationalism have not been wholly overcome. Cumbersome rules of origin, discriminatory government procurement restrictions, complex anti-dumping procedures, intrusive countervailing duty investigations, and other restrictive border measures remain in place, discouraging rational investment decisions and deterring wealth-creating flows of trade and investment. Differences in domestic policy measures further frustrate realization of the dream of a seamless North American market.

This paper outlines what has been achieved as a result of the 1985–87 free-trade negotiations and what is required to finish the task. In so doing, it advances the case for serious consideration of a Canada–U.S. customs union. What would such an agreement entail? What would be its advantages? What would be its drawbacks? In considering these questions, the paper focuses on the trade policy dimensions of the issue. Converting the FTA/NAFTA into a customs union would, obviously, have more than trade and commercial implications. It would also affect political, cultural, and other aspects of the relationship. Any decision to move in this direction, therefore, would need to be based on a careful consideration of such matters.

The Canada–U.S. Free Trade Agreement

At the end of 1987, after sometimes difficult and frustrating negotiations, Canada and the United States succeeded in concluding a far-reaching, new kind of bilateral trade agreement. Billed as a free trade area agreement rather than as a customs union or common market; in reality it partook of features of all three. Negotiators had sought to find the most appropriate instruments to respond to a variety of old and emerging problems and conflicts while, at the same time, addressing the inevitable political sensitivities that had precluded a comprehensive bilateral agreement for more than three generations. The asymmetry in power and interests ensured that negotiators on both sides needed to be nimble and creative if the agreement was to satisfy the economic needs and political sensitivities of both sides.[1]

---

[1] See Michael Hart, with Bill Dymond and Colin Robertson, *Decision at Midnight: Inside the Canada-U.S. Free Trade Negotiations* (Vancouver: University of British Columbia Press, 1994) for a detailed account and assessment of the negotiations and resulting agreement.

The result was an agreement firmly ensconced within the structure and values of the multilateral system embodied in the General Agreement on Tariffs and Trade (GATT). In all respects, the provisions dealing with trade in goods followed the contours of earlier free-trade area agreements negotiated under the auspices of GATT article XXIV, arguably at a more honest level than some earlier agreements. The agreement also addressed issues that went well beyond a conventional FTA, including some that would normally be found in customs-union or common-market agreements. Characterized as "new" trade issues, they were in reality the kinds of issues that need to be addressed as economic integration deepens and the potential for cross-border commercial friction intensifies. Even for these, however, there was a scrupulous effort to negotiate rules that would fit into a GATT-plus mold.

The agreement also included some innovative provisions aimed at re-ducing conflict and resolving disputes. In addition to a more robust version of the GATT approach to dispute settlement, in some ways anticipating reforms adopted during the Uruguay Round negotiations, it included a special dispute resolution regime related to anti-dumping and countervailing duty procedures. The two sets of provisions responded well to the original concerns of Canadian business with increasing bilateral trade skirmishes. However, rather than an agreement limited to a dispute settlement mechanism, as business leaders had originally sought, Canada succeeded in embedding these mechanisms within a fully articulated set of rights and obligations related to trade and investment.

Not all the issues, however, were resolved to the mutual satisfaction of both sides. The United States wanted to go further on investment, but had to be satisfied with an initial first set of rules. It sought an intellectual property chapter and did not get it. It pursued rules on subsidies and had to be satisfied with continuation of the status quo. It was not satisfied with the progress on agriculture. Canada similarly did not meet all of its objectives. It had been prepared to negotiate rules on subsidies, in return for greater discipline on countervailing duties. It wanted to eliminate anti-dumping procedures on bilateral trade and replace them with bilateral rules about competition. It sought much greater access in government procurement markets. The final package represented as much as the two sides could accept in 1987. Subsequent bilateral and multilateral negotiations would test how much will there was to go further.

From an FTA to a NAFTA and a WTO

Within two years of the FTA's entry into force, Canada and the United States were again involved in regional negotiations as Mexico succeeded in convincing first the United States and then Canada that the FTA model should be expanded to include Mexico. Like Canada, Mexico had concluded that the extent of Mexico–U.S. economic interaction required rules and procedures more capable of addressing cross–border commercial conflicts than the GATT. Trilateral negotiations succeeded not only in transforming the bilateral FTA into the trinational North American Free Trade Agreement (NAFTA), but also in improving and expanding its scope and coverage.[2] Nevertheless, it too remained firmly within the parameters of a GATT–plus agreement.

Concurrent with the negotiation of the FTA as well as NAFTA and consistent with the theme of negotiating their regional agreement within the structure of the GATT, Canada, the United States, and Mexico participated actively in the launch and pursuit of a new round of multilateral trade negotiations. They also played key roles in their successful conclusion at the end of 1993. Canada, for example, was instrumental in the establishment of the World Trade Organization (WTO) to administer the results of the negotiations. Throughout this period, all three governments saw the two sets of negotiations as complementary efforts to reach essentially the same set of objectives: rules and procedures that would stimulate new trade and investment opportunities and facilitate the management of conflicts and disputes that might flow from growing trade and investment. In effect, they saw their regional and multilateral negotiating efforts as part of a continuum of complementary rights and obligations.

The Uruguay Round succeeded in setting up an expanded and revitalized GATT–based trade relations system, reversing the gradual shift from multilateral agreements to regional ones, and re–establishing the primacy of a universal set of rules and institutions. The WTO provides a stronger framework for the continued evolution of a trade relations system based on the principles of nondiscrimination, transparency, due process, and progressive liberalization. Joint consultation lays a solid foundation for continuing the process of applying these principles to a wider range of international economic transactions. It should continue the transition from

---

[2] The government's explanatory documents listed some 22 ways in which NAFTA represented improvements over the FTA. See Government of Canada, *NAFTA: What's It All About* (Ottawa, 1993), 13-16.

a set of broad principles and general rules aimed at shallow integration to a much more detailed and complex set of rules capable of fostering deep integration.[3]

The results of NAFTA and Uruguay Round negotiations completed or advanced some of the issues left unresolved at the conclusion of the FTA negotiations. Much progress was made in both negotiations, for example, on intellectual property rights. Both negotiations improved access on government procurement. The WTO strengthens rules on subsidies and deals with some of the abuses in the application of anti-dumping and countervailing duties. The WTO dispute settlement provisions are modeled on those of the FTA and NAFTA, but with further improvements and the benefit of a permanent Secretariat and a multilateral organization to help make them work. The NAFTA chapter on investment marked a major step forward. Nevertheless, even after fifteen years and three sets of negotiations, there remain significant areas where trade and investment between Canada and the United States continue to be hampered by policies and measures susceptible to further negotiations. More about that later.

Canadian and U.S. officials emphasized in 1985–88 that an FTA would allow the two countries to resolve issues between them more quickly and more thoroughly than would be possible within a multilateral negotiation. Has the multilateral system now caught up? Yes, to some extent, but not completely. NAFTA's most significant continuing advantages include:

- Access for goods is tariff free; this benefit, however, is offset to some extent by the transaction costs created by strict rules of origin.

- Customs rules are better and customs–based conflicts are more easily resolved.

- NAFTA's investment chapter provides the best rules available, particularly its provisions for investor–state arbitration, although as recent cases suggest, it might be useful to reconsider what the two governments consider to be an "expropriation."

- NAFTA's services chapter is more liberal and covers more sectors.

---

[3] For a survey of the evolution of the multilateral trading system, culminating in the Uruguay Round negotiations, see Michael Hart, *Fifty Years of Canadian Tradecraft: Canada at the GATT 1947-1997* (Ottawa: Centre for Trade Policy and Law, 1998).

- The provisions governing temporary business travel are unique to NAFTA.

- The chapter 19 bi-national panel provisions for anti-dumping and countervailing duty cases are a major benefit but should be seen as no more than a temporary solution; the real issue is the continued availability of measures that should have no place in an integration agreement.

- Some sectoral rules provide some advantages as well as some problems, e.g., for autos, textiles and clothing, and agriculture.

Offsetting these NAFTA advantages is the fact that the WTO is a multilateral set of rules implemented with the help of a strong, independent Secretariat. Its general dispute settlement provisions are now more than the equal of NAFTA chapter 20, particularly in view of the independent legal advice provided to panels by the WTO's legal staff. The appellate review body has added further precision and credibility to the WTO provisions. Nevertheless, for the foreseeable future, NAFTA will remain an important feature of the regime governing cross-border Canada–U.S. trade and investment. It is for consideration, however, whether it can remain an important feature without further negotiations to resolve bilateral problems that are unlikely to be resolved satisfactorily at the multilateral level in the near to medium term. Part of that consideration must be the extent to which the two governments are satisfied with the economic and commercial impact of the regional accords.

The Impact of the FTA and NAFTA

Looking back now from the vantage point of 1998, many of the specific objectives Canadian officials identified in the early 1980s have been achieved. Their subsequent influence on corporate behaviour and economic performance has generally been as expected: painful at first but more and more positive as the changes took hold. Economic analysis leading up to the FTA negotiations and immediately thereafter indicated that the Canadian economy would need to go through a period of painful adjustment. Nevertheless, to the extent that firms and governments alike would allow these adjustments to take hold, the economy would benefit in increased efficiency, leading to more specialization and export–led growth. The FTA would not solve all the problems faced by the Canadian economy, including problems of fiscal profligacy and constitutional uncertainty, but it could help address problems of industrial structure, productivity, and competitiveness, and it has.

Economic studies over the past few years suggest that the positive effects are becoming increasingly evident, offsetting the earlier but expected negative indicators.[4] Indeed, over the course of the past decade, Canada experienced one of the strongest periods of trade–led growth in its history. Over this period, merchandise exports to all sources more than doubled at market prices. Total trade— exports and imports, goods and services— rose from less than 50 to about 80 percent as a proportion of GNP. The United States accounted for the preponderance of this trade, as it has for most of the postwar years. In 1997, in nominal terms, merchandise exports to the United States represented 82 percent of the total, while U.S. imports accounted for 67.5 percent.

Of course, there is always some ambiguity about measuring or assessing the impact of a major policy initiative. It is difficult to isolate one factor and try to attribute specific changes in behaviour and performance to that factor. Nevertheless, there has been a pattern of behaviour and performance over the past decade which suggests a strong correlation between changes in Canada's trade and investment performance— both outgoing and incoming— and changes in trade and investment policy. The cause and effect relationship, however, is more difficult to determine. Did Canada pursue more outward–oriented trade and investment policies in response to changing trade and investment patterns, or vice versa? Did policy changes lead to changes in the patterns, or did changes in the patterns lead to changes in policy?

The relationships probably ran in both directions and reinforced one another. Policy changes facilitated and sometimes even stimulated changes in trade and investment patterns. Concurrently, changes in trade and investment patterns induced by technological and other factors were instrumental in convincing governments to make the rules more responsive. Changes in the intensity and nature of Canada–U.S. trade were

---

4 Daniel Schwanen of the C. D. Howe Institute has provided the best continuing analysis of the trade impact of the FTA and NAFTA. His analysis demonstrates that protection matters, and so does its removal; trade and investment grew most rapidly in sectors where protection was high and has now been removed. In *Trading Up: the Impact of Increased Continental Integration on Trade, Investment, and Jobs in Canada* (C.D. Howe Commentary no. 89, March 1997), his third report, he concludes that "the pattern of trade between the two countries has shifted roughly in the direction of pre-FTA expectations, and the competitive position of Canadian and U.S. producers in each other's markets has improved relative to those in third countries in many sectors that were liberalized under free trade."

placing inordinate strains on the management of the relationship. By catching up, through a process of bilateral, regional, and multilateral negotiations, the forces of proximity and technology were allowed to function more effectively and perhaps even accelerate what was already taking place. Because the technological changes were profound and the need for policy changes had been resisted, the FTA was publicly perceived to have been a bigger deal than it probably was. On the other hand, continued resistance to the forces of technology and proximity could have had very negative results. Policy does matter.

An interesting illustration of the impact of the agreement on bilateral trade flows is the extent of improvements both governments have made to the border infrastructure, some with the help of the private sector. To accommodate the more than a billion dollars worth of goods that now cross the border on a daily basis, roads, bridges, tunnels, and customs facilities needed to be expanded. At the Sarnia–Port Huron crossing, for example, the Bluewater Bridge has received a second span, the railroad tunnel has been enlarged, and customs facilities have been modernized. In the air, the Open Skies air agreement has greatly facilitated the cross-border movement of people and goods. Missing, however, is a willingness to recognize that the scale of cross-border trade now taking place needs new immigration and customs attitudes. Similarly, not all authorities in the two countries have wholly embraced the full implications of free trade. The willingness of some border–state governors to use state troopers to harass legitimate cross-border trade in agricultural products is a case in point, as is the reluctance of U.S. federal officials to step in and end such election–year grandstanding.

Have the new agreements helped the management of Canada–U.S. relations? Yes, to the extent that governments have been prepared to use their rules and procedures. The existence of international agreements does not mean there will not be conflicts, only that there is a better basis for resolving them; they make it possible to bring conflicts to an end and to resolve issues. A profound misreading of the FTA and NAFTA led to popular Canadian complaints about the rash of Canada–U.S. trade disputes in the late 1980s and early 1990s. The existence of rules and procedures does not end disputes, and in fact, may increase the number of issues that need to be resolved on the basis of rules using formal procedures.

The FTA did at first seem to multiply disputes, as players on both sides of the border tested the will of the two governments to live by the new rules. Procedures under Chapter 19 dealing with anti-dumping and countervailing duty cases proved particularly popular and have continued to engage parties in all three countries under NAFTA. Under the FTA, a total of 35 cases were litigated, with a variety of results, some favouring Canadian parties, some American parties. As William Davey concludes in his study of the FTA cases: "The dispute settlement mechanisms of the [FTA] have worked reasonably well, particularly the bi-national panel review process. The basic goal of trade dispute settlement . . . is to enforce the agreed–upon rules. By and large, these dispute settlement mechanisms have done that."[5] Chapter 19, which was much less than Canada had originally sought, proved a pleasant surprise in reducing the cross–border temperature in trade remedy disputes. It required administrators on both sides of the border to mind their Ps and Qs, and reduced the capacity of U.S. legislators to move the goal posts or to pressure tribunals to favour the home side.

The more general dispute settlement provisions of Chapter 18 of the FTA (20 of NAFTA) have been used less frequently but as usefully. A variety of difficult issues were resolved with the help of high–quality panels and the procedures of the FTA or NAFTA. Additionally, the much improved multilateral procedures under the WTO are now available to help resolve conflicts. In all of these cases, the application of clear rules within a set of binding procedures that ensure the equality of standing of both parties has greatly facilitated the management of relations between the two countries. Canada has not won all the cases, in part because Canada's policies have not always been consistent with its obligations. The purpose of dispute settlement is not to guarantee "wins," but to ensure that issues are resolved on the basis of agreed rules and procedures rather than power politics.

The exception that would seem to prove the rule is the continuing saga of softwood lumber. Originally written out of the FTA, it has bedeviled Canada–U.S. relations for more than a decade and a half. Canada's current agreement to restrain exports of softwood lumber appears to have been based on a political judgment that, while Canada had right on its side, the cost of proving this point, both economically and politically, outweighed the benefits of restraining imports and thus ensuring peace in the industry for five years and keeping the scarcity rents in Canada. Reasonable people can differ about the wisdom of this political judgment and its long–term impact on the integrity of a rules–based approach to managing relations. With this single exception, the new era of more certain rules and procedures has proven its worth.

---

5 William Davey, *Pine and Swine: Canada-United States Trade Dispute Settlement – The FTA Experience and NAFTA Prospects* (Ottawa: Centre for Trade Policy and Law, 1996), 288-9.

Nevertheless, there remain areas for improvement, if only because changes in the structure of international trade and commerce continue to push the envelope and challenge governments to adapt and strengthen the existing framework of rules.

From Shallow to Deep Integration

International trade negotiations often seek to catch up to the reality of international business. That reality is changing rapidly. Developments in communications technology and transportation facilities have made borders more porous and distances less daunting, leading to fundamental changes in business organization and techniques. At the same time, revolutionary changes in the organization and technology of production are further hastening the transformation of domestic economies. Multinational firms are giving way to truly global corporations whose decisions about what to buy and sell, where to manufacture, whose money to use, and what ideas to pursue are less and less dictated by national frontiers. The rules of the game need to catch up more fully to these deeper levels of commercial integration. They need to address not only the old agenda of liberalization within a fixed–rule regime, but also the much more complex set of issues that have developed as a result of this integration. The issues raised by this second phenomenon include the full range of laws, regulations, and policies that determine what competition authorities call the "contestability" of markets.

Contestability involves the embrace of a much broader approach to market access than that which prevailed even as recently as the Uruguay Round. It straddles the continuum of trade, investment, and competition policy. It emphasizes the need to stem practices that may impede the ability of producers to contest a market, whether such practices stem from public policy or private behaviour. It means that border restrictions, investment conditions, regulatory obstacles, or structural barriers, whether public or private in origin, do not unduly impede effective market access and presence. An agreement dedicated to the attainment of full contestability should provide a seamless web of trade and investment disciplines governing both private actions and public policies affecting the ability of internationally active firms to contest markets anywhere on the globe.[6]

---

[6] See Michael Hart, "A Multilateral Agreement on Foreign Direct Investment – Why Now?" in Pierre Sauvé and Daniel Schwanen, eds., *Market Access After the Uruguay Round* (Toronto: C.D. Howe, 1996) for a more complete discussion of the issues involved, and references to the work of other analysts.

Achieving such an ambitious agenda will likely involve constructive interaction between multilateral and regional approaches. Customs unions and free trade areas have historically been negotiated and implemented among neighbours in order to reinforce and secure economic links established as a result of geographic proximity and historical ties. Fears that regional arrangements will lead to a dismantling of the multilateral trading system have proven to be greatly exaggerated. Instead, we have seen the development of a multi–tier trading system. The WTO now represents a far–reaching and widely applied universal code of conduct conditioning a wide range of transnational transactions as well as creating a more uniform approach to an increasing array of domestic economic regulations and policies. At the same time, a number of regional experiments are simultaneously widening liberalization and deepening integration, ranging from rules attuned to the deep integration of the EU to the shallow integration of NAFTA and other newer arrangements.[7]

A Canada–U.S. Customs Union

Over the past fifteen or so years perceptions about the objectives of the Canada–U.S. free–trade negotiations have subtly changed from relatively narrowly conceived negotiating objections to a growing realization that the negotiations formed part of a larger whole. At first, the objectives were informed by concerns that had emerged within the specific context of Canada–U.S. trade and investment and a conviction that these concerns could not be addressed either thoroughly enough or quickly enough at the GATT. With the conclusion and implementation of the agreement, and the desire of Mexico to achieve a similar set of objectives, there emerged a growing realization that Canada's problems with the United States had not been unique and might be part of a larger pattern. With the successful conclusion of the Uruguay Round, this metamorphosis was complete. The FTA had been an early manifestation of a much larger phenomenon, which was placing demands on Canadians that went well beyond what some had originally envisaged in the FTA negotiations, but which had been anticipated in the desire to conclude a "national treatment" agreement. Such an agreement, however, remains to be realized and is unlikely to be realized within a realistic time frame on anything but a bilateral basis.

---

7 See Michael Hart "Doing the Right Thing: Regional Integration and the Multilateral Trade Regime," Occasional Paper no. 39 (Ottawa: Centre for Trade Policy and Law, 1996) for a more complete discussion.

Until the early 1980s, successful regional integration agreements were largely a European phenomenon. Experiments in Africa and Latin America did not prove very successful while Asia and North America had largely eschewed regional approaches to liberalization and rule making. That changed in the 1980s to the point where there are now working examples of regional agreements in every part of the globe. Not all regional agreements, however, are the same. For the United States, regional negotiations complemented its global trade agenda, one that was largely achieved with the establishment of the WTO. The EU, on the other hand, has been working on a much more differentiated dual track: one set of negotiations has concentrated on regional integration while the other has focused on multilateral issues. For the members of the EU, deepening the EU formed the basis for addressing intra–European trade, economic and, increasingly, political issues, while the multilateral WTO negotiations concentrated on extra–European commercial concerns.

As a result, the Europeans have moved furthest along the path of experimenting with the demands of deep integration and they have done so on the basis of a customs union. The EU customs union— in its rules and institutions— is a much more integrative agreement than either NAFTA or the WTO. The EU has developed a scheme of regulation that has allowed a group of now fifteen countries to maintain their separate identities and political priorities while creating a single market as integrated as that of the fifty U.S. states or the ten Canadian provinces. There are *no* customs procedures, no anti-dumping provisions, no buy–national procurement preferences, and no market–limiting product standards; there *are* EU–wide rules about competition, subsidies, and restrictive business practices; and there is a Commission, a Parliament and a Court to enforce these provisions.

In NAFTA, on the other hand, there *are* customs procedures, anti-dumping provisions, buy–national procurement preferences, and market-limiting product standards; there are *no* NAFTA–wide rules about competition, subsidies, or restrictive business practices; and there is no independent commission, parliament, or court to enforce NAFTA's provisions. In short, NAFTA is a WTO–plus regional liberalization agreement rather than an EU–like regional integration agreement.

This is not an accident. In the original Canada–U.S. FTA and then in the NAFTA negotiations, the parties did not set out to negotiate a regional integration agreement. They set out to liberalize trade among them and at the same time address some of the newer issues that would, of necessity, move them closer to an integration agreement. The United States sought to make progress on services, investment, and intellectual property while

Canada and Mexico wanted to pursue competition–type issues. Progress was made on these issues, but in a cautious, GATT–like manner.

Moving NAFTA into a deep integration direction analogous to the EU would require that its members adopt a similar, more differentiated dual track, and negotiate at least some of the following improvements:

- For *government procurement*, the rules would have to change from the limited, WTO–like entities approach to a full national–treatment approach, placing government procurement throughout the region on a non–discriminatory, fully competitive basis.

- For *trade remedies*— anti–dumping and countervailing duties— the rules would have to evolve beyond WTO–like procedural safeguards to common rules about competition and subsidies.

- For *product and process standards*, much more progress would have to be made in developing either common standards or greater acceptance of equivalence, mutual recognition, common testing protocols, and similar provisions.

- For *services*, the rules would have to evolve from WTO–like commitments, albeit based on a negative rather than positive list, to common standards and mutual recognition.

- For *financial services*, greater progress will need to be made to develop stronger surveillance and common fiduciary requirements.

- For *investment*, provisions would need to move further down the track of enforcement by the domestic courts of jointly agreed rules of behavior.

- For the *cross–border movement of people*, more effort is required to develop policies and procedures that facilitate rather than frustrate cross–border traffic.

- *Institutionally*, the agreement would need to move beyond ad hoc intraregional arrangements to supranational arrangements involving an EU–like commission and court–like structures.

Each of these developments, of course, would have major political as well as trade and economic implications, suggesting that such issues are unlikely to be pursued quickly or without major debate. At the same time, none of these issues is likely to be addressed this thoroughly in multilateral negotiations in the foreseeable future. Canada and the United States have proven that they can accomplish matters bilaterally that are not yet ready to be pursued more widely. It is important that they show that they are prepared to make the effort to resolve such issues not only because of the direct benefit to Canadians and Americans, but also because of its positive demonstration effect for the rest of the world.

For Canada, the United States and, perhaps, Mexico, the extent of their existing regional integration, as well as the structural pressures flowing from the forces of globalization, suggest that early movement in this direction would make sense. Canada, for example, has long indicated that it would like to deepen some— but not all— aspects of NAFTA. In particular, Canadian officials have identified the rules related to trade remedies and government procurement as priority areas for attention between Canada and the United States. Mexico appears to share some of these interests, but with less conviction and urgency, largely because it has had less experience with trade agreements and with managing trade relations with the United States on the basis of such an agreement. Some U.S. officials may share these interests at an intellectual level, but so far there is little evidence that intellectual arguments can be translated into political interest. Indeed, there appears to be strong resistance. Rather, U.S. officials have expressed a preference for seeing NAFTA used as a model for expanding reforms based on the U.S. model to Latin America in such areas as intellectual property protection and investment. More importantly, the United States is showing increasing signs of being ambiguous about accepting new international trade obligations; U.S. officials remain interested in expanding U.S. rights, but is less certain about deepening U.S. obligations.

To be frank, the United States— using the phrase widely to encompass not only official thinking in Washington but also academic and think-tank work around the country— is a deeply conservative country, less than willing to grasp the full implications of the new realities and opportunities. The United States tackled the so-called new issues of the 1980s, for example— issues that Jacob Viner identified as shortcomings of the GATT as far back as 1947[8]— in very conventional terms. In neither the FTA/NAFTA nor the WTO did the United States put forward proposals that recognized the need for integrative rule making. Resistance to replacing anti-dumping rules with competition rules remains indicative of this old-fashioned thinking.[9]

---

[8] Jacob Viner, "Conflicts of Principle in Drafting a Trade Charter," *Foreign Affairs,* (July 1947).

[9] See Michael Hart, ed., *Finding Middle Ground: Reforming the Anti-dumping Laws in North America* (Centre for Trade Policy and Law, 1997) for a survey of different attitudes toward reforming the anti-dumping laws.

Nevertheless, given developments in the global economy, and the intensification of private-sector led integration in North America, movement along each of the fronts identified above is critical to underpinning the continued success and benefits of that integration. They are unlikely to be addressed as long as significant political and negotiating energy is devoted to the expansion of NAFTA to countries in Latin America. Moving toward a customs union is, to a large extent, incompatible with continuing efforts to expand NAFTA's reach to the rest of the Americas through the Free Trade Agreement for the Americas (FTAA) initiative. NAFTA is not the vehicle for expanding and consolidating trade liberalization throughout the Americas. Rather, it is the vehicle for moving further along the path of economic integration within North America. It is too difficult to find the necessary political commitment and negotiating coinage to move simultaneously to deepen NAFTA, expand liberalization on a regional basis to countries only beginning to open their economies, apply the rules of the multilateral trade regime, and launch a new round of multilateral negotiations at the WTO. Canadian— and U.S.— trade interests would be better served by merging the FTAA process, as quickly as possible, into a new WTO round. At the same time, as they did between 1986 and 1988, Canada and the United States— and perhaps Mexico— should explore the parameters of going further by negotiating a bilateral or trilateral customs union.

A regional or bilateral trade agreement should no longer be little more than a tariff-preference agreement or WTO-plus agreement. Indeed, it would be far preferable if governments moved more rapidly to eliminate tariff preferences and achieve tariff-free trade on a most-favoured-nation or universal basis as soon as possible. If nothing else, the early achievement of tariff-free trade on an MFN basis would eliminate one of the most troubling aspects of free-trade agreements, rules of origin. The continued existence of low tariffs, coupled with rules-of-origin, impose a transaction cost on cross-border transactions that is out of all proportion to the purported benefit to protected industries. It is time to admit that the era of the tariff is over and get on with other, more pressing and difficult issues. It would also constitute a strong affirmation of the MFN rule and thus point regional trade agreements more clearly toward the frontiers of rule making. Regional agreements should be in the vanguard of defining the contours of free trade in the new, post-tariff global economy. Governments can then concentrate limited negotiating coinage on the newer issues. They should use regional trade agreements as laboratories to determine how best to address these issues. For example, while it might be preferable to make progress in eliminating anti-dumping measures on a multilateral basis, the United States and others are not yet ready for such an ambitious undertaking. By default, therefore, Canada will need to keep its major trading partner, the United States, engaged on this issue on a bilateral or regional basis.

Proceeding in this direction, of course, would have implications that go beyond trade and commercial considerations. Canadians, for example, are concerned that moving toward a common external commercial policy might drag them into applying U.S. geopolitical trade barriers that are inimical to Canadian values and interests. They worry that closer trade and commercial integration could further undermine their ability to nurture Canadian culture and identity. They fear that a customs union could require them to share their resources and leave them without adequate capacity to ensure that Canadians benefit from this asset. They are suspicious that their approach to health care, education, and other defining policies could be compromised.

These are serious concerns to which there are serious answers. Some of these fears relate more to the forces of proximity than to the nature of the rules in place to manage the flow of cross-border exchanges. Canadians benefit from but can do little about the negative aspects of living next door to the world's largest, most energetic economy; the negotiation of better rules, however, provide an improved basis for managing the frictions created by proximity. Other concerns are matters that would need to be addressed with care in the negotiation of the terms and conditions that would apply. Like Canadians, Americans also have worries that would need to be addressed. As in the 1985–87 FTA negotiations, the essence of any negotiation involves resolving such issues and finding mutually acceptable compromises. They can only be determined, however, by engaging each other and analyzing the issues.

Conclusions

A foreign government, no matter how friendly and neighbourly, only rarely rises to the status of a special interest in Washington. To reduce the natural disadvantages that a small, trade-dependent country has in dealing with its superpower neighbor and ensure that legitimate Canadian interests are not too quickly sacrificed on the altar of political expediency, Canada needs the clout that comes from formal agreements with binding procedures. As Derek Burney, one of the principal architects of the FTA, concluded: "Canada's pursuit of trade agreements, of rules and of dispute settlement mechanisms is not a matter of high-mindedness. It is a matter of survival. It is a reality that is brought home to us on a daily basis. As a small country living next door to a global power, we need these rules to reduce the disparity in power and thus allow us to reap the benefits of our proximity."[10] The reciprocal trade agreements of the 1930s, the GATT throughout the postwar years, the FTA and NAFTA in the 1980s, and the WTO in the 1990s, all satisfied this need. Each raised the legal status enjoyed by Canadian interests to new heights and each proved a critical step toward the further negotiation of even better rules and procedures.

The time may have come to raise the stakes once again and to take a serious look at the next level of rule making. Canada and the United States need to consider how a customs–union agreement that completes the work started in the early 1980s: to achieve a seamless market governed by a single set of rules implemented and administered by the two governments to achieve their common interest in a well functioning North American economy. It is the best way for Canada to manage its deepening economic relations with its giant neighbour to the south. It is also the best way for the United States to demonstrate to its other trading partners that it remains committed to rules–based internationalism and is prepared to adapt that system to the challenges and demands of deeper integration.

---

[10] Donald W. Campbell "Lecture in International Trade," Wilfrid Laurier University Chancellor's Symposium, Toronto, 14 June 1995.

TRADE IN SERVICES

Geza Feketekuty[*]

As we look ahead at future multilateral trade negotiations in the World Trade Organization, it could be useful to ponder on the relationship between NAFTA and the WTO with respect to some of the issues that are likely to be on the negotiating agenda. This paper will largely focus on the negotiations in the area of services.

A discussion of the relationship between future negotiations in NAFTA and the WTO on services might also usefully provide an opportunity to reflect more generally on the relationship between regional and multilateral trade negotiations and agreements. The trade distorting and trade creation effects of regional trade agreements has been widely treated in the academic literature, and there is little value of reviewing that body of analysis here. It is useful for purposes of this paper, however, to review the major operational linkages between regional and global trade negotiations, and to examine how agreements at the regional and global level might best complement each other as part of a functioning global trading system.

Linkages Between Regional and Multilateral Trade Negotiations

Regional trade negotiations can serve as building blocks and laboratories for global trade negotiations by providing the officials involved the opportunity to construct agreements on new types of trade issues in a less complex setting. They can facilitate and help pave the way for multilateral negotiations by changing the status quo. Once domestic industries and domestic regulatory officials have come to terms with the need for change

[*] Geza Feketekuty is a professor at the Graduate School of International Policy Studies at the Monterey Institute of International Studies and President of the International Commercial Diplomacy Project. He served for 21 years with the office of the U.S. Trade Representative and has taught at Princeton University, Johns Hopkins University, and at Cornell University.

accept such change in a multilateral context. Moreover, the political coalitions that are formed by stakeholders in favor of a bilateral liberalization of barriers to trade can also be used to advance a multilateral liberalization process. Finally, any domestic regulatory reforms that are carried out as a prerequisite for bilateral trade liberalization, can serve equally well in most circumstances as a basis for a subsequent multilateral liberalization of the same barriers to trade.

The advantage of tackling issues in a bilateral or regional context before tackling them in a wider multilateral context is that bilateral negotiations inevitably raise fewer complexities than multilateral negotiations that involve a much wider group of countries with more varied interests. Moreover, negotiations with neighboring countries that share similar values raises fewer problems than negotiations with countries that have widely divergent values, institutions, laws, modes of governance and domestic regulatory systems. In this sense, the negotiation of the Canada–U.S. Free Trade Agreement (CUSTA) posed fewer problems than the subsequent negotiation of NAFTA, though by the same token, the negotiation of NAFTA raised fewer problems than would a similar agreement with say India or China. Bilateral and regional agreements are also frequently easier to sell domestically because domestic stakeholders are able to make a more concrete assessment of the potential benefits and costs, thus reducing the political asymmetry which normally serves to retard liberalizing negotiations. Uncertainty about costs tends to exaggerate public assessment of the cost by leaving too much room for unfounded fears, while uncertainty about benefits tends to discount the potential value of the benefit in the eyes of stakeholders who stand to gain from the negotiations. For all these reasons, it is often easier to negotiate a bilateral than a multilateral agreement.

While bilateral and regional negotiations can help facilitate and pave the way for multilateral negotiations, they could also help retard subsequent multilateral efforts to liberalize trade by creating a new, regional vested interest group. Such regional interest groups are likely to be as interested in preventing the loss of rents associated with barriers *viz à viz* the rest of the world as the previous national interest groups were in preventing the loss of rents associated with greater bilateral or regional competition. Regional agreements can also serve to Balkanize and fragment regulatory systems, where a new regional effort creates a wider departure from the global norm than was the case for the independent national systems.

This possible restrictive impact of regional agreements on multilateral trade liberalization can be minimized by minimizing the period of time that elapses between the conclusion of bilateral/regional and multilateral negotiations, thus giving regional interest groups or regulatory officials little time to develop entrenched interests.

The Systemic Role of Regional and Multilateral Agreements

It is generally taken for granted by economists that multilateral trade agreements are preferable to regional trade agreements because they introduce less discrimination. This need not necessarily be the case where liberalization requires a degree of regulatory harmonization in order to establish the basis for an integrated market. Trade negotiations in recent years have increasingly focused on government regulation, and it is not at all clear that the global level is always the preferable level for dealing with trade-distorting regulatory issues. In fact, application of the subsidiarity principle in many cases can lead to the opposite conclusion.[1]

In general, the principle of subsidiarity holds that any particular form of regulation should be carried out at the lowest level of governance consistent with the achievement of various social goals. In effect, this principle establishes a downward bias in favor of keeping regulation at the lowest level of governance consistent with the achievement of various social goals, including regulatory effectiveness, economic efficiency and political legitimacy. In other words, the optimal level of governance with respect to any particular type of regulation varies based on factors affecting regulatory effectiveness, economic efficiency and political legitimacy.

The optimal level of governance from the point of view of regulatory effectiveness is determined by the geographic scope of the problem to be regulated. An effort to deal with air pollution in Mexico City may not need to extend beyond Mexico City, while an effort to prevent harm to the global ozone layer requires global regulation.

Economic efficiency in a market economy is determined by the actions of individual consumers and producers, acting either as individuals or as enterprises. The better adapted regulations are to the conditions facing individual economic actors, and the preferences of such actors as either

---

[1] For a fuller treatment of the subject by the author, see *Defining Subsidiarity In The Global System: Economic, Legal, And Political Criteria.*

consumers or producers, the more such regulations are likely to be economically efficient.

The optimal level of governance from an economic efficiency point of view depends on the cost imposed by differences in local, national or regional regulations, as compared to the cost of imposing a uniform rule in the face of widely differing circumstances. Differences in regulations, whether at the local national or regional (continental) level, introduce economic costs by reducing potential economies of scale and scope, or by forcing producers to pay the added costs associated with meeting different regulations. Put another way, regulatory decisions at a high level of governance make it possible to remove the loss of economic efficiency and growth associated with differences in regulations. On the other hand, decisions at a high level of governance introduce added economic costs by leading to the adoption of regulations that do not suit different local conditions, and by making it more difficult to change the regulation when changed circumstances call for such a change. Decisions at higher levels of governance are more difficult to change because a larger number of people have to agree to the change, and accommodating the views and interests of a larger number of people is not only more difficult, but also takes more time.

In summary, an economic cost of pushing regulatory decisions to a higher level is increased rigidity in decision making, and an inability to adapt regulations to fit local conditions. The economic benefit of pushing regulatory decisions to a higher level is a reduction in the compliance costs associated with meeting different regulations in different jurisdictions, and an expansion of the potential economies of scale and scope.

Political legitimacy for regulation is created by public understanding of the rationale and objective of a regulation on one hand, and equal application of the regulation in similar circumstances, on the other hand. There is an inevitable tension between these two requirements of political legitimacy in an integrating global economy. The higher the level of governance, the longer the distance between the regulator and the citizen affected by the regulation, and the less obvious to an individual citizen the compelling need for any particular regulation. Citizens living in a heavily littered neighborhood may well understand the need to pay a deposit on glass bottles, but that may be less obvious to someone living in a rural area. At the same time, citizens in one heavily littered locality may not be very enthusiastic about the deposit requirement if a neighboring locality has no similar regulation, and if those who shop in the neighboring community indiscriminately drop their bottles in both communities.

Canada–U.S. Free Trade Agreement—Cutting Edge in Services, Investment & Labor Mobility

An interactive, two–way relationship between regional and multilateral trade negotiations was very much in evidence during the negotiation of the Canada–U.S. Free Trade Agreement. The Canada–U.S. FTA preceded the launching of the Uruguay Round of Multilateral Trade Negotiations by a few years, and received part of its political impetus from the difficulties encountered in launching the Uruguay Round. The United States felt stymied by the reluctance of many developing countries to include trade in services and investment on the agenda of a new round, and was looking for other venues for advancing its commercial interests in these areas when the Canadian government, for its own reasons, proposed the negotiation of a bilateral Free Trade Agreement.

In putting forward their proposals for the scope of the FTA, U.S. negotiators assigned a high priority to the inclusion of both trade in services and investment in large part because they wanted to signal to the rest of the world the U.S. determination to address these issues in a new round of multilateral trade negotiations, and wanted to provide some models for the multilateral negotiations. The President's message to the Congress, which accompanied the transmission of the legal texts at the conclusion of the negotiations, underlined the importance the United States assigned to the services provisions as a precedent for subsequent multilateral negotiations by noting that "This Chapter is a successful step in U.S. efforts to fully integrate services into the international trading system, and provides impetus for multilateral negotiations on services."

The provisions on trade in services and on investment were included in Chapter Fourteen (Services), Chapter Fifteen (Temporary Entry for Business Persons), Chapter Sixteen (Investment) and Chapter Seventeen (Financial Services). In the minds of American negotiators, these provisions helped demonstrate that services trade issues could be addressed in an operationally viable and useful way in trade agreements. While the services provisions of the U.S.–Israeli Free Trade Agreement preceded the services provisions of the Canada–U.S. FTA, the latter provided a more comprehensive and far–reaching model which the negotiators in the Uruguay Round could examine for insights. It also gave trade negotiators and domestic regulators in the two countries an opportunity to work out some of the challenges that the negotiation of trade–oriented agreements in services provided for both sets of bureaucracies.

The services provisions of the Canada–U.S. Free Trade Agreement did not modify existing regulations which created barriers to trade, but committed the two countries not to adopt any new measures that would discriminate against suppliers from the other country or services produced in the other country. The agreement also included three annexes, which elaborated on the basic provisions with respect to architectural, tourism, and enhanced telecommunications–network based services. The rather odd collection of three annexes reflected both targets of opportunity and current interests of key industries, and reinforced the role of the agreement in setting a precedent for subsequent regional and multilateral negotiations.

What Was Achieved in the Uruguay Round

The negotiations in services were successful in developing a comprehensive legal framework for trade in services, the General Agreement for Trade in Services (GATS). The GATS covers the full range of issues critical to the achievement of effective market access, including provisions covering domestic regulations, establishment of a local presence, foreign investment and labor mobility. While the provisions of the GATS does not establish substantive, across the board commitments on such issues as market access and national treatment, it provides a legal framework for the negotiation of such commitments, and spells out the obligations assumed by countries with respect to negotiated commitments.

The GATS provisions establish an across-the-board obligation on the transparency of laws and regulations affecting trade in services. Transparency is important for several reasons. Full information about the laws and regulations that will apply to a particular transaction is critical for an assessment of the costs associated with that transaction, and therefore the economic viability of that transaction. Without such information, the potential risks associated with the pursuit of an economic opportunity might be unacceptably high. Accurate information about current laws and regulations is also an essential prerequisite for any effort to change laws and regulations that create market access barriers for foreign businesses. Full knowledge of the conditions and costs associated with any particular international transaction is the first requirement for trade, because without such knowledge importers and exporters cannot calculate whether such trade is likely to be profitable. The framework also explicitly obligates governments to inform private parties that have submitted requests for operating licenses of the precise status of their applications.

Like the Canada–U.S. Free Trade Agreement, the GATS agreement also contains a telecommunications annex that establishes significant commitments with respect to the use of telecommunication networks for the provision of services covered in the national schedules and for intra-corporate communications. Business users are assured access to public telecommunication networks and private leased circuits on reasonable and non-discriminatory terms and conditions. They are also given the right to acquire and attach equipment, to connect private leased line networks to the public switched network, and to use operating protocols of the service supplier's choice.

The Canada–U.S Free Trade Agreement and the Uruguay Round Agreements Compared

The General Agreement on Trade in Services built on the services chapters and annexes of the FTA. Unlike the FTA, and subsequently NAFTA, the GATS Agreement, and its accompanying annexes and national schedules of commitments, did not provide a comprehensive ban on new barriers to trade and investment in services, and fell far short of the commitments on labor mobility in the FTA. The GATS went further than the FTA in elaborating key principles and concepts for the regulation of services, established a more institutionalized procedure for the liberalization of regulatory measures that hampered trade in services, and pushed further in defining the scope for negotiated commitments. Unlike the FTA which focused exclusively on discrimination in regulatory measures as a barrier to trade, the GATS agreement also provided for the negotiation of market access commitments where nondiscriminatory domestic regulatory measures impede competitive entry or conditions of doing business by both domestic and foreign enterprises.

Bilateral negotiations since the conclusion of the Canada–U.S. Free Trade Agreement have liberalized bilateral trade and competition in some sectors, particularly in the area of air and land transportation. On the other hand, negotiations in the WTO on basic telecommunication services since the conclusion of the Uruguay Round have pushed the boundaries of trade and investment liberalization in this sector beyond either the FTA or the initial GATS agreement. The bilateral FTA, as well as NAFTA and the GATS Uruguay Round Agreement, covered access to and use of the telecommunications network, and the competitive provision of enhanced telecommunications services, but not the provision of basic telecommunication services. Subsequent negotiations in the WTO, however, led to the conclusion in the spring of 1997 of the General Agreement on Basic Telecommunications (GBT), which establishes an internationally competitive framework for the provision of basic telecommunication services.

This negotiating history tends to show a complementary relationship between negotiations on trade in services in a regional North American context and a global WTO context, based largely on targets of opportunity.

There has been little discussion of the systemic relationship between regional and global agreements on trade outside of tariff negotiations. In the tariff area, the relationship is relatively clear, in as much as a regional negotiation is supposed to provide an opportunity for the complete elimination of tariffs among a group of countries, in contrast to the more piece-meal process of dismantling tariffs on a global basis. No similar organizing principle has emerged in the area of services, and the relevant provision on regional agreements in the GATS remains relatively nebulous and is full of inconsistencies.

A systemic pattern may nevertheless be reflected in the greater progress made on land and air transportation, and on labor mobility in the North American context, as compared to the global GATS context. The heavier density of traffic and border crossings in a North American context may make it reasonable to argue that these issues were best addressed, initially at least, in a North American regional context, much as they have also been addressed in a regional European context. Similarly, the negotiation of an agreement on value-added or enhanced telecommunication services in the FTA context preceded the negotiation of a similar, though more robust, agreement in the GATS. In contrast, negotiations on basic telecommunications jumped immediately to a global level. The existing global regime for basic telecommunication services was rapidly breaking down, and it undoubtedly made more sense to address this issue on a global rather than a purely regional basis.

Whither NAFTA?

The ambitious potential agenda for the next round of negotiations on services under the GATS in the WTO leads to the question on the future role of NAFTA. In what areas could negotiations under NAFTA serve as a useful catalyst for the multilateral negotiations by establishing new models or precedents? In what areas could negotiations advance the framework for trade in services within North America, both over the near term and over a longer time horizon? Over the longer term, what should be the role of NAFTA in a globalizing world economy?

The first place to look for a potential contribution by NAFTA to the global negotiations is in the areas where NAFTA has made greater progress than the global negotiations— namely transportation and labor mobility. In both of these areas some progress has been made in a North American context, but progress that falls short of a comprehensive and well functioning set of disciplines.

Progress in transportation has been piecemeal, and much remains to be accomplished in all areas of transportation. A viable framework for competition in transportation services in North American would make a substantial contribution to both the expansion of North American trade and to the multilateral negotiations in this area. Such an agreement could build on the GBT model, and go beyond it in dealing with such transportation-specific issues as the licensing of truck and bus drivers, as well as pilots, and the labor rights of drivers and pilots. It could also deal with the inspection of vehicle safety for all types of trucks, buses, trains, planes and ships. It would also need to deal with issues of coastal shipping, including the Jones Act. These are all sensitive issues, but that is precisely why negotiations in a NAFTA context might break useful ground.

The FTA agreement on labor mobility broke major new ground, but its implementation has not been anywhere near as smooth as the negotiation of the agreement. A great deal of ambiguity regarding required documentation and arbitrary actions by agents at the border has made the operation of the agreement much less smooth than the equivalent agreement within Europe. An effort to evaluate problems associated with the implementation of the agreement, and the subsequent negotiation of expanded provisions in areas subject to arbitrary interpretation by border agents, could make an important contribution to both trade within North America and multilateral negotiations in this area. One option to consider might be the development of a standardized document that would entitle its bearer to move across the borders in pursuit of professional activities without further challenge.

Another area where negotiations in a NAFTA context might plow useful ground is in the area of professional services. The agreement on architectural services in the FTA broke new ground, but has not been followed by any other agreements in the FTA or NAFTA context. The GATS agreement on accounting has added a multilateral agreement on professional services, albeit one that did not go far in establishing a framework for mutual recognition of professional competence and for licensing of qualified professionals.

The most important area, however, where negotiations in North America could make a contribution to regional and global cooperation on trade in services is in the area of culture. This issue is a major source of conflict that continuously threatens to poison trade relations between the two countries. Moreover, if the United States and Canada, with their similar cultural background and history cannot work out a viable agreement, there is much less hope of overcoming the hurdles in this area on a global basis. Any agreement in this area requires some flexibility on both sides. The United States must recognize that access of local communities to cultural media is even an issue within the United States, where governments at all levels regularly require media companies to set aside channels for various local groups and public service programming. On the other hand, Canada needs to recognize that some ground-rules are needed in this area. With good will on both sides it should be possible to come up with an agreement that gives Canadian authors and artists some form of preferential access to Canadian media outlets, while protecting the commercial interests of U.S. media companies.

This brings us the question as to the longer-term role of the FTA or NAFTA in a globalizing world economy, where multilateral efforts over time will remove barriers to trade on a global basis. On the basis of the principle of subsidiarity, the most useful role of NAFTA can be to provide an institutional framework for cooperation on regulatory issues of a regional nature, and in some cases, for the negotiation of a harmonized set of regulatory standards where that is necessary to accomplish regulatory objectives. The density of economic linkages across the North American borders may well make it desirable from the point of view of either economic efficiency or the effective achievement of regulatory objectives to establish close cooperative relationships, or the development of common regulatory standards in some areas of public policy. In practice, a great deal of such cooperation already takes place on an informal basis on an issue-by-issue basis. NAFTA could in the long run provide a more coherent institutional framework for such cooperation.

Conclusion

The Canada–U.S. Free Trade Agreement and NAFTA have played a useful catalytic and pioneering role in paving the way for multilateral negotiations on trade in services, and in establishing a framework for dealing with regional issues ripe for negotiated solutions. At the same time, trade in services within North America has simultaneously benefited from the negotiation of the GATS agreement in the Uruguay Round and subsequent negotiations within the GATS/WTO umbrella. The new round of GATS negotiations scheduled to commence in 2000 can be expected to expand trade opportunities in services and the legal framework for international competition in services even further. At the same time, further negotiations in a FTA/NAFTA context could serve as a useful catalyst for the multilateral negotiations in areas such as transportation, labor mobility, professional services, and cultural issues, while at the same time reducing friction and expanding trade opportunities within a North American context. Over the longer term, it would be useful to explore how NAFTA could advance regulatory cooperation within a North American context on public policy issues of a regional nature.

REGIONAL DOMINOS AND THE WTO: BUILDING BLOCKS OR BOOMERANG?

Sylvia Ostry[*]

There has been an enormous proliferation of regional agreements in the 1990s after the completion of the Uruguay Round. The issue of the relationship between these preferential arrangements and the multilateral-based system (based on non-discrimination) has generated an enormous literature. The debate, increasingly rancorous, was couched in a beguiling metaphor. Are these regional integration agreements (RIA's) building blocks or stumbling blocks to the creation of a global rule-based system? But the question itself was misleading. There is no one-size-fits-all RIA—think of the European Community; the Canada-U.S. Free Trade Agreement (CUSTA), the North American Free Trade Agreement (NAFTA), Mercosur, Asean, etc. And worse, the metaphor is static—a building block in the 1960s might be a stumbling block in the 1990s. A better metaphor is the game of dominoes; the use of RIAs as part of a broader, evolving geoeconomic policy template. The ultimate objective of the domino play is to broaden and deepen the global system—and, as I will argue here, part of the game involves knowing when to change strategy.

The argument for a domino policy is twofold. First, it is easier to achieve progress in regional arrangements because they are more flexible, less time-consuming than the larger, more cumbersome multilateral negotiations and, because of this flexibility, they are easier "to customize." You can have different goals for different regions. And the second argument is that progress at the regional level then serves as a catalyst for

* Sylvia Ostry is Distinguished Research Fellow at the Munk Centre for International Studies at the University of Toronto. She has served as Ambassador for Multilateral Trade Negotiations and the Prime Minister's Personal Representative for the Economic Summit. Dr. Ostry also has served as Head of the Economics and Statistics Department of the OECD, Paris.

"competitive liberalization," both in other regions, and ultimately in the World Trade Organization (WTO).

The main architect of the regional domino policy has been the United States which initiated its multi-track trade policy in the 1980s with CUSTA when the Uruguay Round talks were stalled because of the fight with the Europeans over agriculture and with the so-called G-10 hard liners, led by Brazil and India, over the new issues: services, intellectual property and investment. The main other player in this, and, indeed, all subsequent domino games was the European Union (EU). Indeed, for the most part, regional dominos is a game for big players only. Yet, as will be discussed below, a small player (Canada) negotiated a unique dispute settlement arrangement which has already had a significant impact on the trading system.

This paper will focus on the regional domino game as it has evolved in CUSTA and NAFTA, tracking the interaction with the multilateral system and the WTO. It is not intended to provide an analysis of these agreements, which are available in many publications, but rather some stylized facts that highlight the overall strategy of customization and competition. While APEC is also part of that overall strategy, given the context of this conference the analysis will be largely confined to the Western Hemisphere.

Finally, the paper will consider the broader question of the impact of the game on the system as a whole, especially the operation of the WTO. It will be argued that the original version of the game has run out of steam and may now be counterproductive. To be effective in promoting global liberalization, the game will have to be adapted to the changing global environment. Any effective adaptation, however, will require a strengthening of the WTO.

First Domino: CUSTA

The negotiation to launch the Uruguay Round negotiation took almost as long as the entire Tokyo Round of the 1970s. The Americans had been trying to initiate a new round since the early 1980s because of dissatisfaction with the results of the Tokyo Round and with GATT itself as a weak "institution" and also to stave off the rising protectionist fury in Congress (mainly because of the overvalued dollar). The Europeans were blocking the launch to avoid coming to grips with the Common Agricultural Policy (CAP) and a number of developing countries were bitterly opposed to including the so-called "new issues" of services, intellectual property and investment. Yet without these new issues, in which the U.S. was a world leader, it seems highly improbable that the American business community or politicians would have continued to support the multilateral system for much longer.[1] The response of the U.S. administration was to launch a new trade policy: regionalism *via* the CUSTA and unilateralism *via* Section 301 of the 1974 Trade Act in order to achieve multilateralism *via* the Uruguay Round.

A major objective for the U.S. in the bilateral negotiations with Canada (announced in the Canadian house of Commons on September 26, 1986) was to demonstrate to the Europeans that bilateralism was a feasible alternative that would be actively pursued if the foot-dragging at the GATT continued. To send a message to the so-called G-10 hard-liners, the agreement must include the new issues. For the developing countries, the implied threat was strongly reinforced by a new "tough policy" announced by President Reagan on September 23, 1986 that included his support, the first by an American president, for self-initiating the little-used section 301 of the 1974 Trade Act on unfair trade practices. The notice was clear: the new issues are part of the trade agenda and only the venue of negotiation remains open to choice— Geneva or Washington (or Brasilia or New Delhi or . . .).[2]

Was the ploy successful? Of course it's not possible to "prove" that the E.C. finally decided to grapple with reform of CAP because of fear of U.S. regionalism. Still, it may have helped by adding to the internal pressure for agriculture reform within the Community from countries like the U.K. and the Netherlands. Moreover, international business support for a round which included the "new issues" was effectively mobilized by the American multinationals.[3] The Uruguay Round was launched in Punta del Este in September, 1986.

What's the score card on the other major objective of this first play— the inclusion of the new issues in CUSTA? A quick summary would be one out of three. Services were included for the first time in any international trade agreement, but, for a number of reasons related to Canadian

---

[1]   Sylvia Ostry, *The Post-Cold War Trading System: Who's on First?*, University of Chicago Press, 1997, pp. 105-108.

[2]   For a fuller exposition, see Sylvia Ostry, *Governments and Corporations in a Shrinking World*, Council on Foreign Relations, New York, 1990, pp. 25-29. See also, Geza Feketekuty, "U.S. Policy on 301 and Super 301," in Jagdish Bhagwati and Hugh T. Patrick, (eds.), *Aggressive Unilateralism: America's 301 Trade Policy and the World Trading System*, University of Michigan Press, Ann Arbor, 1990, pp. 91-96.

[3]   Ostry, *Governments and Corporations*, Chapter 2, pp. 17-52.

domestic policy and politics, intellectual property was not included and limited progress was made on the investment issues.[4]

Comparison of Two Regional Agreements and the General Agreement on Trade in Services

Table 1: A Brief Comparison of Regional Agreements and the GATS

Agreements Criteria	CUSTA	NAFTA	GATS
Modalities and instruments of liberalization	National treatment for all modes of supply. Right of non–establishment. Grandfathering of all existing non–conforming measures. No general procedures for harmonization of regulations or mutual recognition. No disciplines on non–discriminatory QRs.	National treatment, 'reverse' MFN, freedom of mode of supply, including right of non–establishment (no local presence). No grandfathering. Allows for exemptions to national treatment, MFN and local presence. No disciplines on non–discriminatory QRs, but all such measures to be listed. Ratcheting provision for unilateral liberalization. Abolition of residency requirements for professions. Generic blueprint for use by service providers seeking recognition agreements. Work programmes on foreign legal licensing of engineers. Work programs on standards harmonization (land, transport and telecoms). Accession clause.	All modes of supply covered in principle. Transparency, MFN, and dispute settlement as basic general obligations. No general right of non–establishment. Encouragement of recognition agreements for licensing and certification requirements. No general disciplines on non–discriminatory QRs, but a number are prohibited under the market access article unless explicitly reserved.

It's important to underline, however, that CUSTA must be regarded as a major breakthrough by establishing trade in services (an oxymoron at the creation of GATT) as part of a new trade agenda, the agenda of deepening integration as it is now termed. The main purpose— to include services in the Uruguay Round— was achieved. In terms of liberalization, however,

---

[4] For a full review of the agreement, see *The Canada–U.S. Free Trade Agreement*, External Affairs, Ottawa, 1988. See also Michael Hart, with Bill Dymond and Colin Robertson, *Decision at Midnight: Inside the Canada–U.S. Free Trade Negotiations*, UBC Press, Vancouver, 1994. See also, Gordon Ritchie, *Wrestling with the Elephant: The Inside Story of the Canada–U.S. Trade Wars*, Macfarlane Walter and Ross, Toronto, 1997, Chapter 5, pp. 93–120 for a discussion of pharmaceuticals and investment in the context of the bargaining dynamics.

CUSTA results were less impressive. A useful summary evaluation of outcomes is presented in Table 1, which compares CUSTA, NAFTA and the GATS.

Comparison of Two Regional Agreements and the General Agreement on Trade in Services

Table 1 (continued)

Agreements Criteria	CUSTA	NAFTA	GATS
Sectoral Coverage	Positive list approach to coverage. Some 60 service activities covered. Sectoral annexes on value–added telecommunication and computer services; tourism services; and mutual recognition for architects. Separate chapters on financial services and temporary entry of business people.	Negative list approach to coverage. Universal coverage, except for air services subject to bilateral air agreements. Annexes on: reservations of existing non–conforming investment and cross–border services measures at federal and state/provincial levels; 'unbound' reservations in sensitive sectors; activities reserved for the state; exceptions to MFN; and existing non–discriminatory QRs. Separate chapters on telecommunications (access to and use of public networks and services); financial services; temporary entry of business people. Timetables for the liberalization of land transport and specialty air services.	Positive list of scheduled sectors. Most air transport services excluded via an annex (indefinite). Other annexes deal with telecommunications (access to and use of public networks and services); financial services (complemented by an understanding of commitments on financial services); movement of natural persons.
Agreements Criteria	No disciplines for procurement of services—except for services incidental to sale of a covered good. No rules for subsidies to service industries.	Government procurement of services and construction covered. Positive list for entity coverage; negative list approach for services coverage. No disciplines on subsidies for services.	No disciplines for government procurement or subsidies. MFN obligation for subsidies. Subsidy disciplines to be negotiated in future. Services and construction procure-ment included in GATT code on government procurement.

Source: Bernard Hoekman and Pierre Sauve, "Regional and Multilateral Liberalization of Service Markets," *Journal of Common Market Studies*, Vol. 32, No.3, Sept. 1994, pp. 303–305.

This may be seen from table 1, CUSTA established national treatment as the main liberalizing norm applied to service providers; freedom in principle for service providers to use any mode of supply; and the reduction of impediments to effective access by all modes. However, the effect was minimal since all existing nonconforming measures were "grandfathered," although a "standstill" which precludes new discriminatory laws and regulations was also agreed. CUSTA established the concept of a "positive list" approach to sectoral commitments, i.e. its obligations applied only to sectors explicitly listed in the annex and one key sector not listed was basic telecommunications. Services were also excluded from the CUSTA's government procurement agreement. As may be seen from the Table, the GATS adopted the basic CUSTA template, but with some additions: for example, specifying each mode of delivery to which the basic norms of the agreement apply. Thus in the GATS framework (unlike that of CUSTA) national treatment can be applied selectively on specific modes, sector-by-sector. An annex to GATS also permits an MFN exemption. The main reason for these "adaptations" of the basic rules was the concern with "free riding," especially in sectors like telecommunications and financial services. Finally, as Table 1 demonstrates, NAFTA builds on CUSTA and GATS, especially by adopting a "negative list" approach which is more supportive of liberalization. Thus unlike CUSTA, NAFTA establishes a general liberalization of trade in services except where reservations are listed.

Thus the geoeconomic strategy of the regional domino game started with CUSTA, moved to GATS, and then to NAFTA, with improvements in design in each play. Still, the most important breakthrough in NAFTA was really not services, but investment, the second domino. But before turning to that subject, it is useful to look at another part of the CUSTA agreement, the innovative dispute settlement arrangements in Chapter 19. This domino was played by Canada, which made it rather unusual in a game normally reserved for big players.

Major players have greater political and economic power in their own regions and can therefore determine the main objectives of any agreement. Smaller countries are usually driven by what are called safe-haven concerns, or insurance against future protectionism in the large market. The more uncertain is security of access, the greater the need for a safe-haven.[5] In the case of Canada, the greatest threat to predictability and

---

5   For a discussion of safe-haven RIA's, see John Whalley and Colleen Hamilton, *The Trading System After the Uruguay Round*, Institute for International Economics, Washington, D.C., July 1996, pp. 103–111.

security of access to the U.S. market stemmed from the trade remedy laws: anti–dumping and countervail against subsides. When it proved impossible to eliminate or replace these laws in CUSTA an innovative new dispute settlement arrangement, designed to constrain their use for protectionist purposes, was agreed. CUSTA thus included (more by accident than design) the first example of international administrative law.[6]

Beginning in the 1970s, changes in U.S. trade remedy laws facilitated easier use by domestic industries against foreign exporters. Among the procedural changes undertaken at the behest of Congress was the incorporation of judicial review into antidumping and countervailing duty practices— a generic feature of the U.S. litigious administrative law model. The rapid rise in "administered protectionism" in the 1970s and 1980s was not due to this procedural change, but nonetheless represented a major threat to Canadian exporters. In lieu of any other policy option, the Canadians proposed and the U.S. (reluctantly) accepted that judicial review of antidumping and countervailing duty actions be undertaken by bi-national "dispute settlement" panels on which Canadians would be represented equally with Americans. As spelled out in Chapter 19 of the CUSTA, panels would be required to apply the domestic laws of the country but also to determine whether those laws were correctly and fairly applied. Private parties have a right to request a panel review and can represent themselves before panels. Findings are binding on both governments. This is thus a unique example of international administrative law since the role of the bi-national panel is to *review the procedure* of the *domestic* administrative agency. Canadian and American trade remedy laws are very similar, although there are differences in the "standard of review" applied in both countries. So, while Chapter 19 was opposed by some Americans as an undue invasion of sovereignty, for the most part it was accepted as a "trade–off" in the bilateral negotiations. When Chapter 19 became part of NAFTA, however, it required significant changes in the Mexican legal infrastructure. This aspect of the CUSTA "domino effect" is worth spelling out.

Canada and the U.S. have very similar trade remedy laws and also administrative procedures systems based on their shared common law heritage. The situation in Mexico was very different, stemming, as it does,

---

6   See Gilbert R. Winham, "NAFTA Chapter 19 and the Development of International Administrative Law: Application in Anti–Dumping and Competition Law," *Journal of World Trade*, Geneva, 32:1, February, 1998, pp. 65–84. Canada scored a major hit in the binational panel arrangement. For an analysis of decisions see Alan M. Rugman and Andrew D.M. Anderson, "NAFTA and the Dispute Settlement Mechanisms: A Transactions Costs Approach," *The World Economy*, 20(7), November, 1997, pp. 935–950.

from a civil law heritage. In the present context, the most important difference was *procedural* (although there were also some substantive differences in the trade remedy laws). The essence of the procedural difference related to the *transparency* of the administrative process, which for both Canada and the U.S. was essential to the due process rights of *individuals* (i.e. *firms*) and "not from the presumed sovereignty of national states."[7] We shall return to this issue below.

Thus a condition for Mexico to benefit from Chapter 19 was to change both it's trade remedy laws and regulations and its related administrative law procedures. The most important aspect of change was to increase the transparency of operations of the agency in change of the trade remedy laws, in effect to import the U.S.–Canada model.[8] And this import was not like any other, since legal systems are a fundamental part of the institutional architecture of a sovereign state. To ensure that the import was "permanent," moreover, NAFTA allows withdrawal of benefits if any partner fails to implement a Chapter 19 panel award. Finally, while CUSTA had provided that Chapter 19 would remain in effect for five years plus a two year extension (during which the two parties would try to develop a substitute for the trade remedy laws) NAFTA made it permanent. The implication is quite clear: if other countries accede to NAFTA and are to benefit from the innovative dispute settlement mechanism they will have to import the key elements of the legal system on which it is based. In this instance those key elements are transparency and the due process rights of *individual firms*.

These same elements are also important in the NAFTA domino play of the U.S.— a path-breaking agreement on investment. CUSTA and the Uruguay Round produced meagre results on this key "new issue" but NAFTA provided the opportunity to change all that.

Second Domino: Investment Rules in NAFTA

The NAFTA negotiations began in 1990 at the request of Mexico. For Mexico, the motive was less a desire for a safe-haven than a need to lock-in domestic reforms. By way of contrast, Canada felt it essential to join the negotiations as a defense mechanism against a hub and spoke continental

---

7   Winham, p.76.

8   See NAFTA Annex 1904.15. Schedule of Mexico. This details changes in Mexican antidumping and countervailing duty statues and regulations and in other statutes and regulations relevant to the operating procedures of the responsible administrative agency. Of the 21 amendments specified, all but six relate to transparency.

trading system, centred on the U.S., which would erode the preferential access gained in CUSTA. For the United States, NAFTA provided an opportunity to finish the unfinished new issues agenda of CUSTA. A second regional domino play would give a push to the lagging Uruguay Round, which was clearly going to miss the 1990 target date set in Punta.

NAFTA, as noted above, built on and improved the services agreement of CUSTA. In intellectual property, the U.S.–Canada dispute over compulsory licensing (which had blocked an agreement in this area) was settled; Mexican reforms on patent and copyright laws were locked in; and the U.S. won a battle on "pipeline protection" for pharmaceutical and agrichemical products already patented elsewhere— a battle lost in the Uruguay Round. But the really big victory was in investment, a key issue which produced meagre results in CUSTA and in Geneva.

The absence of a global regime for foreign direct investment (FDI) is an excellent example of the propensity of governments to "make policy in a rearview mirror." Almost precisely at the time the Uruguay Round was launched, the international economy was beginning a process of dramatic transformation, spawned by an investment surge and by the time the Round ended, the agents of globalization— the multinational enterprises (MNE's)— were the main channels for trade, finance and technology flows.

Since, for a number of reasons, the multilateral negotiations on investment rules seemed less and less likely to produce significant results[9] and since U.S. MNE's were world leaders in the ongoing globalization of the world economy, and the major investors in both Canada and Mexico, it is plausible to argue that NAFTA was more about investment than trade. And the key priority of the domino play was to establish a template for a global investment regime.

NAFTA establishes the basic norms for an investment regime, including national treatment for investors from the three countries, as well as MFN to ensure that NAFTA investors are treated as well as any other foreign investors; the right of establishment by prohibition of a wide range of performance requirements (the original American wish-list for the Uruguay Round); and prohibition of restrictions on capital movements (except for prudential or balance of payments reasons). But by far the most innovative element— a first in a trade agreement— was the investor protection provisions and a new dispute settlement arrangement. Designed for the purpose of protecting American and Canadian investment in Mexico (and reflecting the long-held fear of Americans concerning

---

9   See Sylvia Ostry, *A New Regime for Foreign Direct Investment*, Group of Thirty, Occasional paper 53, Washington, D.C., 1997, pp. 3–7.

expropriation by Latin American governments). This centrepiece of the NAFTA accord was considered a precedent–setting breakthrough.

The investment provisions of NAFTA included procedures for resolving disputes by which private parties may seek binding arbitration rulings against a host government in an international forum and adopted a broad definition of expropriation which could include investor claims against government regulation in, say, environmental areas, which negatively affect the value of investment. In the U.S., property rights are protected by the Constitution and this meaning of "expropriation" is not uncommon in jurisprudence concerning "regulatory takings." In international law the "taking" versus "expropriation" distinction exists but the jurisprudence mainly covers conventional expropriation. In Canada (and probably also Mexico) the jurisprudence in the area of "takings" is different from that in the U.S. Since in a sense, any regulation might alter the relative costs and opportunities of companies but only a foreign company can seek compensation, several challenges by American companies in Canada have raised a political firestorm.[10] And, indeed, it was the adoption of NAFTA language on expropriation in the multilateral agreement on investments (MAI) which provided a powerful rallying point for opponents of the OECD negotiations. A domino that boomeranged?

Because it was too late to improve the investment provisions of the Uruguay Round, negotiations on an MAI were launched in the OECD in 1995. Led (or pushed) by the U.S., with only reluctant support from the European Union, the negotiations were intended to produce a "high standard" agreement which could provide the model for a global accord in the WTO. And indeed at the first Ministerial Meeting of the WTO in 1996, the formation of a working group on investment and competition was agreed.

Although an OECD agreement was to be open to accession by non–member countries (who could sign on but not fully participate in the negotiations) the OECD initiative provoked rancor among many WTO members. There were also difficulties among the OECD countries themselves over numerous exceptions and derogations. But it was the international non–governmental organizations (INGOs) led by the environmentalists (ENGOs) which proved most effective in bringing the negotiations to a halt. The arcane legalism of regulatory "taking" was effectively transformed into an argument which touched the exposed nerve of sovereignty. However, the due process rights of firms, which was the

---

10   Sylvia Ostry and Julie Soloway, "The MMT case ended too soon," *The Globe and Mail*, Toronto, 24 July 1998.

norm established by CUSTA's Chapter 19, is now embedded in the international trading system and it seems unlikely that a global regime for investment could be established without some version of it.

It's important to underline the role of INGOs, and especially ENGOs, in today's policy process. It's no accident that the ENGOs were the first to play a significant role in trade policy, since NAFTA included specific environmental provisions—the first in trade history. The influence of the INGOs has been greatly enhanced by the revolution in information and communication technology (ICT), both through agile and skilled use of the media (especially television), and the low cost and global span of communication linkages such as e-mail. The policy process has become much more contestable than in the past: marching in cyberspace is far easier than traditional interest group lobbying and, as the MAI boomerang demonstrates, can be very effective.

The Regional Domino Game: What's next?

This paper has concentrated on the game in North America, i.e. the domino play between CUSTA and NAFTA and the multilateral system. However, a fuller exploration (beyond the scope of this discussion) should also include the regional policy in East Asia, specifically APEC. There are several examples of skilled domino plays by the U.S. such as the push to complete the basic telecommunications agreement and the international technology agreement. These carefully orchestrated show-pieces in APEC were then taken to Brussels (to bring the EU on board) *en route* to Geneva and the WTO. The November, 1994 Bogor "vision" of free trade by 2010 (for developing countries) and 2020 (for developed countries) was echoed in the December, 1994 Miami "vision" of Western Hemisphere free trade by 2005 for the Free Trade Agreement of the Americas (FTAA). The effort to export the 2020 "vision" to the first WTO ministerial meeting in Singapore in 1996, however, didn't work.

It's important to underline once again that a regional domino strategy is primarily a game for big players. Thus the ultimate target is the WTO, then the EU must be the partner in the end game. However, with two big players, the game now is getting complicated. The EU-Mercosur negotiations, for example, or ASEM (EU-Asean) will make U.S. overall geoeconomic strategy more difficult since it is unlikely to be fully in accord with that of the EU. Further, with the EU engagement, the bargaining clout of the smaller countries could be enhanced, which would make the domino (a choice by the large country) more difficult to achieve.

These complications are bound to add to uncertainty and hardly seem conducive to generating a clear "vision" of the future world trading system.

But that's not the only problem with the regional domino policy of the U.S. The lack of fast track certainly diminishes the credibility of American leadership in the FTAA, especially since other countries (such as Brazil) are building coalitions as a counter-weight to U.S. regional dominance. The Asian financial turmoil is hardly conducive to significant results in Malaysia this year in the Early Voluntary Sectoral Liberalization announced at last year's Vancouver Summit. In any case, one would have to say that the APEC approach to liberalization within the region (concerted unilateralism) has been a complete failure to date.[11]

So, to get back to the "What's Next?" question, if the momentum to regional liberalization is flagging, are there other options for a new version of dominos? Both the FTAA and APEC sponsor a range of activities other than, but related to, trade and investment liberalization. These can be grouped into two broad policy domains: trade facilitation and community-building, or cooperation. And these two policy pillars should be the focus of a new regionalism.

Trade facilitation covers cooperative action in the administration of product and other technical standards as well as customs and immigration procedures. Negotiating internationally harmonized standards or mutual recognition agreements requires hard slogging, but this improved "plumbing" is essential to effective market access by both trade and investment, and, of increasing importance, as production processes become more technologically complex. Indeed one might argue that as transparent border barriers have come down, these invisible barriers have become major impediments to trade flows. While the WTO has recently sponsored a symposium on trade facilitation, there is in fact little multilateral action in this area. Whatever has been accomplished has been bilateral (US-EU) or regional. But the regional initiatives in both the FTAA and APEC, have been poorly focused and poorly funded, in part because of weak overall coordination. Yet this is one area where clear "deliverables" could be specified which by definition must involve business participation. This in turn would provide an ideal venue for business networking. And since, in many of the member countries of both the FTAA and APEC, facilitation will of necessity involve the redesign of the regulatory institutional infrastructure, it opens up opportunities for

---

[11] See, Ippei Yamazaiva, "APEC and WTO in Trade Liberalization," *Whither APEC? The Progress to Date and Agenda for the Future*, C. Fred Bergsten (ed.), Institute for International Economics, Special Report 9, October 1997, Washington, D.C., pp. 61–69.

strengthening intergovernmental links through technical assistance. In order to ensure that the different regional initiatives are coherent, the WTO could provide a central information repository.

Community-building or cooperation is a vast and vague domain in both FTAA and APEC. Projects range from sustainable development, women's rights, corruption, money laundering, education and technical training to building civil society, etc. While activity seems extensive, the process is not transparent and almost impossible to monitor.[12] Without more specificity of objectives the outcomes can't really be monitored and evaluated. Yet this vague and nebulous domain could be transformed if the activities were contained and clustered and efforts launched to undertake the extremely complex task of defining outcomes. A primary focus should be technical assistance to improve "soft infrastructure" such as regulatory system capabilities, and administrative and trade law regimes. If *facilitation* is the plumbing, institutional infrastructure is the *foundation* of sustainable trade and investment liberalization. Again, this activity is best carried out at a regional level (since it can be better adapted and customized) and should involve cooperation with the regional development banks. But, once more, it must be coordinated at a global level by the WTO in cooperation with the International Financial Institutions. And the WTO capability in technical assistance is virtually non-existent except for minimal resources for trade policy training, mainly in the least developed countries. Yet if this proposal for a new regionalism is to strengthen and not disrupt the global system, the WTO itself must be reinforced.

Reinforcing the WTO

The WTO is *au fond* like GATT in being a member-driven organization without a significant knowledge infrastructure, i.e. a secretariat of highly qualified experts able to undertake research directed at policy analysis, as in the OECD, the IMF and the World Bank. This analytic deficit virtually precludes policy discussion, and the important peer group pressure it generates. Without the instrument of peer group pressure the transactions costs of achieving consensus in the WTO can be so high that more flexible and therefore speedier alternatives (regional or bilateral) will always be desirable. Moreover, the size and disparate interests of the membership greatly add to the difficulty of achieving consensus. Equally important,

---

12   For a first effort at evaluation of FTAA Summitry by an independent group, see The Leadership Council for Inter-American Summitry, *From Talk to Action: How Summits Can Help Forge a Western Hemisphere Community of Prosperous Democracies*, North-South Center, University of Miami, March, 1998.

with the entry of new members such as China and Russia, the lack of "transparency" threatens a serious overload of the already stretched and new evidentiary–intensive dispute settlement system.

Although the notion of a shared vision of the postwar trading system is part romantic myth, the postwar elites did share enough basic ideas to serve as a context for policy dialogue and, of course, the Cold War was a powerful fount for cohesive purpose. While some may argue that there is far greater support for trade liberalization today than in 1948, as always the devil is in the details— what do we mean by "trade liberalization"? The most basic issues facing democratic countries— the domestic balance between market efficiency and other social and political objectives and the balance between these domestic objectives and international rules— were hardly a matter of vital concern in the border barrier liberalization after the war. Further, while the deeper integration policy agenda was and will continue to be determined not only by governments but also by MNE's, and as noted above, by the INGOs and ENGOs, the increasingly influential new global actors too. The traditional politics of trade in GATT–land involved the Olsonian distributional coalitions concerned with the division of the pie. Some of the INGOs may have similar objectives but their message today is more easily sold either on TV or by e-mail, pitched to an audience sensitive to the globalization issue. And, more importantly, where there are genuine and significant *systemic* differences in a global optic based on ecology and one based on efficiency, consensus will require difficult debate and dialogue. The point of all this is not to discuss trade and the environment, but to illustrate the radically changed politics of trade policy in WTO–land.

So what reforms would be necessary to strengthen the WTO and ensure the sustainability of the multilateral rules–based system? There will be a wide range of views on this matter and my suggestions are not intended to be exhaustive— but perhaps may stimulate discussion.

The first requirement to enhance the flexibility and adaptability of the WTO is to establish a smaller body or executive committee akin to the IMF Interim Committee or the World Bank's Development Committee. A Uruguay Round attempt to establish a successor to the 1975 Consultative Group of Eighteen (CG18) unfortunately failed, mainly because of opposition from a number of developing countries who feared exclusion. But given the change in atmospherics since the late 1980s, in particular the much more widespread appreciation of the need for a global rules–based system, the time is now ripe for another effort.

The next WTO Ministerial Meeting (to be held in the U.S.) should propose that an Executive committee of Ministers be established to provide overall guidance to the WTO in promoting the ongoing liberalization of the world trading system. The Executive Committee would be able to meet on a regular basis and, with the assistance of the Director-General and the secretariat, review current and prospective policy issues in order to advise the biennial Ministerial Conference, which would retain full decision-making authority. With such a forum, at both a Ministerial and Senior Official level, the *norms* and *principles* of liberalization rather than the *specifics of legalistic detail* could be discussed and debated. It is essential to underline that forging a consensus in a smaller group aided by expert policy-analytic information is facilitated by peer group pressure. The Executive Committee can then play a role in promoting the extension of that consensus to the entire membership.

In establishing such a Committee, the most difficult problem, of course, is membership and various formulae tried out in the Uruguay Round failed to secure agreement. But in establishing the Trade Policy Review Mechanism (TPRM), the Round created a precedent for a possible formula. Thus different countries were subject to different review schedules on the basis of the member's share of world trade. This same formula could be used for establishing a committee of reasonable size and rotating membership which would ensure that all countries and regions would be represented within a given time frame.[13]

Another function of the Executive Committee supported by a high quality (although not necessarily large) expert secretariat would be the diffusion of knowledge in national capitals, another essential ingredient of consensus-building. Further, in order to keep up to date and reasonably small in size, the WTO could not possibly generate all its policy analysis in-house. Like most research bodies today, the WTO secretariat would have to establish a research network linked to other institutions such as the OECD, the Bretton Woods institutions, private think tanks, universities and the like. Knowledge networks are key elements in promoting cooperation and coordination. This networking should also include INGOs such as business groups (the International Chamber of Commerce, for example); transnational environmental groups; international labour associations and intergovernmental organizations such as the ILO. And, of course, the regional networks which are now evolving. This symbiotic relationship between the WTO and the regions is essential, as noted above, to the integrity of the global system.

---

13   Robert Wolfe, "Global Trade as a Single Undertaking: The Role of Ministers in the WTO," *International Journal*, LI:4 (Autumn 1996).

In the area of soft infrastructure (regulatory reform, competition policy, effective and transparent administrative law regimes and other institutional issues), some increase in WTO facilities for technical training would be required. But even under the most optimistic scenario of enhanced resources, the WTO capabilities in training would be dwarfed by the technical assistance resources of the World Bank and increasingly, the IMF. So some cooperative arrangement would be essential— a good and practical example of "policy" coherence— but hardly sufficient.

Because of recent changes in the policy orientation of the Fund and Bank, the problem of improved policy coherence has taken on very different dimensions. Both institutions (albeit for different reasons and not entirely in harmony) are shifting policy focus to issues of institutional infrastructure — domestic regulatory policies; "transparency"; the role of government; trade policies— essentially the same broad range of issues as the WTO. It's probably not an exaggeration to assert that 'IMF and— World Bank programs not just in East Asia but in India, Latin America, Central Europe and Africa, have led to more systematic trade liberalization than— bilateral or multilateral negotiations have ever achieved."[14] But real cooperation between the WTO and its sister agencies would require significant reinforcement of the WTO. This is the same condition as that presented earlier to ensure a healthy and sustainable regional–global interface. Put simply, if the centre doesn't hold, will the system?

---

[14] Lawrence Summers, "Why America Needs the IMF," *Wall Street Journal*, 27 March 1998, pp. A22. This is hardly the best route since none of the measures are bound in the WTO.

THE FUTURE OF REGIONAL TRADING ARRANGEMENTS IN THE WESTERN HEMISPHERE

Gary Hufbauer* & Barbara Kotschwar**

Many changes have altered the trade relationships in the Western Hemisphere over the past decade. Latin America has opened up and North America has taken a greater interest in commerce with South America and the Caribbean. The United States has moved away from its previous insistence that multilateral negotiations were the only show in town, and Canada has realized that there is life— and even market activity— south of the United States. Countries in the Americas are trading more intensively with one another— of the $1.5 trillion exported in 1997 by the countries of the Western Hemisphere, over 55 percent was sold within the Americas. Not only is there more trade, there are more trade arrangements. Starting in the late 1980s, existing regional integration arrangements were rejuvenated to fit new economic conditions. Moreover, new arrangements— a variety of customs unions, free trade agreements and hybrids— have been put into place. The culmination of this new regionalism is the Free Trade Area of the Americas (FTAA), proposed at the First Summit of the Americas held in Miami in December 1994. The FTAA has as its objective an agreement by the year 2005, on a schedule for the elimination of barriers to trade in goods and services and restrictions on investment among the 34 democratic countries of the Americas— the entire Hemisphere minus Cuba. Negotiations were launched in April 1998 at the Second Summit of the Americas, and talks have begun in the negotiating groups.

---

*Gary Hufbauer is the Reginald Jones Senior Fellow at the Institute for International Economics. He served as Deputy Assistant Secretary for the U.S. Treasury responsible for trade and investment during the Tokyo Round and was Director of the International Tax Staff.

**Barbara Kotschwar is the Coordinator, Foreign Trade and Information System, with the Trade Unit of the Organization of American States. She was formerly with the Institute for International Economics and has written a number of articles on trade and regional integration.

To predict the future, we must examine the past and consider the present. Our aim in this paper is to reflect on the evolution of regionalism in the Americas and to set out a scenario for the next decade of trade relations among the FTAA countries.

Latin America: A Clouded Past

Latin America has historically tended towards regionalism. From Simon Bolivar to Raul Prebisch to modern day technocrats such as Fernando Henrique Cardoso, the wisdom has been that unity is better— although not always feasible. While most integration plans did not include the area north of the Rio Grande— in fact, most were construed as means to balance the power of the United States— the idea of a Pan-American Union has been batted around for ages, even in periods when protectionist policies dominated the daily agenda.

In fact, Latin America's post–war regional integration arrangements were conducted within the framework of import substitution industrialization (ISI). ISI served as an economic development model in the context of declining commodity prices and neglect from the United States (at the time, the United States was concentrated on reconstructing Europe and limiting the spread of communism in Asia). The aim of ISI was to buffer Latin America from worsening terms of trade following the commodity boom sparked by the Second World War. By erecting high walls against manufactured imports, countries would develop their own industries and reduce their dependency on the advanced countries in general and the United States in particular. To overcome scale limitations,

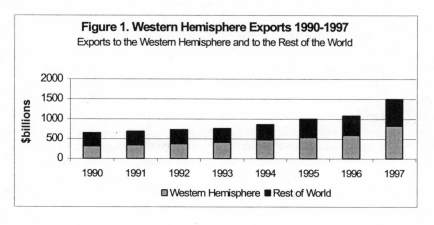

Figure 1. Western Hemisphere Exports 1990-1997
Exports to the Western Hemisphere and to the Rest of the World

ISI was expanded regionally, in theory creating larger markets for regionally produced goods. Regional agreements were often supplemented by production sharing arrangements in which countries would divide the production process among and within industries. To illustrate the theory, using the example of automobile production, one country might produce steel and stamp out auto bodies, another make engines, a third would make transmissions, and a fourth would assemble all the parts into autos.

Regional integration was thus seen as a means to surmount the inherent scale limitations of small domestic markets in Latin America, to allow industries to become competitive on a regional level, and to encourage industrial development within a cooperative framework. Regional markets with high levels of protection *vis à vis* the United States and Europe could be used to shift local firms from solely making consumer goods towards the production of intermediate and capital goods as well.

Early attempts at regional integration date back to the late 1950s when, under the guidance of the United Nations Commission for Latin America (ECLA), a group of South American countries initiated discussions on the means to foster greater regional integration. These proposals were predicated on the need to go beyond the domestic import–substitution strategies, which had been embraced by most Latin American countries. However, the integration agreements that emerged were really anti–trade agreements in that they emphasized the regulation of investment and production and the restriction of imports from the rest of the world.

Early Integration Agreements

The Latin American Free Trade Agreement • LAFTA/ALALC was founded in the early 1960s, and LAFTA eventually embraced all the South American countries plus Mexico. In LAFTA, high barriers to external trade were maintained despite the Kennedy and Tokyo Rounds–and LAFTA was used to justify their continuance. Incoming investment was licensed and soft attempts were made to divide commercial and governmental functions between members. Within LAFTA, the reduction of tariffs and other barriers were negotiated on the basis of product lists, which limited the extent of cross–sector trade offs. Other subjects were likewise addressed on a piecemeal rather than a comprehensive basis; the members sought to regulate economic specialization by agreement rather than the market.

Countries were initially enthusiastic about exchanging preferences within LAFTA, but the game was up once all of the easy items— usually goods that were not produced at home— were liberalized. The process stalled when difficult sectors— e.g., automobiles, other consumer durables, agriculture, and textiles— came up for discussion. In other words, the theory of industrial rationalization broke down in practice. On the whole, LAFTA served political rather than economic purposes. By 1980, LAFTA had been replaced by the less ambitious Latin American Integration Association (LAIA/ALADI), which was largely structured around bilateral trade preferences.

Andean Pact • Partly due to the limited progress on LAFTA's economic front, and partly to a feeling that Argentina and Brazil were grabbing all the LAFTA gains, in the late 1960s, six of the eleven LAFTA members established their own new arrangement, the Andean Pact. This new agreement included Bolivia, Colombia, Ecuador, Peru and Chile (which left in 1976) and was later joined by Venezuela (1973). This highly institutionalized structure was modeled after the European Economic Community (EEC), but unlike the EEC, the Pact did little to liberalize trade between members. In fact, severe external barriers were maintained by all members except Colombia. Production–sharing arrangements between the Andean countries were a major focus of negotiation, buttressed by a highly restrictive investment regime (the notorious Decision 24).

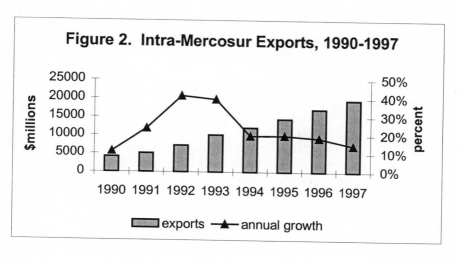

Figure 2. Intra-Mercosur Exports, 1990-1997

Central American Common Market (CACM) • Another early regional trade arrangement, made up of the five Central American countries, was the Central American Common Market (CACM). While early liberalization measures produced trade growth among the members, the CACM turned out to be a paper arrangement with little implementation. Efforts at production–sharing led to acrimonious debate among the members. By the 1980s, CACM was totally overshadowed by political and military conflicts within the region.

Caribbean Common Market • In 1968 several Caribbean countries launched their own integration system, the Caribbean Free Trade Area (CARIFTA). In 1973 CARIFTA was replaced by the Caribbean Community and Common Market (Caricom).[1] Caricom never came close to a common market, in part because the individual islands relied heavily on tariff revenue; in part because the trade between them was extremely limited.

The Move Toward a New Regionalism

In the mid 1980s, as a complement to the disciplined macroeconomic policies adopted in the wake of the international debt crisis, Latin American countries moved away from protectionist policies. They opened their economies, reduced trade barriers and tried export promotion strategies. Unilateral trade liberalization was carried out by simplifying tariff structures and reducing rates from astronomical to merely high levels, and eliminating many nontariff barriers, except on agriculture. Trade policy liberalization was part of a larger outward–oriented development strategy, which replaced the old import substitution approach. Among other features, foreign investment was invited instead of licensed. In the 1980s and 1990s, new agreements were negotiated in the spirit of open regionalism, designed to be complementary with, and a prod to, GATT/WTO negotiations for freer trade on a multilateral basis. This period of hemispheric relations is remarkable not only for the dramatic reorientation of the Latin American approach towards regional integration, but for the heightened participation of North America in hemispheric trade matters. We now turn to these developments.

---

1   Caricom members include Antigua and Barbuda, Bahamas, Barbados, Belize, Dominica, Grenada, Guyana, Jamaica, Montserrat, St. Kitts and Nevis, St. Lucia, St. Vincent and the Grenadines, Suriname, Trinidad and Tobago.

Latin America: from Import Substitution to Open Regionalism

Ironically, ECLAC, the institution that was founded by and housed Raul Prebisch is now the major exponent of *open regionalism*, a strategy by which countries simultaneously participate in two or more trade and integration arrangements as long as each participatory step is driven by liberalization both among the member countries and with the rest of the world.[2] Domestic policies turned decidedly pro-market, and countries embarked on the new generation of regional agreements. Pro-market translated into lower external tariffs (unilaterally as well as within the Uruguay Round), privatization, disciplined macroeconomic policies (such as small budget deficits and low inflation) coupled with harder currencies, and democratic elections.

While many champion the new attitude of trade agreements in the Hemisphere, there are those who are troubled by the numerous

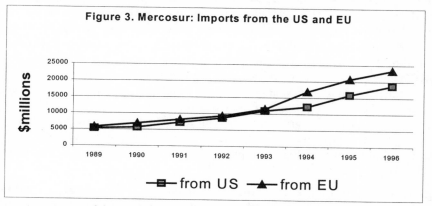

Figure 3. Mercosur: Imports from the US and EU

agreements—and have described the hemisphere as resembling a spaghetti bowl. A kinder term would be network—and the networking continues. In Summer 1998, both the Central American countries and the Caricom signed a Free Trade Agreement with the Dominican Republic. Mexico has signed a free trade agreement with Nicaragua and is negotiating with the other Central American countries. The Mercosur is talking to the Andean Community and the Andeans are considering negotiating with the Central Americans. And so it goes. Chart 1 lists the various plurilateral and bilateral agreements in force today.

---

2   CEPAL, *El regionalsimo abierto en America Latina y el Caribe. La integracion economica al servicio de la transformacion productiva con equidad*, Santiago de Chile, 1994.

MERCOSUR • The most important new arrangement is the Mercosur, which includes Brazil, the largest South American country, Argentina, Uruguay, and Paraguay. Like the original European Common Market, the Mercosur served an important political purpose, namely defusing tensions between Argentina and Brazil.[3] Unlike earlier Latin American regional agreements, the Mercosur countries reduced their external barriers, liberalized investment, and tackled difficult sectors. This arrangement proved extremely successful at stimulating trade: as seen in Figure 2, intra-Mercosur exports grew by an average of 30 percent per year in its first five years of existence. Mercosur has not visibly restricted its trade and investment with the rest of the world— both EU and U.S. exports to these countries have grown at respectable rates (figure 3).

Challenges remain to be tackled within the Mercosur, on the monetary as well as on the trade front. Argentina is highly vulnerable to a possible Brazilian devaluation, and both countries depend on the credibility of the real plan for their economic stability. The Asian financial crisis has drawn speculation— by policymakers as well as bankers— about the staying power of Mercosur. So far Brazil is holding on. Brazil's central response to the crisis has been constructive fiscal austerity, coupled with an IMF package of $42 billion and "voluntary" stretch-outs by the private banks. In addition, Brazil has put into place new trade restraints, consistent with the WTO. This means tighter sanitary and phytosanitary inspections, licensing, more anti-dumping cases and some manipulation of exceptions to the Common External Tariff (CET). In past crises the Mercosur partnership survived because the partners were willing to forgive each other's policy lapses— as long as these transgressions were not too damaging. This pattern should hold in 1998–99, provided that Brazil keeps its derogations within reasonable limits.

Andean Community • The Andean Community is the Andean Pact in modern packaging. Still highly institutionalized, the Andean Group discarded the more trade-discouraging measures, and replaced the notorious Decision 24 with a more investor-friendly regime. The result is genuine investment liberalization and free trade in some sectors, less bureaucracy, and an approach that is half FTA, half customs union. Trade among the members has grown considerably as the countries have liberalized their trade regimes and has the Andean Community has been reformed (Figure 4). Yet puzzles remain. Trade is free from tariffs and nontariff barriers among only four of the five (Peru apart). Three share a

---

3   In the 1970s both countries toyed with nuclear aspirations. Unlike India and Pakistan, they instead
     pursued a path of cooperation— a path that culminated in the formation of Mercosur.

common external tariff— although there are exceptions even among these three. Meanwhile, Bolivia and Peru are outside the common external tariff. Bolivia is now an associate member of Mercosur, and has been allowed to maintain its flat external tariff rate by the Andean Community. Peru's membership came into question in 1992, when the other Andean countries condemned the Fujimorazo— President Fujimori's 1992 closing of Congress and suspension of Constitutional rights. Venezuela broke relations with Peru, and Peru's membership in the Andean Group was suspended. Although Peru has now been reinstated, and in fact houses the Secretariat, Peru's membership remains open to question. Peru also maintains its own bi-level tariff schedule and has bilateral free trade agreements with each of the Andean countries.

Despite all its growing pains, the Andean Community is moving forward with its integration goals, and is expanding trade relations with

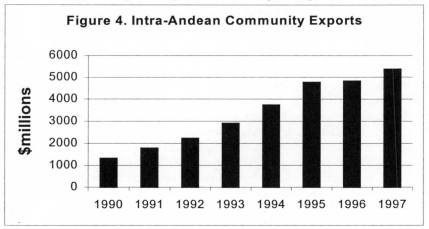

Figure 4. Intra-Andean Community Exports

other countries. The Andean Community members speak with one voice in the FTAA negotiations-and are in the process of negotiating as a unit with a number of other Latin American partners. At this time, the Andean Community is negotiating a free trade area with Mercosur— which has already accepted Chile and Bolivia as associate members. If these negotiations succeed— still a far-off proposition, but not an impossible one— a true South American Free Trade Area-or SAFTA— would exist.

CACM and CARICOM • There is some new energy in these arrangements, especially among the Central American countries that have resolved their civil wars. Both arrangements, however, lack unity of purpose and strategy. The Central American Common Market is far from a common market. Members have been negotiating together, but signing and implementing separately. The Caribbean countries continue to focus on Lome negotiations with the European Union. For the most part, Caribbean countries are waiting for an invitation to join NAFTA, or more U.S. unilateral liberalization, via extension of the Caribbean Basin Initiative (CBI). They place far more value on their dealings with the European Union and the United States than on the creation of a free trade area between the islands.

Chile • In the early 1990s, Chile sought membership in NAFTA; when Washington politics proved too much of a hurdle, Chile negotiated a series of bilateral FTAs with Mexico, Mercosur, and others. Mexico, Canada, and Chile have been particularly active in promoting bilateral FTAs within the Western Hemisphere, sometimes one-on-one arrangements (e.g., Chile–Mexico), sometimes one-on-one-plus (e.g., Mexico with Colombia and Venezuela in the Group of Three (G-3) Arrangement). Usually these bilaterals are designed to be NAFTA and/or Mercosur consistent.

Cuba • In addition, there is the sidelines player, Cuba. While the United States continues its embargo, Cuba trades substantially with the countries of the Caribbean as well as with Mexico and Venezuela. Canada and Mexico invest in the Cuban economy, especially in tourism and mining. The Association of Caribbean States (ACS), which includes Cuba in its membership, is considering a proposal for a wider Caribbean Free Trade Area. When Cuba once again joins the inter-American system, the implications will be significant. A large island with rich natural resources and a talented workforce, Cuba will be a frontrunner in the Caribbean. Cuba has potential in mining, pharmaceuticals, sugar, rum and bananas. Added to this is the pent-up desire of many Americans to spend their tourist dollars in Cuba-a factor that will undoubtedly boost Cuba's tourism sector— potentially at the expense of its Caribbean neighbors.

The opening of Cuba could have a major impact on the FTAA. The passing of the Castro government in Cuba may prompt a U.S. rush to bring the new Cuba into NAFTA, and the potential dislocation in the Caribbean and Central America could sweep CACM and Caricom into NAFTA in the same breath. In turn, this could set the stage for a NAFTA-SAFTA bargain that will culminate in the FTAA.

NAFTA countries • The Canada-U.S. FTA proved to be the forerunner of the North American Free Trade Agreement (NAFTA) and other pacts within the region. CUSTA was consciously viewed as a template for the Uruguay Round of GATT negotiations— and was in fact used as a template at least twice, once for the Uruguay Round and again for NAFTA. NAFTA in turn served as a welcome mat for Mexico into the world trading system, and marked a sharp turn from historical U.S.–Mexican political and commercial antagonism.

In addition, as a consequence of the bilateral agreements negotiated by Canada and Mexico, NAFTA's rules and disciplines have been indirectly "exported" to other Latin American countries. All of Mexico's post-NAFTA agreements are built upon NAFTA disciplines. The G–3 agreement between Mexico, Colombia and Venezuela, as well as Mexico's bilateral agreements with Bolivia and Costa Rica, incorporate NAFTA-type rules, and the Canada–Chile Free Trade agreement even goes beyond NAFTA in certain areas (notably, it rules out anti-dumping proceedings between the parties). Mexico and Chile are currently renegotiating their 1992 free trade agreement, in keeping with this trend. Within the Western Hemisphere, in addition to the three NAFTA countries, Bolivia, Chile, Colombia, Costa Rica and Venezuela have also accepted NAFTA-type rules and disciplines in important areas. For example, all these countries will grant investors national treatment and accept international arbitration for the resolution of investment–related disputes. This is a far cry from the old Calvo Clause, which asserted that investor disputes had to be adjudicated by local courts. In the service sector, these countries have agreed to undertake liberalizing measures which exceed those called for in the Uruguay Round, using a "top-down" approach to free trade in all services.[4] They have also agreed to national treatment-based rules in government procurement and have updated their intellectual property rights regimes. Finally and importantly, these agreements have adopted NAFTA-type dispute settlement mechanisms to resolve trade disagreements.

Increasing commonality in bilateral and plurilateral agreements bodes well for trade and investment relations within the Americas. Common rules and procedures and a strengthened legal framework will smooth the way in future negotiations. NAFTA may not serve as the path to the FTAA, but it will continue to play a significant role in structuring the framework for trade and investment liberalization in the Americas.

The Free Trade Area of the Americas: Choices Ahead

What will happen to existing subregional economic integration arrangements when the FTAA comes into effect? The Declaration of San Jose

---

4   In a "top down" approach, the country agrees to implement the principles of liberalization unless an activity is specifically reserved. This is also called a "negative list" approach.

states that the FTAA, will coexist with arrangements that are already in place. However, since the FTAA is to be WTO-consistent and "balanced and comprehensive in scope," it will in substance supersede many of these arrangements. One can imagine that existing bilateral agreements will be folded into the FTAA in the sense that every commitment in the FTA will be restated in stronger form in the FTAA. In other words, looking to the future, we see the FTAA as a way to unravel some of the spaghetti, while keeping the networking going.

What about the structure of negotiations? Currently, the FTAA talks are being conducted partly by blocs, partly by individual countries. Mercosur negotiates as one. The Andean Community, the Central American Common Market and the Caricom for the most part speak with one voice per regional arrangement. The NAFTA countries, by contrast, negotiate individually.

The FTAA process has now been underway for three years and much of the preparatory work has been done. Twelve working groups, with the assistance of the Tripartite institutions (the IDB, OAS and ECLAC) have built databases, prepared studies on a range of trade and investment disciplines, and have compared national and regional legislation in the relevant FTAA negotiating areas. The FTAA negotiations were launched in April 1998 at the Santiago Summit, and in September 1998 hundreds of negotiators descended upon the University of Miami conference centre to begin talks. Nine negotiating groups were set up—in market access, agriculture, investment, services, intellectual property rights, competition policy, government procurement, subsidies, anti-dumping and countervailing duties and dispute settlement. Consultative groups have also been established to study electronic commerce, smaller economies and civil society.

The question now is to what end? It is easy to imagine dead-end scenarios in which nothing comes of the grand design launched at the Miami Summit. The Asian financial crisis gave new arguments to those, especially in the United States and Brazil, who already oppose free trade agreements. Unless the major countries summon the political will, little free trade will result from the FTAA. The next U.S. President—be it Al Gore, George W. Bush or someone else—will have to work hard to muster support for a hemispheric trade initiative. Otherwise, the FTAA vision could easily blur into political summits with economic nuggets (a path that APEC seems to be following), and lose its focus on free trade. We put forth three scenarios for the future FTAA.

The Minimalist Scenario • Not much happens in the Americas, but the FTAA process stimulates some trade activity in other fora. The EU, eager to preserve its large market in South America, hastens a free trade agreement with Mercosur, with a limited degree of agricultural liberalization. At the same time, a new round of trade talks is launched at the multilateral level. Within the WTO, agricultural talks began in 1999, and countries started services negotiations in the year 2000. Many, including Sir Leon Brittan, called for the "Millennium Round." In this scenario, the FTAA acts as a spur to the Millenium Round. Even if the free trade focus is maintained in the FTAA, there may be little substance to distinguish the FTAA from the WTO talks—and thus to make it worthwhile diverting skilled human resources and political capital to the pursuit of freer hemispheric trade. In a minimalist scenario, the first few years of the FTAA negotiations are spent pushing WTO initiatives, and the FTAA eventually folds into the multilateral negotiations.

The middle-of-the-road scenario • In a middle-of-the-road scenario, the FTAA moves beyond the WTO in certain areas, but it falls short of achieving ambitious goals. A likely area of accomplishment is "civil society". Since the Americas are inevitably linked—by geography, history and culture as well as by commerce, immigration and drugs –as environmental and labor issues (and perhaps a few other civil society questions) are built into the agenda. If the FTAA comes up with a creative way of addressing these contentious issues, then it will have made a significant contribution.

The Maximalist Scenario • In the maximalist scenario, the FTAA moves well beyond the WTO and eliminates the barriers to trade and investment among the 34 participating countries on a much faster schedule than the WTO timetable. Indeed, without a surprising great leap forward, the Millennium Round will not produce anything like a world free trade agreement. China and Russia remain to be ushered into the system, and, along with many other countries, they don't seem ready for free trade in the next two decades. Hence, the FTAA can make a contribution above and beyond the multilateral realm through faster liberalization of traditionally protected sectors—notably agriculture, textiles and apparel, autos, and a range of services. Also, the FTAA could move towards deeper integration, addressing sensitive issues such as labor and environmental conditions well before the multilateral level is ready to deal with them.

Supporting this scenario, the FTAA is currently addressing novel issues: government procurement (currently the plurilateral WTO agreement has the participation of only two countries in the Americas), competition policy (not yet the subject of a multilateral framework), and the formation of a mechanism to hear the views of nongovernmetal actors. On this last item, the FTAA countries have formed a Committee on Civil Society to diffuse the sort of tensions that resulted in the burning of cars and spraying of graffiti at the 1998 WTO Ministerial meeting. This committee is designed to serve as a bridge between policymakers and their most vocal constituents.

Chart 1. Trade and Integration Agreements in the Western Hemisphere

	Entry into Force
Customs Unions	
Mercosur	1995
Andean Community	1969, rev. 1998
Central American Common Market (CACM)	1961
Caribbean Community (Caricom)	1973
Free Trade Arrangements	
Plurilateral arrangements	
NAFTA	1994
Group of Three (G–3)	1995
Mercosur–Bolivia	1997
Mercosur–Chile	1996
Bilateral FTAs	
Bolivia–Mexico	1995
Canada–Chile	1997
Caricom– Dominican Republic	1998*
Central–America–Dominican Republic	1998*
Chile–Colombia	1994
Chile–Ecuador	1995
Chile–Mexico	1992
Chile–Venezuela	1993
Costa Rica–Mexico	1995
Mexico– Nicaragua	1998*
Preferential Trade Agreements**	
CARICOM	
CARICOM–Colombia	1995
CARICOM-Venezuela	1993

* date of signature

** The trade agreements between Colombia and Venezuela and the Caricom initially offer Caricom preferential access to Colombian and Venezuelan markets, but will be renegotiated to become fully reciprocal.

Source: Miguel Rodríguez Mendoza and Barbara Kotschwar "Latin America: Expanding Trade Opportunities" in *SAIS Review*, June 1997.

Especially in the United States, the twin issues of labor and the environment have been linked to the trade agenda and served as lightning rods for opponents of free trade agreements. One creative solution that could be put into place by FTAA members would be a hemispheric wide labeling system, along the lines of the ISO 9000 for labor and environmental standards in the manufacture of traded goods and services. Under this approach, business firms would subscribe to labels that attest to the working and environmental conditions under which goods and service are made.[5]

A companion "market approach" to promoting labor standards is the adoption of codes of conduct, which typically specify minimum labor and environmental standards. The firm that adopts the code would then advise its subcontractors that if they violate the same code, they lose the contract. Code language is often vague and enforcement can be lax, but steps have been taken to address those problems, starting with the establishment of a universal standard for ethical sourcing.

In our crystal ball, the maximalist scenario describes the future. We think the momentum behind hemispheric integration will be stronger over the next decade than the push for rapid global integration. Just as a combination of economic and political considerations carried the day in Europe, so too, in our opinion, will they result in a full-blown FTAA.

---

[5]   U.S. consumer groups are pushing this approach, and some labels already exist. A famous example is the Rugmark label for carpets which guarantees that the carpet was not made with child labor.

CONFERENCE SPEAKERS

Biographical Summaries of Conference Participants

as of September 11–12, 1998

M. Jean Anderson is a partner in the law firm of Weil, Gotshal & Manges LLP and is head of the firm's Washington, D.C.–based International Trade Group. Ms. Anderson and the International Trade Group have represented companies in Europe, Asia, Latin America and the U.S. They also have been principal legal advisors to the Government of Canada on NAFTA and the negotiation and implementation of the WTO agreements.

During the FTA negotiations Ms. Anderson was Chief Counsel for International Trade at the U.S. Department of Commerce. In that position she was a principal negotiator of the FTA and a primary architect of the Chapter 19 dispute settlement system.

Ms. Anderson has chaired the International Trade and Canada Committees of the International Law Section of the American Bar Association. She has taught international trade law at Georgetown University Law Center. She holds degrees from *l'Institut d'Etudes Politiques* of the University of Paris, Northwestern University, and Georgetown University Law Center.

James A. Baker, III is a senior partner in the law firm of Baker & Botts and Senior Counselor to The Carlyle Group, a merchant banking firm in Washington, D.C. Mr. Baker served as the United States Secretary of State from 1989 to 1992. At the time the Agreement was negotiated, Mr. Baker was U.S. Secretary of the Treasury, a position he held from 1985 to 1988. As Treasury Secretary he was also Chairperson of the President's Economic Council. Mr. Baker served as Chief of Staff to President Reagan (1981–85), and he was Chief of Staff and Senior Counselor to President Bush in 1992–93. He is Honorary Chairperson of the James A. Baker, III Institute for Public Policy at Rice University.

Mr. Baker graduated from Princeton University and holds a J.D. from the University of Texas. Among his many awards for distinguished public service, Mr. Baker received the Presidential Medal of Freedom in 1991.

James J. Blanchard is a partner in the Washington, D.C. law firm of Verner, Liipfert, Bernhard, McPherson and Hand. From 1983 to 1991 he was Governor of Michigan and from 1975 to 1983 he was a member of the U.S. House of Representatives from Michigan.

From 1993 to 1996 Mr. Blanchard served as United States Ambassador to Canada. During his tenure as ambassador he managed a broad range of issues as they applied to U.S.–Canadian relations. These issues included trade, natural resources, environment and national security. He also provided critical support to the passage of NAFTA and the Open Skies Agreement. He is a graduate of Michigan State University and holds a law degree from the University of Minnesota. Mr. Blanchard is the author of a forthcoming book entitled *Behind the Embassy Door: Canada, Clinton and Quebec.*

Derek H. Burney is Chairperson and Chief Executive Officer of Bell Canada International. Prior to joining Bell Canada International, Mr. Burney served as Canada's Ambassador to the United States. During the FTA deliberations, Mr. Burney was Chief of Staff to Prime Minister Mulroney and was directly involved in the negotiation of the Agreement. From 1990 to 1992 he was the Prime Minister's personal representative in the preparations for the Houston, London and Munich G–7 economic summits.

Mr. Burney graduated from Queen's University and also received a master's degree in political science from the University. In 1993 he was named an officer of the Order of Canada.

William A. Dymond is Senior Trade and Investments Negotiator and Chief Air Negotiator for Canada's Department of Foreign Affairs and International Trade. From 1992 to 1995 Mr. Dymond was Ambassador from Canada to Brazil. During the FTA negotiations Mr. Dymond was Minister Counsellor, (Commercial) at the Canadian Embassy in Washington and from 1986 to 1987 was Senior Advisor to the Trade Negotiations Office in Ottawa.

Among Mr. Dymond's publications are: "Canada–U.S. Trade Options," in the *Canada U.S. Law Journal* (1985); "Lord Ronald and U.S. Trade Policy," Centre for Trade Policy and Law (1990); "Mercosur: Southern Partner for NAFTA" in Policy Options, Institute Research Public Policy (1995); and *Decisions at Midnight*, an account of the Canada–U.S. Free Trade Negotiations, University of British Columbia Press 1994. Mr. Dymond is a graduate of the University of Toronto and also received an M.A. from the University.

John Engler is Governor of Michigan. Prior to being elected Governor in 1990, he served in the Michigan Legislature. He was first elected to the House of Representative in 1970 at the age of 22. He served in the House and subsequently in the Senate where he was elected Senate Majority Leader. In 1996 Mr. Engler was selected as chairman of the Republican Governors Association, the Council of Great Lakes Governors and the Education Governors Panel. He is currently a member of the executive committee of the RGA and serves on the National Governors Association Human Resources Committee. He also serves on the board of the NGA Center. Mr. Engler is a graduate of Michigan State University and holds a law degree from Thomas M. Cooley Law School.

Geza Feketekuty is a professor at the Graduate School of International Policy Studies at the Monterey Institute of International Studies. He also writes and lectures on a wide range of trade policy topics and customized courses in trade policy and international trade negotiations. Mr. Feketekuty previously served for 21 years with the office of the U.S. Trade Representative in various senior trade policy positions. Among his responsibilities were coordination of U.S. participation in the Tokyo Round of Multilateral Trade Negotiations and also the domestic and foreign agenda development for the Uruguay Round.

Mr. Feketekuty has held various teaching positions at Princeton University, Johns Hopkins University and Cornell University. He holds degrees from Columbia University and Princeton University. His publications include the book *International Trade in Services: An Overview and Blueprint for Negotiations* (1988), Ballinger Publisher with the American Enterprise Institute.

Michael Hart is Professor of International Affairs at the Norman Paterson School of International Affairs at Carleton University and Senior Associate at the Centre for Trade Policy and Law. He is also Visiting Professor at the Trade Center of the Monterey Institute for International Studies. At the time the Agreement was negotiated, Professor Hart was co-chair of the task force that prepared for Canada's participation in the negotiations with the U.S. and was a senior member of the actual negotiating team. During various other assignments in Ottawa and at the Canadian Permanent Mission to the GATT in Geneva, he pursued agricultural trade issues, the negotiation of textile and clothing restraint agreements, commodity agreements and bilateral air agreements and the legislation and implementation of Canada's trade remedy laws. Professor Hart is also an independent analyst of trade policy issues.

Alan F. Holmer is President of PhRMA, which represents research-based pharmaceutical and biotechnology companies. Prior to assuming that position he established the international trade practice for the law firm of Sidley & Austin. In 1985 Mr. Holmer was appointed General Counsel to U.S. Trade Representative, Clayton Yeutter, and in 1987 was promoted to Deputy U.S. Trade Representative. In 1983 after serving in the Reagan White House, he was named Deputy Assistant Secretary for Import Administration at the Commerce Department.

Mr. Holmer is a graduate of Princeton University and holds a law degree from Georgetown University. He has also served as an Adjunct Professor of Law at Georgetown University. He is the co-author with Judith H. Bello of the *Guide to the U.S.-Canada Free-Trade Agreement*, Prentice Hall Law and Business (1990).

Gary C. Hufbauer recently returned to the Institute for International Economics as the Reginald Jones Senior Fellow. Prior to his return to the Institute he was Vice President, Maurice Greenburg Chair and Director of Studies at the Council on Foreign Relations. Dr. Hufbauer served in the U.S. Treasury Department as Deputy Assistant Secretary responsible for trade and investment during the Tokyo Round and was Director of the International Tax Staff.

Dr. Hufbauer graduated from Harvard University, holds a Ph.D. in economics from Kings College at Cambridge University and a J.D from Georgetown University. His recent publications include *Flying High: Liberalizing Civil Aviation in the Asia Pacific* (co-editor, 1996), *Fundamental Tax Reform and Border Tax Adjustments* (1996), *Western Hemisphere Economic Integration* (co-author, 1994), *Reviving the European Union* (co-editor, 1994), *NAFTA: An Assessment* (co-author, 1994), and *Economic Sanctions Reconsidered* (co-author, second edition, 1990).

Barbara R. Kotschwar is a Senior Trade Specialist at the Trade Unit of the Organization of American States. She is responsible for analyzing regional integration trends in the Western Hemisphere and for providing technical and analytical support to the Free Trade Area of the Americas process, in particular to the FTAA Negotiating Group on Market Access and the FTAA Advisory Committee on Smaller Economics.

Prior to joining the Trade Unit, Ms. Kotschwar worked on trade issues at the Institute for International Economics. She has authored or co-authored (including several with Gary C. Hufbauer) a number of articles on trade and regional integration. She is a graduate of McGill University and holds a M.A. from Johns Hopkins University.

Mordechai E. Kreinin is University Distinguished Professor of Economics at Michigan State University. Dr. Kreinin is past president of the International Trade and Finance Association and has been a consultant to many institutions including the United Nations, the U.S. Department of State and the U.S. Department of Commerce. Dr. Kreinin is the author of many articles and nine books including the widely used text *International Economics*. He has been visiting professor at 10 universities in the U.S., Canada, Europe and Australia. He has also been active in university governance issues and policies. Dr. Kreinin holds a Ph.D. in economics from the University of Michigan.

Richard G. Lipsey, FRSC, OC is Professor Emeritus of Economics at Simon Fraser University and fellow of the Canadian Institute for Advanced Research and member of its large-scale international research project on Economic Growth and Policy. Dr. Lipsey has authored several textbooks that are used worldwide and have been translated into fourteen foreign languages. He has published over 150 articles in learned journals and books on various aspects of theoretical and applied economics.

From 1983 to 1989 Dr. Lipsey was senior economic advisor for the C.D. Howe Institute where he co-authored monographs on Canada's Trade Options and on the Canada-U.S. Free Trade Agreement. He also wrote more than a dozen journal articles and pamphlets on various aspects of the free-trade debate.

Dr. Lipsey is a graduate of the University of British Columbia, holds an M.A. from the University of Toronto and a Ph.D. from the London School of Economics. He has held a chair in Economics at the London School of Economics, was Chairperson of the Department of Economics and Dean of the Faculty of Social Science at the University of Essex and was Sir Edward Peacock Professor of Economics at Queen's University. Dr. Lipsey is an officer of the Order of Canada and a fellow of the Royal Society of Canada.

Peter McPherson is President of Michigan State University, a position he has held since 1993. Prior to arriving at MSU, he held senior executive positions with the Bank of America including Group Executive Vice President of Investment Management.

From 1987 to 1989 Mr. McPherson was Deputy Secretary of the U.S. Treasury focusing on trade, tax and international issues. He was a senior negotiator during the FTA deliberations. His other governmental positions include Administrator of the Agency for International Development, General Counsel to the Reagan–Bush transition and Special Assistant to President Ford. Mr. McPherson graduated from Michigan State University, holds an MBA from Western Michigan University and a J.D. degree from American University.

William S. Merkin is Senior Vice President, International, Strategic Policy, Inc., specializing in international trade issues. From 1980–1989, Mr. Merkin served in the office of the U.S. Trade Representative. He was the Deputy Chief U.S. Negotiator during the negotiation of the FTA and is an acknowledged expert on U.S.–Canadian bilateral trade and investment issues. Prior to the FTA negotiations Mr. Merkin represented the U.S. at international meetings of the Customs Cooperation Council and at meetings of GATT.

From 1970 to 1980, Mr. Merkin served in the U.S. Department of Commerce and was a member of the U.S. negotiating team for the Tokyo Round of Multilateral Trade Negotiations.

G. Mustafa Mohatarem is Chief Economist for General Motors Corporation where he is one of four leaders of the corporation's Public Policy Center. General Motors' Economic team is responsible for assessing the impact of worldwide economic development on the corporation and advising the corporation on various economic policy issues.

Mr. Mohatarem was the lead contact for GM with the United States and other governments during the Uruguay Round of GATT negotiations as well as the FTA and NAFTA. He interacts regularly with domestic and foreign officials on trade–related issues.

Mr. Mohatarem is a graduate of Denison University and holds an MBA and a Ph.D. from the University of Chicago. He has served as visiting professor at the University of Notre Dame and adjunct assistant professor at the University of Michigan and at the University of Detroit.

Sylvia Ostry is Distinguished Research Fellow, Centre for International Studies at the University of Toronto. Among her positions with the Federal Government were Ambassador for Multilateral Trade Negotiations, Prime Minister's Personal Representative for the Economic Summit, Deputy Minister of International Trade, Chairperson of the Economic Council of Canada and Deputy Minister of Consumer and Corporate Affairs.

Ms. Ostry was also Head of the Economics and Statistics Department of the OECD in Paris and Volvo Distinguished Fellow at the Council on Foreign Relations. Mrs. Ostry has a Ph.D. in economics from McGill and Cambridge Universities. Her publications include, *Who's on First? The Post-Cold War Trading System*, University of Chicago Press, Chicago, (1997) and *Asia–Pacific Crossroads: Regime Creation and the Future of APEC*, Vinod K. Aggarawal and Charles E. Morrison (editors), St. Martin's Press, New York, (1998). In 1990 Mrs. Ostry was made a Companion of the Order of Canada.

Roger B. Porter is IBM Professor of Business and Government and Director of the Center for Business and Government at the Kennedy School of Government, Harvard University. He is a Senior Scholar at the Woodrow Wilson International Center for Scholars and Faculty Chairperson of Harvard's Program for Senior Managers in Government. His teaching and research focus on the relationship between business and government, strategic management, and domestic and international economic policy.

In the Bush Administration, Mr. Porter served as Assistant to the President for Economic and Domestic Policy. In the Reagan Administration he served as Deputy Assistant to the President and Director of the White House Office of Policy Development. He also served as Executive Secretary of the Economic Policy Council and as Counselor to the Secretary of the Treasury. He was Executive Secretary of the Cabinet Council on Economic Affairs from 1981 to 1985. He also served in the Ford Administration.

Mr. Porter is a graduate of Brigham Young University. He was a Rhodes Scholar and received a B.Phil. from Oxford University. He received his MA and Ph.D. degrees from Harvard University. His publications include the books *Presidential Decision Making* and *The U.S.-USSR Grain Agreement*.

S. Simon Reisman is President of Trade and Investment Advisory Group in Ottawa. At the time of the FTA Deliberations, Mr. Reisman was brought back into government service by Prime Minister Mulroney to be the Ambassador for Trade Negotiations and Chief Negotiator for Canada.

During his career in government Mr. Reisman held a number of Senior positions. Among those positions: Chief Negotiator for the Canada–U.S. Auto Pact; Deputy Minister of Finance; Secretary of the Treasury Board; and Deputy Minister of Industry. He was a member of the Canadian delegation at the first session of GATT in 1948 and at a number of subsequent sessions. Mr. Reisman graduated from McGill University, received an MA from the London School of Economics and LL.D from Carleton University. He is the author of *Canada–United States Economic Relations, Canada's Export Trade* and *Canadian Commerical Policy*.

Charles E. Roh, Jr. is a partner in the Washington office of the international law firm of Weil, Gotshal & Manges. Mr. Roh specializes in international trade and investment issues for domestic and foreign associations and governments. Mr. Roh served as Assistant U.S. Trade Representative for North America and was also the Deputy Chief Negotiator of NAFTA for the U.S. Mr. Roh was previously Associate General Counsel of the Office of the U.S. Trade Representative and the legal counsel for the USTR mission to GATT in Geneva. In those positions he represented the U.S. in GATT dispute settlement proceedings and in the drafting and negotiation of numerous international agreements. Mr. Roh is a graduate of Princeton University and holds a J.D. from Harvard University.

Douglas A. Schuler is Assistant Professor of Management at the Jesse H. Jones Graduate School of Management at Rice University. Professor Schuler's research focuses on the antecedents and results of corporate political activities particularly in the context of trade policies, drawing from management and political science. Professor Schuler's National Bureau of Economic Research paper with Professor Stephanie Lenway on steel industry trade policy also appears in a Conference volume *Empirical Studies of Commercial Policy*, University of Chicago, 1991. His recent work has appeared in *Academy of Management Journal, Business: Society* and the *International Trade Journal*.

David B. Schweikhardt is an Associate Professor in the Department of Agricultural Economics at Michigan State University. He specializes in agricultural and trade policy. His recent research has included an examination of the impact of the FTA and GATT on Michigan and U.S. Agriculture. From 1988 to 1992 Mr. Schweikhardt was an assistant professor of agricultural economics at Mississippi State University where he conducted research on the impact of the FTA on the U.S. cotton industry. His research also examined the problems of financing agricultural research in a federal system of government. Mr. Schweikhardt is a graduate of Purdue University and holds an M.S. and Ph.D. from Michigan State University.

Michael B. Smith is Vice President of Global USA, Inc. and leads the firm's international trade and investment practice. At the time the Agreement was negotiated, Mr. Smith was Senior Deputy United States Trade Representative. Prior to that he was the first U.S. Ambassador to GATT, Deputy USTR in Geneva, and Chief Textile Negotiator of the U.S. His work in international trade was influential in establishing the conceptual and structure foundations of the Uruguay Round and the FTA. Mr. Smith is a graduate of Harvard University.

Ann M. Veneman is the Secretary of the California Department of Food and Agriculture, an agency which regulates the largest agricultural economy in the United States. Ms. Veneman was Deputy Secretary of the U.S. Department of Agriculture from 1991–1993 and prior to that was Deputy Undersecretary of Agriculture for International Affairs and Commodity Programs. During the FTA negotiations, Ms. Veneman was Associate Administrator for USDA's Foreign Agricultural Services, where she was actively involved in the Uruguay Round of GATT negotiations, NAFTA and the FTA negotiations. Ms. Veneman graduated from the University of California at Davis, earned a master's degree from the University of California at Berkeley and a J.D. from the University of California, Hastings College of Law.

Konrad von Finckenstein, Q.C. is the Director of Investigation and Research for Industry Canada's Competition Bureau. He is responsible for the administration and enforcement of competition law in Canada, as well as three labeling statutes. Mr. von Finckenstein was, at the time the Agreement was negotiated, Senior General Counsel for the Trade Negotiations Office. His other positions include Senior General Counsel at the Department of Regional Industrial Expansion, Assistant Deputy Minister for Trade Law at the Department of Justice and Free Trade Policy and Operations at External Affairs. He also served as Assistant Deputy Attorney General for Tax Law and Coordinator for the Implementation of the FTA. Mr. von Finckenstein is a graduate of Carleton University and holds a law degree from Queen's University. He was appointed Queen's Counsel in 1984.

Michael H. Wilson is Chairperson of Michael Wilson International Inc., a Toronto firm which advises and assists companies in expanding their international business activities. He is also Vice Chairperson of RBC Dominion Securities with responsibilities in domestic and international investment banking. During the FTA negotiations, Mr. Wilson was

Minister of Finance. As Minister of International Trade, he participated in the negotiation of NAFTA, guided Canada through GATT negotiations and pursued Canada's trade and investment interests in 26 countries. Mr. Wilson has also held senior Federal cabinet posts in Industry, Science and Technology.

Mr. Wilson also represented Canada at six G-7 Economic Summits, the International Monetary Fund, The World Bank, the Organization for Economic Cooperation and Development and the Asia Pacific Economic Cooperation.

Paul Wonnacott is Alan R. Holmes Professor at Middlebury College. Mr. Wonnacott was previously a Professor of Economics at the University of Maryland, and he was a member of the President's Council of Economic Advisors from 1991 to 1993. He has also held positions with the U.S. Department of State, the Board of Governors of the Federal Reserve System, Columbia University and the Canadian Royal Commission on Banking and Finance.

Mr. Wonnacott's publications include *Free Trade between the United States and Canada: The Potential Economic Effects*, with R. J. Wonnacott Harvard Economic Series (1967), a book which helped to reopen the debate over free trade within North America and to set the stage for the U.S.-Canadian Free Trade Agreement of 1988, and "Beyond NAFTA: The Design of a Free-Trade Agreement of the Americas," a chapter in *The Economics of Preferential Trade Agreements* (1996) by Jagdish Bhagwati and Arvind Panagariya, eds. Mr. Wonnacott graduated from the University of Western Ontario and received a Ph.D. from Princeton University.

Clayton Yeutter is Counsel to the Washington, D.C., law firm Hogan and Hartson. Prior to joining the firm, he served as President Bush's Secretary of Agriculture, Chairperson of the Republican National Committee and Counselor to the President. From 1985 to 1988 Mr. Yeutter served as the U.S. Trade Representative. While in this position he helped to initiate the 100-nation Uruguay Round of GATT negotiations and led the American team in negotiating the FTA.

From 1978 to 1985, Mr. Yeutter was President and Executive Officer of the Chicago Mercantile Exchange. He also served in several subcabinet positions in the Nixon and Ford administrations. Mr. Yeutter received a law degree and Ph.D. from the University of Nebraska.